# Minds in Play

## Computer Game Design
### as a
## Context for Children's Learning

# Minds in Play

## Computer Game Design
## as a
## Context for Children's Learning

Yasmin B. Kafai

*University of California, Los Angeles*

**LEA** LAWRENCE ERLBAUM ASSOCIATES, PUBLISHERS

1995    Hillsdale, New Jersey                    Hove, UK

Lawrence Erlbaum Associates, Inc., Publishers
365 Broadway
Hillsdale, New Jersey 07642

**Library of Congress Cataloging-in-Publication Data**

Kafai, Yasmin Bettina.
  Minds in play : computer game design as a context for children's learning / Yasmin Bettina Kafai.
     p.  cm.
  Includes bibliographical references and index.
  ISBN 0-8058-1512-0.—ISBN 0-8058-1513-9 (pbk.)
  1. Computer-assisted instruction—United States—Authoring programs—Case studies.  2. LOGO (Computer program language)—Case studies.  3. Microcomputers—United States—Programming—Case studies.  4. Video games—United States—Case studies.  5. Constructivism (Education)—Case studies.  I. Title.
LB1028.66.K34  1994
372.13'34—dc20                                                94-30219
                                                                    CIP

Books published by Lawrence Erlbaum Associates are printed on acid-free paper, and their bindings are chosen for strength and durability.

Printed in the United States of America
10  9  8  7  6  5  4  3  2  1

*To my parents*

# Contents

# Preface

## Games to be Played—Games to be Made

In the wake of the advent of inexpensive microcomputers in the late 1970s came the first wave of nonprofessional programmers. Children, older students, teachers, and computer hobbyists took to the keyboard to find an experience that nobody had been able to have in previous generations. And in the wake of the interest in programming came a search for programmable project areas—you can't program without programming something. By the early 1980s, habits had set in. In the schools, the presence of the Logo turtle favored projects involving graphics. Teachers learning to program often looked for topics that would have an instructional function. Adult hobbyists implemented on their little computers simple forms of "system programs" that existed on the big machines but had not yet permeated down as they have today. Across the board a scattering of these new programmers embarked on projects to create another kind of entity that had come into being with the microchip. In popular parlance the video game was almost becoming synonymous with the idea of a home computer and the challenge of making one's own had an obvious appeal.

It is interesting to reflect on why making video games did not become a more important part of the school computer culture. The superficial answer is technical. Think back 10 years to the situation in a typical school computer lab. The machines are Apple II computers. The programming language is Apple Logo. With this combination it is *possible* to make a playable game, but the threshold of skill and effort needed is very high and the final result needs a stretch of imagination to be classed as a "real game." No wonder making a game was something that would be undertaken mostly by the exceptionally bold students and was seldom promoted by teachers as the thing to do.

This technical explanation certainly tells a part of the story, and is reinforced by noting that an increase in game-making is coming about simply as a result of improvements in hardware and software. I have observed many students and teachers in computer labs or workshops taking advantage of the fact that MicroWorlds Logo running on the newest Mac or IBM makes games as easy to program as the static graphics that became identified with the use of Logo 10 years ago. But there is much more to the story of video games in educational than technological evolution. Indeed, something that will more powerfully, and more deeply, facilitate a more massive entry of video game programming into schools is Yasmin Kafai's initiative in bringing this activity into the arena of central concerns of contemporary education theory.

As a background to this remark, it is instructive to note an oversimplification inherent in using the evolution of the technology as an explanation of what happens in schools. There is a two-way street: The evolution of the technology has, to a significant degree, been influenced by (as well as influencing) the culture of educational computing. To see an example, let me recall that in the very early 1980s computers with names like Atari and TI 99/4 were at least as well represented in schools as the Apple II; and because these computers were designed to serve also as game machines, they had hardware features that facilitated programming dynamic actions needed by games but also by other kinds of animation that open to children the opportunity to manipulate and understand many key concepts in science and mathematics. The Apple II was a wonderful workhorse that we all came to love for what it could do. But there was so much these other machines did better that the development of educational computing was significantly retarded by Apple's market victory. Clearly the world of education (which includes research communities and the Washington bureaucracies as well as schools), did not value what these machines could do enough to fight for them.

What I value most in Kafai's work is its contribution to valuing the activity of making a game. I don't mean this merely quantitatively. Articles about computers vie with one another in telling their audience how very exciting such and such an activity is for the students—or even how important it is for society that children should be engaged in this or that. Kafai also does some of that; but what differentiates her writing from the general "run" is paying serious attention, not only to the detail of what exactly these students are doing, but especially to the categories of theoretical inquiry that should be brought to bear on understanding these details. And by doing this well she also makes a contribution in the other sense: in the end her writing will serve to show education theorists a new domain from which to enrich their ideas. Game-making emerges not only as important to the children (and others) who do it, but also to theorists who want to understand the process of intellectual doing, thinking, and learning.

Perhaps the most important way in which game-making is a theoretically important domain is the emphasis it lays on *importance* as a category in thinking about what situations are good for learning. Literature on school improvement is full of exhortations to make the content of instruction "relevant." In this theoretical perspective the Kafai's work highlights the need for more discussion about what constitutes relevance for a ten-year old. Certainly not connecting school arithmetic with the supermarket! Connecting school science with environmental activism is a much better way to invest learning with importance. But if one does belong to a culture in which video games are important, transforming oneself from a consumer to a producer of games may well be an even more powerful way for some children to find importance in what they are doing.

My point here is not to argue about which source of a sense of importance is best but to note how reflection on game-making is an excellent medium for exploring multiple dimensions—psychological, cultural, mathetic—of this aspect of the learning environment. It is also an excellent medium for highlighting the issues raised by posing an opposition in educational thinking between instructionism and constructionism.

Every educator must have felt some envy watching children playing video games: If only that energy could be mobilized in the service of learning something that the educator values. But the envy can take very different forms. Instructionists show their orientation by concretizing the wish as a desire for games that will teach math or spelling or geography or whatever. The Constructionist mind is revealed when the wish leads to imagining children making the games instead of just playing them. Rather than wanting games to instruct children they yearn to see children construct games.

Accepting the honor of writing a preface carries the obligation offering some advice to readers. These two examples of connections made by this book between games and fundamental theoretical issues will suffice to give meaning to mine which I'll state as an appeal to read this work on the multiple levels given it by the richness of its author's mind. The book offers a very practicable model from which teachers can draw inspiration in their work with computers. It should embolden them to see importance in what some might dismiss as mere games. The book also offers a model to researchers (and I say this without presuming that teachers and even students should not be included here) in developing thick descriptions of the process of doing a project. Finally to theorists (and again the term is inclusive) it offers not only its author's theoretical insights but also a rich field in which to grow their own.

—Seymour Papert

# Introduction

## Minds In and At Play

Games, more than any other media, have brought technology into children's homes, and children have received them enthusiastically. Games capture children's imaginations and engage them in fantasy worlds. Whereas most research efforts have concentrated on discussing the effects of game playing, this book takes a different stance—it looks closely at games as a context for learning by placing children in the roles of producers rather than consumers of games.

As a starting point, this book describes and analyzes a rather unusual learning experiment, called the Game Design Project, which took place in an inner-city public elementary school (Kafai, 1993). A class of 16 fourth-grade students were programming games in Logo to teach fractions to third graders. The children transformed their classroom into a game design studio for six months, learning programming, writing stories and dialogues, constructing representations of fractions, creating package designs and advertisements, considering interface design issues, and devising teaching strategies. In this context, programming became a medium for children's personal and creative expression: In the design of their games, children engaged their fantasies and built relationships with other pockets of reality that went beyond traditional school approaches. In other words, the ideas and observations described in this book are not about computers in education; they are about what children can do and how they can learn with computers.

The following scene captures the first 20 minutes of one day in the Game Design Project, when two students discuss their games, design ideas, and fraction questions as they work at the computer:

On a Wednesday morning, 10 weeks into the project, two students, Amy and Trevor, sit next to each other at the computers while working on their games. The computers are arranged in two circles, with 16 computers each, outside of their classroom. The notebooks in which the students write every day about their ideas, plans, and designs are stacked between their computers. Trevor sits with both his legs folded on the chair and types in the name of a Logo procedure to start his game. The introduction to his game, called "The Island of the Goon," reads: "You are a monkey. You are going to Island Snow. There are blue birds at a lake and a mountain. First go to the lake, then to the mountain. and last to the GOLDEN MOUNTAIN. You have to get the Golden Snow from the GOLDEN MOUNTAIN to cure the king monkey, Contrae, because he is sick. At the island, you will meet the monkey you just saw turned into a goon by the evil wizard. Use the arrow keys to move. He will ask you a fraction problem. If you get it wrong, you will become mentally deformed. Good Luck!!!"

While the turtle begins drawing on the screen, Trevor looks over to Amy's computer screen, which displays a page full of turtle shapes. He points to one of her shapes and asks, "Why do you have a question mark?" then leans back waiting for Amy's answer.

Amy replies, "It's for my game. What do you have done so far in your game?"

On Trevor's screen, the turtle draws the outlines of a circle and fills the background with color. Trevor responds, "I have an island."

Amy retorts: "That's it?! Why don't you tell what's going on?" She then comments on the player figure placed on the bottom of the Trevor's screen: "You can't see that's you."

"How do you know?" Trevor asks.

Amy replies, "Because I can read it, if I look very close. It just doesn't look good because it lies on top of the line." Pointing to Trevor's screen, she suggests a new place: "I'd just put 'You are' here."

Even though Trevor challenges Amy's observation—"So? It works for me"—he selects the page with all his shapes. He starts working on the player shape by moving a cursor over a grid of squares. By deleting some of the squares, he changes the outline of his player's shape and explains: "I'm cleaning him up, so you can see the line."

When Trevor returns to his page with the island map, the new shape appears in the player's place. Amy congratulates Trevor on his improvement: "See, very good."

After Trevor has completed the revisions of his player figure, he looks again at Amy's screen and points to one of her shapes that shows six small squares, three of which are shaded in and comments, "This is one half."

Amy replies, "No, three sixths. I can't make them [the third graders] reduce. You know, I can't make them reduce it."

"Why can't you make them reduce it?"

"Because they don't know how to do it." Amy then starts playing her own game. She reads aloud the introduction: "You want to go to the home of Zeus but the map was ripped up by the Greek God Hades. All of the Greek Gods and Godesses have a fraction of the map. You are to go to the Gods and Godesses one at a time and they will ask you a fraction problem. If you get it right you will get a fraction of the map. When you get the whole map you will be at the gate of Zeus' home. The bull at the gate will ask you three hard fraction problems. If you get them right you will go inside Zeus' home and get to become the God or Godess of fractions and meet Zeus!"

As Amy continues to play her game, she answers one fraction question after the other and collects the different parts of the map. After she has correctly answered the third fraction question, she realizes that the third quarter of the map is not in the right place; it partially covers other parts. "This isn't right. This is messed up," she complains. She stops her program by pressing the control and S keys, then flips to the page where she can see all her procedures. She reads aloud the Logo code while scrolling down the page: "There is something wrong with SETSHAPE. SETPOSITION 60 50. It has to be 60 10."

Meanwhile, Trevor has been working on a new shape. Several times, he tries to get Amy's attention: "Now, does this look like a stick figure? Does this look like a stick figure? Answer me! Does this look like a stick figure?"

Amy briefly turns her head and says: "Yes. Shhh, I am trying to figure something out! SETSHAPE 11. SETPOSITION 75 10. Oh Oh." She slaps herself on the head: "75 10. I am on the wrong page! That's it! Heh, it worked." Amy and Trevor continue working on their games.

This book describes and analyzes the Game Design Project as a learning environment. It follows closely the game designers over a period of six months as they worked every day on designing their games. Constructionist theory motivated the project's implementation (Papert, 1980, 1990a, 1990b): A major emphasis was placed on the learners' being the generators, not the recipients, of knowledge. Children were given the opportunity to show and develop their abilities in design and to learn at their own pace while creating complex software products—games—for use by others (Harel, 1991; Perkins, 1986).

Constructionist theory guided the three distinct but mutually supportive inquiries of this book. The first inquiry is of a pedagogical nature and describes the Game Design Project as a constructionist learning activity. The intention is to provide one model of what students and teachers can do with computers in school. My second inquiry focuses on the nature of games and what they have to offer to education. Of course, any pedagogic agenda must include some theoretical foundation: I would neither expect nor want a reader to appropriate my model (or any other model) without insight into the cognitive and social processes through which it works. Hence, the last inquiry addresses the issue of students' thinking and learning in the context of a long-term enterprise. I state these inquiries here separately although they are interrelated and overlap each other.

My first motivation is to create one model for constructionist activities that can be applied to other learning contexts. I provide one model, namely game design, that describes the learning environment created together with the students and the teacher. It furthermore describes how programming can be integrated with other classroom work. This model assigns a particular epistemological role to work with computers in general and programming in particular. Programming is seen as a construction tool for personal expression and knowledge reformulation. Here I ask: Is the computer good for children? What things can children do with computers? What does programming tell us about children's learning, thinking, and feeling? (Papert, 1990a). Contrasting approaches often see computers as agents of change in schools and emphasize the computer's instructional function. In this context, educators and researchers ask questions such as: Does the computer promote or enhance cognitive growth? Does the computer produce mechanical thinking? The Game Design Project adopts the first line of inquiry and asks what children can learn when designing games and, similarly, what we can learn about them in this process. Learning through design considers programming not only valuable for its computational and technological knowledge, but also supportive of other learning. It proposes an environment in which the computer becomes a tool that allows children to express their personal thoughts and ideas in the form of a product.

My second motivation is to explore the issue of whether making games can become a powerful source for children's thinking and learning in the school context. Playing video games is an activity of great importance in children's culture and social life. The increasing presence of computers and video games in homes has initiated many discussions in the media and educational circles about their value and influence on children's affective, social, and cognitive well-being (Kinder, 1991; Provenzo, 1991). In this book, I address the issue of game playing from a different perspective. Instead of focusing on the effects of game playing, I look at children's learning and thinking while they are engaged in the process of game making. In the design of my research, I take advantage of the fact that children are interested in and knowledgeable about games. I capitalize on this interest by asking them to design games. I see programming games as a medium for children's personal and creative expression. This exploratory inquiry provides insights into what can be learned about children's fascination with games from the perspective of making them, and will help broaden the general discussion.

The third motivation is to investigate the development of students' thinking and learning in the context of a long term-learning enterprise. My theoretical interests go beyond what is directly relevant to practical work in the classroom. This effort is aimed at understanding what I saw and placing what I did in the context of other trends of inquiry. I am looking for insights into the different ways in which students engage in designing a complex piece of interactive software and what knowledge they build and connect to in this process. I combine two different approaches to describe and analyze these processes. First, when I focus on the evolution of the project as a whole, my purpose is to make sense of the different transition points students pass through as they concretize their ideas in the implementation of a game. One aspect of particular interest is the question of how students approached this task of designing a computer game during the extended time frame of the Game Design Project. Second, when I focus on the development of individual students, I describe in a microgenetic fashion how they worked on a daily basis, encountered and mastered challenges, and appropriated programming concepts and fractions. My conclusions here contribute to the understanding of how students individually develop in the context of such a learning enterprise. Diversity in styles of thinking and learning, also called *epistemological pluralism*, has been dealt with in other academic fields such as feminist theory (Gilligan, 1982), theory of science (Keller, 1983, 1985) and computational theory (Turkle & Papert, 1990). The attention to diversity therefore seems a necessary and timely inclusion in the analysis. The particular setting and time frame of the Game Design Project offer an opportunity to examine some of these issues and contribute to the ongoing process of defining further situations, objects, styles, and mindsets in constructionist theory.

These three inquiries motivated the investigation of making games for learning from distinct yet overlapping perspectives.

The six chapters of the book can be divided into three sections. The first section, chapters 1 and 2, introduces the research and theoretical issues, design rationale of the learning environment, and research methodology. The second section deals with the results of investigating the Game Design Project and includes chapters 3, 4, and 5. Each chapter can be read on its own, yet the students' whole learning experience can only be appreciated by combining the results of all three chapters. The third section, chapter 6, presents the discussion of results and conclusions.

Incidentally, the title of this book, *Minds in Play* is a play on words. Eleven years ago (1983), Elisabeth and Geoffrey Loftus, two psychologists, wrote a book called *Minds at Play* in which they investigated the effects of playing video games. I chose a variation on this title, because I investigated the effects of making games: children's minds were as much in as at play while programming their games.

# Chapter 1

# Learning Through Design:
# Review of Theory and Research Issues

In the Game Design Project, I created together with the students and the teacher an environment that used the design of computer games as a context for learning. Sixteen fourth-grade children worked for six months making games in Logo to teach fractions to younger students. They met every day for one hour and wrote in their notebooks about their ideas, plans, and designs. They also discussed issues related to fractions, teaching, programming, and games. They gave presentations to each other and met once a month with their prospective users. In addition, they created advertisements and cover designs and wrote documentation for their games. All taken together, the students designed a fully finished product.

It was my intention to implement the Game Design Project as one model of a constructionist learning environment—a place where children, each at their own pace, could learn through building a complex product for use by others. The following sections describe the research issues pursued with the implementation of this project, the theoretical foundation of the pedagogy learning through design, and a review of the research on learning Logo programming and fractions.

## RESEARCH ISSUES PURSUED
## IN THE GAME DESIGN PROJECT

This rich and multifaceted learning environment provided the background to examine different research issues: (a) individual styles and processes and transitions in learning; (b) social practices in a learning cultures; (c) the characteristics of "learning through design"; (d) making games as an approach to promote the learning of programming; and (e) constructing mathematical representations as a new approach to the learning of fractions. The following overview presents a more detailed discussion of each research issue.

## Individual Styles and Processes and Transitions in Learning

Learning and thinking over long periods of time touch on the fundamental question of how we come to know and learn about things. There are few longitudinal studies that document and analyze learning processes and developments of individuals or groups. Exceptions are, for example, individual cases such as presented in Lawler's (1985) book or the snapshot portraits of Piaget's children (1955). In most cases, learners are observed at different time points. Quantitative and qualitative differences may point toward the existence of different developmental patterns, yet the time period between the beginning and experienced learner has been unclaimed territory. Within the Game Design Project, I attempted to follow the students' learning and thinking as closely as possible for a period of six months. My investigation addressed what patterns, transitions, or shifts can be observed in the process of making games, and how individual students deal with the task at hand.

Within in the process of designing a game I intended to look at how individual differences are reflected in the product as well as in the process. Current school work usually presents assignments in a form that assumes that there is only one right way to do it. Designing an educational games, however, presents a task that has several possible solutions. I assumed that an open-ended task such as making a game will to allow for a variety of solutions and approaches to create the final product. Several theoretical approaches ask for the acceptance of multiple ways of knowing (see Gilligan, 1982; Keller, 1985; Turkle & Papert, 1990). I assumed that the diversity with which the students think about fractions, integrate them into their games, choose game ideas, and use a particular style of programming would be reflected in the processes of constructing or implementing features in their games. Furthermore, games elicit great diversity in how people think about them and how they play them. Gender differences seem to play a role in the choice of game themes. How will knowledge and skills become embedded in and connected to an individual's own personal system? Where and how in the game design process will I find evidence for the establishment of these connections? How consistent are these developments within each individual? These are some of the questions I hoped to answer with this study. I looked at individual cases in the design process as well as the whole class of students to identify the differences and the commonalties that emerge.

## Describing the Social Space of a Learning Culture

One purpose of the Game Design Project was to create a learning culture in which thinking and talking about fractions, games, and Logo would become the daily currency. Papert (1980) defined learning cultures as places where learning comes in natural and unobtrusive ways. One of his examples was the place where one best learns a foreign language—the country where the language is spoken every day. If France is one of the better places to learn to speak French, then a math land, or a mathematics culture, in which one can learn "to speak mathematics" would be a better place to learn mathematics. One of the pressing issues in education is to find ways to describe the design and implementation of a learning culture.

I intended to investigate which particular features define the Game Design Project and make it a learning culture. The routines and rituals of the project draw from another important source that has also been described as a place of learning—the design studio. In the traditional design studio, students learn knowledge about the domain, its rules and reasons; skills involved for producing design products, which include the deduction from general principles to concrete cases; and to reflect in action on what they have learned. The design studio, then, is a learning culture in which the objects to be designed—a house, a car, or a theory— become the focus and the objects of conversation in the designers' multiple roles as builders, testers, evaluators, and presenters. With the Game Design Project, I hoped to create such a learning environment resembling the design studio and answer the following questions among others: Which are the ways to describe the intervening variables of such a learning environment? How does a community of practice become established? What particular roles do the students, but also the teacher and the researcher, play in this context? What impact do they have on the growth of such a culture?

## Learning about "Learning through Design"

Learning through design proposes a new pedagogy in which children are placed in the position of producers of knowledge. Compared to most school assignments, design tasks seem rather open-ended in nature because the constraints are set by the designer. In the case of game design, this means that the students have to develop a game format that fulfills both the instructional purpose of teaching the user something and the purpose of engaging the player at the same time. The format of the game depends on whether one chooses a fantasy game, a game of chance, or a game of skill. The expectations about the format of instructional lessons can range from drill and practice to exploratory environments, depending on the students' chosen educational philosophy. The combination of the educational format with the game format poses a challenging task for the students. This challenge is counterbalanced by the fact that children are quite knowledgeable in games, more than adults, through their constant exposure and engagements.

One goal with the Game Design Project was to establish to which extent the design task engages the designer in the learning of the subject matter at hand, namely fractions. It is an open question whether designing computer games will facilitate the integration of fractions in the same fashion as did instructional design (Harel, 1988). In other words, to follow Perkins' request for creating a design environment for learning, the following questions need to be answered: How does the game design task promote an active and creative use of the knowledge by the learner? How central will the subject matter—fractions—be to the core of the game? Will game design allow for integration? These research issues deal with the nature of design tasks and opportunities offered to different kinds of learners for acquainting themselves with the content matter. A comparison of different design tasks would shed light on this issue.

## Learning Computer Programming as a Tool for Personal Expression and Knowledge Reformulation

In traditional computer courses in schools, the focus has been on learning programming constructs. One of the main assumptions is that the learning of programming would support the acquisition of problem-solving skills. Several limitations characterized previous studies that made these claims: Students did not program intensively, programming was not used in various and meaningful contexts, and the studies did not integrate the programming with the learning of other subject matters (Harel, 1988; Palumbo, 1990).

In the Game Design Project, these previous limitations have been taken into consideration. The project's implementation follows the constructionist view that technological knowledge such as programming is "reflective," valuable not only in its own right, but also capable of enhancing the learning of many other subjects. To design a computer game requires not only extensive programming in order to accomplish the task, but also the consideration of interface design issues, user input, and graphics, among others. In addition, it integrates the learning of other subjects such as fractions and allows children to express their ideas and fantasies. The crucial point of this study is then to examine very closely this reflective role of programming as a tool for knowledge reformulation and personal expression. A number of questions need to be asked in this context: Will the programming of computer games and the design of fractions representations in this context enhance the students' understanding of fractions? Will the programming of instructional sequences lead children to reflect on their own learning experiences and to revisit their own knowledge of fractions? Will these activities place children in a situation that requires them to design, plan, reflect, evaluate, and modify their programs on a constant basis? In which ways will the dealing with games stimulate the children's imaginations? All these questions examine the reflective value of programming. It is my assumption that programming games will allow students to acquire sophisticated programming skills in conjunction with other subject matters.

## Constructing Mathematical Representations for Learning

Representations of concepts and systems play a central role in the learning and understanding of mathematics. Fractions make extensive use of representational systems. Current educational practice assumes that manipulation of external representations, such as Cuisenaire Rods or fraction bars, results in mirrorlike representations in the students' minds. This assumption has been prevalent (although thoroughly questioned), largely because these particular representations are only some of many possible views of a mathematical concept (Cobb, Yackel, & Wood, 1992).

Students extract or construct features based on their prior under-standing and personal styles. The community of mathematics ed-ucators and psychologists has turned lately to the role that the construction of such external representations can play in the stu-dents' learning and understanding (Harel & Papert, 1990; Janvier, 1987; Streefland, 1991).

One of the premises of the Game Design Project is that learn-ing about representations and learning to build multiple represen-tations is important for the students' development of mathemati-cal understanding. It is assumed that the students' flexibility in translating between different representations of fractions (e.g., words, symbols, and pictures) is an indicator of their understand-ing (Lesh & Landau, 1983) and that this can be greatly enhanced by having students build their own mathematical representations. One objective is to investigate how children deal with and inte-grate fractions in their games and how this facilitates their think-ing and learning about representations. In Logo, for example, students can create in the programming process a procedural rep-resentation of the pictorial representations of fractions, among others. But will students who have to merge the domains of games and fractions into their programming of computer games also be engaged with the creation of different representations? What will be the students' conceptual development of fraction representations? In which contexts will the students situate or embed the fractions in their games? In which ways will students create and implement fraction representations? Hence, I compare the processes and products of different designers and see how they lead children to reflect on their own learning experiences and to revisit their own knowledge of fractions.


## REVIEW OF THEORY: LEARNING THROUGH DESIGN

The goals of this section are to introduce the pedagogy of learning through design, and to contribute new insights to the idea that making, building, or programming—in short, designing some-thing—is a good context for learning. For that purpose, I examine some specific cases of design theories in regard to their relevance to learning and the nature of its qualities. In this context, I explore the relationship between two bodies of ideas with very different origins: theories of design and theories of learning. Theories of design are formulated from concerns with "making" rather than "learning." Designing as an activity has rarely been considered an educational process per se. Hence theorists interested in the nature of design appear at first sight to have very different concerns from those of people interested in learning (Jones, 1980; Margolin, 1989; Rowe, 1987; Simon, 1969). The design theorist is interested in the final product as such; for the learning theorist, the product is a spin-off of the process that led to it. With these different interests, theories of design and theories of learning have little to say to each other.

My aim in the following sections is to describe the increasing convergence of both design and learning theories. This convergence began several decades ago with a common interest in models of information processing that served as a background for explaining the processes involved in learning and designing. This interest moved both theories closer to each other but still left a gap. Recent developments in learning and designing theories have placed the construction of meaning in the foreground. To see designers or learners as "constructing meaning" when they build, design, or understand something is to see them engaged in the same enterprise.

## Designing and Learning

In recent developments of theories of both learning and design, there has been a steady movement towards each other (for an extensive review, see Kafai, 1992). One of the overlaps between both sets of theories is their common interest in processes involved in learning and designing. In this context, both learning and designing have been conceptualized as processes of problem solving. This view of design sees the designer as a computer solving a constraint problem: to find a solution that satisfies the given conditions. Simon defined design very broadly as "changing existing situations into preferred ones" (1969, p. 129), involving processes such as planning, search, decision making, reasoning, and managing of mental resources. In the design process, two phases are distinguished: analysis and synthesis. Analysis examines a problem and splits it up into its components, whereas synthesis focuses on bringing all the different parts together to a solution. In both analysis and synthesis, designers develop strategies, such as modularization or generating alternative solutions, when dealing with complex design tasks (Akin, 1984; Kalay, 1987; Rowe, 1987).

A similar movement has been seen in learning theories that are based on models of information processing (e.g., Anderson, 1983; Newell & Simon, 1972). This approach of information processing provides working theories of how learning and thinking processes are involved in the building of knowledge structures. This focus on problem-solving processes in learning and designing has reduced the distance between the two areas. Even when design theorists pay attention to the process, they may be more interested in different aspects of it than the learning theorists are: the design theorist is generally interested in how the process contributes to the product, and the learning theorist is interested in how it contributes to the producer.

The use of information-processing approaches in both theories seems to work well in the realm of well-defined problems where the boundaries of the domain are clearly defined, a solution is possible, and tools and means are known (Simon, 1969). Yet, when faced with an ill-defined or open-ended situation, as applies to many learning and most design problems (Rittel & Webber, 1984; Simon, 1984), information-processing approaches are at a loss. They do not take into consideration how problematic situations first have to be construed. Schön emphasized this point, speaking from the perspective of the designer:

> But with the emphasis on problem solving, we ignore problem setting, the process by which we define the decision to be made, the ends to be achieved, the means which may be chosen. In real-world practice, problems do not present themselves to the practitioners as givens. They must be constructed from the materials of problematic situations which are puzzling, troubling, and uncertain. In order to convert a problematic situation to a problem, a practitioner must do a certain kind of work. He must make sense of an uncertain situation that initially makes no sense. (1983, pp. 39–40)

Hence, modern trends in both design and learning theories place the construction of meaning at the core of this process, thereby moving the two closer to one another. One group of design theories focuses on design as the process of making sense of things and building relationships between the designer and the object (Krippendorf, 1989; Robinson, 1986; Waldman, 1982). This approach carries its interpretation from the original meaning of "design," which goes back to the Latin *de* + *signare*. Here, *design* means making something; distinguishing it by a sign; giving it significance; and designating its relation to other things, owners, or users—a meaning that has been lost in many other design theories. Krippendorf (1989) described *design* as a

> circular cognitive process that may start with some initially in-comprehensible sensation, which then proceeds to imagining hypothetical contexts for it and goes around a hermeneutic circle during which features are distinguished—in both contexts and what is to be made sense of—and meanings are constructed until this process has converged to a sufficiently coherent understanding. (p. 13)

Krippendorf and others, therefore, suggested that we think about design as the process of making sense of things. The relationships that people build with objects or situations constitute the core process, and not the object or artifact itself. Constructing meaning is a relationship through which designers sort out what objects mean to them or to others, where they selectively connect features of an object and features of its context into a coherent unity.

This kind of language is far less removed from the concerns of the educator or the learning theorist. These theorists of design give the designer a more personal role. They talk about how a designer comes to understand not only the objective constraints but also the subjective meanings; design is even seen as looking for or building meanings. Learning, too, could be described as looking for and building meanings. Constructivist theories see the building of relationships and meaning as the core process of learning (Piaget, 1964). Thus, my inquiry into learning through design is at the point of intersection where ideas of development are converging in these two areas. This places me in the company of several other investigators who have seen similar connections (Harel, 1988, 1991; Papert, 1980, 1990b; Perkins, 1986; Turkle & Papert, 1990; Wilensky, 1991). We all share the premise of constructivist approaches to learning, but from different angles.

## Learning Through Design

Constructivist theories assume that knowledge is actively constructed and reconstructed by the learner out of his or her experiences in the world. An extension of this knowledge construction
process is provided by constructionist theories that place the
building or making of actual objects at the core of this knowledge-
construction process, in which learners establish diverse relationships or connections (Papert, 1980). Learning through design offers one example of a constructionist approach in which children
can be engaged in meaningful learning activities. This approach
integrates different features drawn from different sources: designs
as objects-to-think-with (Papert, 1990a), construction of personalized connections (Wilensky, 1991), diversity in building relationships and approaches to learning (Turkle & Papert, 1990), time
frame in learning (Lawler, 1985; Papert, 1993), design nature of
knowledge (Perkins, 1986), learning instrumental to a larger intellectual and social goal (Harel, 1988), learning through design as a
complex integrative process (Schön, 1983), and design activities as
powerful occasions for learning (Harel & Papert, 1990). Taken all
together, they offer a rich and complex description of the processes and characteristics involved in learning through design.

To provide students with this kind of learning experience, it is
important to engage them in constructive activities that are
meaningful to them (Papert, 1980). Papert stressed the role of self-
constructed interactive objects such as computer programs that
may, in turn, become objects-to-think-with "when the learner is
engaged in the construction of something external or at least
shareable . . . a sand castle, a machine, a computer program, a
book" (Papert, 1990a, p. 3). The construction of objects-to-think-
with is personal, because each learner chooses different objects
and builds in this process different relations with them. Papert
(1980) made this point clear when he referred to his own objects-
to-think-with (gears) and how they might not be appropriate for
someone else:

> A modern-day Montessori might propose, if convinced by my
> story, to create a gear set for children. Thus every child might
> have the experience I had. But to hope for this would be to miss
> the essence of the story. I fell in love with the gears. This is

something which cannot be reproduced to purely "cognitive" terms. (p. viii)

Design involves the building of artifacts or objects. The design of a program or a computer game can turn into an object-to-think-with that engages students' thinking, feeling, and learning. Not only the object itself, but also the construction of personalized connections to objects, to each other, and to oneself are part of this process (Wilensky, 1991):

> [C]oncreteness is not a property of an object but rather a property of a person's relationship to an object. Concepts that were hopelessly abstract at one time can become concrete for us if we get in the "right relationship" with them. (p. 7)

> It is through people's own idiosyncratically personal ways of connecting to other people that meaningful relationships are established. In a similar way when learners are in an environment in which they construct their own relationships with the objects of knowledge, these relationships can become deeply meaningful and profound. (p. 13)

Wilensky proposed here that the process of "concretizing" describes the concreteness of an object through the person's relationship with it. Design opens the door to focusing on the processes that can foster the building of such relationships. A game design idea starts out in the abstract and becomes concrete as the designer creates and implements its different features. In this process, the game designer becomes more and more involved with his or her own ideas and renders the project personally meaningful. From this perspective, learning through design emphasizes that learning is most effective when children build personal, meaningful objects.

Another feature of learning through design is the diversity in building relationships and approaches in learning. Students may approach the design task from different ends, choose to emphasize different aspects of the design, and think about it in different ways. One way to characterize the differences in thinking and approaches to solving a problem came from Turkle and Papert (1990). They proposed a distinction between planners and bricoleurs. The former describes an approach to programming that maps out context, content, and structure of a design at the beginning; in the latter, the design of the game emerges in the process of implementing it:

> The bricoleur resembles the painter who stands back between the brush strokes, looks at the canvas, and only after this contemplation, decides what to do next. For planners, mistakes are missteps; for bricoleurs they are the essence of a navigation by mid-course corrections. For planners a program is an instrument of premeditated control; bricoleurs have goals, but set out to realize them in the spirit of a collaborative venture with the machine. For planners, getting a program to work is like "saying one's piece"; for bricoleurs it is more like a conversation than a monologue. In cooking, this would be the style of those who do not follow recipes, but instead make a series of decisions according to taste. While hierarchy and abstraction are valued by the programmers' planner's aesthetic, bricoleur programmers prefer negotiation and rearrangement of their materials. (p. 136)

Turkle and Papert used the term *epistemological pluralism* to question prevalent views in the culture that emphasize a progression from concrete to abstract as reflecting intellectual growth. They suggested that we need to reevaluate concrete thinking, whose core features are proximity and a close relationship to objects. With the request for diversity comes also the demand for activities that are rich enough to allow for different styles of thinking and learning. As Simon (1969) pointed out, a unique feature of design problems is that they do not have a single right solution; there are always alternatives. For example, in building a house, it would seem improbable that each student would construct the same building. My intention with the Game Design Project was to offer a design activity that had multiple avenues for students to approach a complex problem, build a game around the idea of fractions, and find a personal solution.

Another equally important aspect of building relationships and allowing for diversity is that learning takes time. Papert (1993) made a strong argument for the need for time in learning. Using himself as an example when trying to learn about flowers, he reflected on the quantity and quality of his learning encounters:

One contact was not enough to heat up the previously chilly region of flower names. By now as I write two years after the lupine incident, there has been dramatic change in my memory for flower names. It is as if flower names now find a place to stick in my memory. But this did not happen all at once and by the time it did, much more than the ability to remember names had changed in my relationship with plants. (p. 97)

The relationships established to subject matters do not come "all at once," but emerge gradually over time. The process of making connections or associations is crucial to building relationships and cannot be achieved through rote learning. As Papert asserted:

I do not pretend to know exactly how the process of growth happens. But I do know how it did not happen: I tried to commit to rote memory the characteristics of each group taken from a book but repeatedly made mistakes. Perhaps if I had been interested only in these three flowers I would have been able to memorize their formal characterizations. But if I turned to other plants and came back to the three yellow ones I'd get something wrong again. Slowly something different from rote memory of defining characteristics developed sets of associations or connections. (pp. 102–103)

Papert summarized the importance of the time frame for learning to discover and build connections:

My learning had hit a critical level in the sense of the critical mass phase of a nuclear reaction or the explosion of a population when conditions favor both birth rate and survival. The simple moral is learning explodes when you stay with it: a full year had passed before the effect in my mind reached a critical level for a manifestly exponential explosion of growth. The more complex moral is that perhaps some domains of knowledge such as plants are especially rich in varied connections and particularly prone to give rise to explosions of learning. (pp. 103–104)

In the conception of my game design activity, I addressed the issue of time in learning and broke with the traditional concept of a "curriculum unit" (used in the sense of focusing three to four

weeks on one topic). This extended time frame proved to be crucial for many students in their programming and design development of their games.

In relation to Perkins, learning through design assumes his
key insight of the design nature of knowledge. Perkins (1986) distinguished between knowledge as design and knowledge as information, the latter reflecting the use of knowledge as passive,
isolated, and in storage. One of his central arguments was that the
ways we think, learn, and teach knowledge should reflect the active use and its connections with other knowledge elements. He
defined design as "a structure adapted to a purpose" and stated
that much of human activities is directed toward "shaping objects
to purposes," which reflects one of the main ideas of design—to
create artifacts. Perkins used design as a framework for the
learning process—a framework that facilitates thinking and
learning as the designer formulates on what the purpose of the
knowledge is. These questions can be used as guidelines to direct
inquiry and exploration as well as the more goal-directed process
of solving problems and evaluating results. These questions help
the learner to establish connections between what is known and
what is learned, and ask for what purpose it is learned. In
Perkins' terms, creating a design environment for learning means
providing a framework in which asking these questions can be a
meaningful activity. The context of designing a game provides an
analytical framework for students to engage actively with different issues at hand: to ask themselves what is difficult about fractions, how to represent fractions, what theme to choose for their
games, how to integrate fractions into the game context, and how
to accomplish the programming for their games. Furthermore, it
emphasizes the importance of the students' learning how to make
a product instead of just producing short answers.

Most specifically of all, my investigation of learning through
design is closely related to Harel's work (1988, 1991). In the analysis of the Instructional Software Design Project, Harel described
how the interplay of cultural and individual aspects in the construction of interactive objects such as computer programs affected children's thinking, learning, feeling, and socializing. One
of my starting points was to examine the generality of her conclusions by looking at a related but different kind of design project.
In the Game Design Project, students were involved with fractions
and programming by creating external representations of their
thoughts, ideas, and feelings in their games. It was also my inten-

tion to reexamine and extend Harel's theoretical methods. For that purpose, I focused on design as an object of study as well as a context for study, and I examined how the designer designs as well as how the designer learns other things while designing. Accordingly, I paid more attention to the modern literature about design theories.

One feature of Harel's learning through design is that it makes learning instrumental to a larger intellectual and social goal: Products such as instructional software or educational games are explicitly designed for use by others. Shannon, an architect, pointed out "[t]he difference between simply doing something and designing something is in the level and quality of commitment and consideration given to the task, and how one feels in accomplishing it . . . Designing on the other hand cannot be automatic. It always forces critical thinking, judgment—personal involvement" (1990, p. 40). Designing, then, puts students in charge and engages them in a continuous dialogue with their own ideas and with the ideas of intended users and co-designers. Students assume control in their learning through asking questions, gathering information, and putting all this to work by creating an educational game for younger students to learn about fractions.

Furthermore, Harel saw learning through design as a complex integrative process. In Harel's view, design not only integrates problem solving but also problem finding and reflection. Schön (1983; see also Goldschmidt, 1988, 1990a, 1990b) also called design a reflective conversation with situations, materials, or media. In the Game Design Project, a possible description of a game designer could be that he or she starts by finding a problem, then continues with parts of the solution, tries to make sense out of it, considers how to reframe the situation, and continues with problem solving. This description displays succinctly a paradox inherent in design (but also in learning): between making something new and different, and having at the same time something that is understandable and recognizable. In continuously reframing the unfamiliar situation back and forth through different cycles of appreciations and actions, the designer comes to a closer understanding of the new situation. As Schön phrased it: "the unique and uncertain situation comes to be understood through the attempt to change it, and changed through the attempt to understand it" (1983, p. 132). In this process, the designer constructs a particular, personal relationship to the artifact, which undergoes changes as the process continues. This process seems to stop when an artifact has been created; yet it never ends, because existing design solutions are used and reused in new design situations.

One result of Harel's work was to provide a definition of design activities as powerful occasions for learning. Design is a vehicle that promoted the learning of other subjects, such as programming and fractions. Harel and Papert (1990) used the following criteria to characterize design tasks that are suitable for learning: integrativeness, appropriability, and evocativeness. Design activities are integrational when they facilitate interdisciplinary work and thought (see also Feurzeig, 1988; Pea, 1988; Perkins, 1986). Learning in this situation transcends subject borders. In the Game Design Project, learning about fractions was integrated with learning about programming, how to teach others, interface design, and many other aspects. Through this integration, this assignment acquired more of the quality of real design situations. This integrative nature of design has also been recognized by designers: "Designing is planning and making connections. It is putting people and things and situations together" (Shannon, 1990, p. 40).

Another criteria is to the appropriability of design materials, which requires that these materials be accessible to students' different styles of thinking and learning. The diversity of project themes, working styles, and entry paths in design activities was described and discussed by Resnick (1991).

A third aspect is to the evocativeness of materials: Can they be carriers of multiple meaning? Materials such as Cuisenaire Rods, which are often used to introduce students to rational-number concepts, are one of many possible representations (e.g., pattern blocks, fractions bars). Design activities, in contrast, emphasize that students create their own representations and can choose whichever representation they consider appropriate (Harel, 1991, pp. 339 - 340). Instructional design (as in Harel's study) is one example of design for learning that worked well with fractions because the students' understanding of fractions was closely related to their representational characteristics. However, we have little experience and evidence regarding the synergistic nature of other design contexts and activities. The investigation of game design is, therefore, an effort to find out about the impact of different design contexts.

Learning through design, as the pedagogical rationale for the design of my project, incorporates all the features just discussed. Students use their knowledge in an active fashion when designing a product—their educational games—for the use of others. The design of educational computer games puts the students in charge of their own learning by letting them decide what theme to choose for their game, what features of their games to implement at what time point, and what questions to ask about fractions. It allows students to approach this task in their own personal way. One central aspect is the length and intensity of involvement in this project. Students were engaged over an extended period of time in designing and implementing all features of their games. This aspect gave students time to mess around and to build relationships in special ways, not only with their games but also with the subject matters involved. An open question for this study was the extent to which game design would integrate the content matter to be learned, namely fractions. I summarize the most important research findings on Logo programming and fractions in the next section.

## REVIEW OF RESEARCH: LEARNING OF LOGO PROGRAMMING AND FRACTIONS

The learning through design approach in the Game Design Project integrated subjects that are usually studied in isolation in schools. Students learned about two distinct areas: Logo programming, the tool used to create the games, and fractions, the subject of the game. In the following sections, I review and discuss major research and educational concerns about these areas.

### Research of Logo Programming

Programming was brought into schools to introduce students to a broad scope of concepts from computer science and artificial intelligence. Learning to program was expected to enhance the acquisition of critical thinking skills. Many claims have been made about what it means for young students to learn Logo programming (for an extensive overview, see Harel, 1988). A review of the early research results showed that the transfer effects of programming in terms of logical thinking or better problem-solving skills were questionable, and that students experienced a wide range of difficulties with Logo programming and "cognitive transfer" from Logo programming (Carver, 1987; Clements, 1985; Heller, 1986; Kurland & Pea, 1983; Pea & Kurland, 1984; Perkins

& Martin, 1985; Solomon & Perkins, 1987). Harel (1988) identified several explanations for these early results. First, most studies focused on the instruction of formal aspects of programming concepts. Logo was not "integrated" as a tool of expression and representation in a wide range of contexts that were meaningful and personal to students. Students learned programming for the sake of programming in "isolated" contexts. Second, in most studies, students did not program extensively. Rather, students programmed only for short periods of time. Third, most students in early studies wrote short programs and, therefore, never experienced the many complex facets of programming as they exist in the real world. Palumbo's (1990) literature review of studies on learning programming led to the same conclusion: Length and intensity of exposure have a major impact on the success of programming instruction. At the same time, researchers have also started to investigate other aspects, such as creativity involved in programming (Clements, 1991) and how programming experience influences students' perceptions of themselves as learners (Burns & Hagerman, 1989).

Many recent studies have taken the concerns of length, treatment intensity, and subject integration seriously. Two distinct approaches to using Logo in the schools have emerged: as a tool for learning problem-solving skills and as a tool for knowledge reformulation and personal expression.

*Programming as a Tool for Learning Problem-Solving Skills.* In the last five years, some research, has focused on teaching specific problem-solving skills through the use of Logo (Au & Leung, 1991; Dalton & Goodrum, 1991; Many, Lockard, Abrams, & Friker, 1988; Swan, 1991). Students are taught very specific instructional sequences in the context of programming; these sequences are based on theoretical models of the particular problem solving skills. In one of the first studies, Carver (1987) used a production model to explain the debugging skills necessary to be learned in programming. Carver first analyzed the various skills involved in debugging before designing her instructional component. Her instruction provided many explicit occasions for the students to learn and apply the necessary debugging strategies. Clements (1990) adopted Sternberg's theory of metacognitive abilities for the instructional design of executive abilities. He modeled an intensive course of 26 weeks (in total 78 hours), in which different components such as planning, representing, debugging, and problem solving were explicitly taught by embedding them in programming assignments. Another example is Lehrer, Guckenberg, and Sancilio's (1988) approach, which chose to focus on control theory as a model for teaching epistemic and metacognitive aspects in debugging tasks. Epistemic aspects consider any error an opportunity to learn, whereas metacognitive aspects focus on possibilities for generalizing the learning experience to other situations. Two features are central to these studies: Students spent considerable time working on tasks, and instruction was geared toward teaching specific planning and problem-solving strategies. The general trend in these studies indicates that students show mastery of both the instructed skills and of transfer tasks.

*Programming as a Tool for Knowledge Reformulation and Personal Expression.* In her research, Harel (1988) introduced a new approach to learning and using Logo programming. Her approach, following Papert's (1980), emphasized the importance of time commitment, intensity of programming, and a rich context, so that programming could become meaningful and personal to students. In the Instructional Software Design Project (ISDP), children were asked to design software to teach fractions to younger students. Instructional design proposes a complex project that engages students over a long period of time. The complexity of the task becomes clearer if one considers that designing instructional software involves more than the mere production of code: structuring the control flow of the program, maintaining the connections between different procedures and pages, and designing the interface for the prospective user. In addition, students must consider different ideas for fraction representations, how the representations can be implemented in Logo, and pedagogical concerns, among many other issues. One example is Debbie's house scene (as described on page 24; see the section on learning fractions).

In several aspects, Harel's study stands out in contrast to previous Logo research. First, it used Logo for knowledge reformulation. Here, programming was used to learn concepts of another subject domain—fractions. Second, it used Logo for software design as opposed to programming. Software design encompasses more than the mere production of code as emphasized in programming. Third, it used Logo for the purpose of personal expression as students express their ideas, thoughts, and feelings regarding fractions in designing fractional representations in Logo. Using programming as a tool for knowledge reformulation and expression, then, fulfills two purposes: Students learn Logo programming in this process, and students' use of Logo benefits other learning, such as of fractions and software design.

*Programming Games in Logo.* My research addresses these issues of using Logo programming as a tool for knowledge reformulation and personal expression—for the purpose of teaching fractions in the context of a game. Instructional game design proposes a complex project—the programming of games—that engages students over a long period of time. Two claims are associated with designing games in Logo. First, learning programming is instrumental to a larger intellectual and social goal: to design a game intended for the use of others to learn about fractions. Second, the particular learning context of programming a game will encourage the students to learn more programming.

The first claim focuses on the instructional feature of the game design: Students are asked to design a game for others to learn about fractions. Here, students are engaged with a teaching dialogue that involves showing and representing examples. By placing themselves in the role of a teacher, they focus on what needs to be explained and represented in examples. In this process, the designer evaluates in continuous cycles what he or she thinks is difficult for third graders to understand and how to show and explain it. In their programming, student designers will focus on designing fraction representations and providing explanations. These aspects are also characteristic of the learning experiences of students in Harel's (1988) study.

The second claim focuses on the game features and what they contribute to the programming process. Dealing with games will stimulate children's imagination. It places children in a situation where they think about a story context in which the game takes place, the goal of the game, what the features of the main character and other participating figures are, and how their appearances in the game will be choreographed. The game designer has to spend a great deal of time and programming effort to simulate the sequence of events—and the learning experience lies precisely in this process.

One concern that could be raised about young students designing computer games is that this task will be too hard for them. Computer games (as they are currently available on the market) emphasize interactive features such as animation, sound, and feedback. One solution could have been to provide programming primitives such as animation modules or decision branching in order to facilitate the programming of sophisticated game features. However, Logo allows programming these game features in relatively simple ways and it incorporates sound, graphics, color, and text into one document. The actual challenge for the game designers is to combine and integrate the instructional content and game context. I hypothesize that these activities will place children in a situation that requires them to design, plan, reflect, evaluate, and modify their programs on a constant basis. The expected outcome is that these diverse activities will allow students to acquire more sophisticated programming skills in conjunction with other subject matters.

### Research of Learning Fractions

Fractions play a central role in the mathematics curriculum in elementary schools. Fractions, ratios, proportions, decimals, and percentages are some of the subconcepts of rational numbers, one of the first number systems to which students are introduced in school. National assessments of students' knowledge and ability to perform arithmetic operations on fractions show that most students seem not to have learned the mathematical content presented (e.g., Carpenter, Matthews, Lindquist, & Silver, 1984; Hart, 1981; Post, 1981). In the research literature, various reasons are given for students' problems dealing with fractions: for example, the dominance of the whole number system (Behr, Wachsmuth, Post, & Lesh, 1984), the complex operations necessary to understand and manipulate fractions (Noelting, 1980; Piaget & Inhelder, 1951), and students' incorrect generalizations from everyday experiences (Kieren & Nelson, 1978; Kieren, Nelson, & Smith, 1985; Wearne-Hiebert & Hiebert, 1983). As a way of solving this problem, a variety of instructional methods, longer periods of precomputation work with fractions (Lefevre, 1984; Payne 1984; Skypeck, 1984), or even postponing the introduction of fractions into secondary school (Hart, 1981) have been suggested.

In recent years, mathematical educators and psychologists have paid increasing attention to the role of representations for mathematical concepts and how they can assist the learner in the construction of internal representations (e.g., Harel, 1990; Janvier, 1987; Kaput, 1987, 1991; Richards, 1991; Streefland, 1991; von

Glasersfeld, 1987, 1991). The terms *to represent* or *representation* do not have a unified meaning in the literature. Instead, they cover a variety of aspects ranging from individual internal cognitive representations to formal mathematical concepts and external physical embodiments (Goldin, 1991).

*The Role of Representations in Understanding Fractions.* Representations have been used in various forms to help students understand fractions. One way to think about the different approaches is to describe them on a continuum. On one end of this continuum, students are provided with external representations of a concept with the hope that the internal representations constructed by the students reflect in a mirrorlike way the main characteristics of the external representation. For example, teachers try to help students in their conceptual understanding by using manipulatives such as Cuisenaire Rods, fraction bars, or fractions clocks as different pictorial and concrete representations of fractions (Hiebert & Wearne, 1986; Silver, 1986). The research of the Rational Number Project (Behr, Post, Silver, & Mierkiewicz 1980; Post, Behr, & Lesh, 1982; Wachsmuth, Behr, & Post, 1983) argued against the use of one particular representational model for teaching, because students must learn to break away from standard representations in order to move flexibly among different modes of representations. They identified the students' difficulties in transferring among the different modes of fraction representation as one major impediment. Further support for this observation is that students use given models or manipulatives, such as number lines, in different ways. The same features of a manipulative can be interpreted in different ways, depending on students' prior understanding of fractions (Tierney, 1987).

The other end of the continuum emphasizes the learner's active role in constructing external representations of fractions as a way to build internal representations. Little research has been done in the area of students making or constructing their own representations as a way for students to reflect on their current knowledge and to build their understanding of fractions. Janvier, Bednarz, and Belanger (1987) reported that there is neither encouragement nor pedagogical methods in school for students to construct and exploit their own mathematical representations. The results of their research indicated that "children could not produce, on the spot, effective representations to help explore or solve the problems" (p. 120) when they compared different groups of students working with representations or other means to solve problems. However, they found that the teaching of particular strategies helps students become more efficient in the production and use of representations for problem solving.

Two recent studies have promoted learners' building representations for understanding fractions: Harel (1988, 1991) and Streefland (1991). Each researcher used different pedagogical interventions, goals, contexts, and procedures. Because there are few other studies in the same spirit and because these two are relevant for the approach used in my study, I present them here in greater detail and discuss their commonalties and differences.

*Constructing Representations in the Constructionist Perspective.* Harel involved students in building representations as they designed instructional software. In her study, she asked a class of fourth-grade students to design instructional software in Logo to teach fractions to younger students. During the four months of the project, each student produced a piece of software. Harel claimed that the resulting pieces of software embedded students' personal thoughts about what was important and difficult to learn about fractions, and what kinds of representations were helpful for understanding. The assumption behind instructional design is that students become deeply involved and gain deeper understanding of the representational structure of fractions through the process of constructing, programming, and explaining their own representations. The following example shows one particular student, Debbie, in the process of working on her fractions representations. (Fig. 1.1 is a screen printout of Debbie's work.)

> It is Wednesday afternoon at the Hennigan Elementary School in Boston. In a large and open area of Project Headlight, 17 fourth-grade students and their teacher are grouped around two large circles, each composed of about a dozen or so desktop computers. Debbie sits at her computer swinging her legs, her hands poised over the keyboard, completely absorbed into her programming project. To her right, Naomi programs letters on the computer screen in different colors and sizes . . . . Debbie shows Naomi her programming code. "It's a long one," she says, running the cursor down the screen, very proud of the 47 lines of code she has programmed for her "HOUSE" procedure. She

then exits the LogoWriter editor to run her program for Naomi, who moves her chair closer to Debbie's. In a slow quiet voice, pointing to the pictures on the screen, Debbie explains to Naomi: "This is my House scene. I designed all these shapes; each one equals one half. In the house the roof has two halves, the door has two halves, and I will add to this scene two wooden wagons and a sun. I'll divide them into halves too . . . . The halves, the shaded parts, are on different sides of the objects. You know you can use fractions on anything . . . . Do you like the colors?"

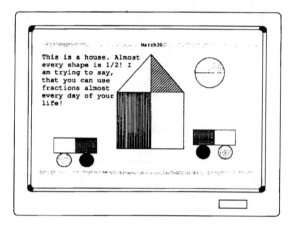

FIG. 1.1. Screen printout of Debbie's House scene.

Note: From "Software Design as a Learning Environment" by I. Harel and S. Papert, 1991, *Constructionism*, (p. 48) Norwood, New Jersey: Ablex Publishing Corporation. Copyright 1991 by Ablex Publishing Corporation. Reprinted by permission.

The idea of representing the halves of different objects, the objects being "regular human things" in a real-life situation, is Debbie's. In the final version of her teaching software, an explanatory text will accompany the pictures on the screen: "This is a house. Almost every shape is one half! I am trying to say that you can use fractions almost every day of your life." Debbie is the only child in the class who has designed and programmed this particular type of lesson to her younger students. She is very clear why she designed it: to teach other children that fractions are more than the strange numbers on school worksheets. She has discovered that fractions can be all around us; they describe objects, experiences, and concepts in everyday life. While

Debbie is working on this representation, the only advice she asks of her friend is about the colors: "Do you like the colors?" Naomi tells her: "It's nicer if all halves are in the same color." They negotiate for a while, but Debbie doesn't agree: "No, it will be boring." Naomi and Debbie continue to work on their projects with their keyboards in their laps. (Harel, 1991, p. XV–XVI)

Debbie's process of creating this particular fraction representation shows her engagement with various details such as the content of the representation (i.e., one half) and the little design details (i.e., colors), which all contributed to deepen her understanding of fractions. It also provides a picture of the design project's social texture, which became a learning atmosphere for students discussing and exchanging their ideas.

*Constructing Representations in the Realistic Perspective.* Streefland developed a two-year-long curriculum providing material related to fractions in real situations for a class of fourth graders. The primary aim of the realistic approach was the insightful reconstruction of the fraction system corresponding to the historical learning process. Students' learning activities were based on constructing different representations of given or individually chosen problems. These curriculum activities incorporated different goals: to initiate students' personal constructions of representations; to intertwine different areas of the rational number concepts, such as fractions with proportions; and to demonstrate the usefulness of symbols, diagrams, or context models as representations. For example, he asked students to create representations of the sharing of various things: pancakes, chocolate bars, or pies. Students then illustrated how a certain number of these things might be shared among a certain number of people. Next, they drew and partitioned a variety of shapes, comparing them and adding fractions to them. Students also wrote numerical expressions corresponding to their particular drawings. Primary emphasis was placed on the students' own productions, using those as a means for the students and their classmates to reflect on chosen approaches and to think about different solutions. The following excerpt of a situation given to the students might serve as an example of how students worked in this learning environment:

The Fractured Family decided to eat one day in a pancake restaurant. They choose De Smickel in Soest, a pleasant place for the whole family. . . . [A picture of the restaurant was included.] At the table next to the Fractured Family there was a party of eight—a woman with seven children. It was a birthday party. The woman ordered six pancakes with eight dishes. No wonder, for the pancakes turned out to be enormous, more than enough for eight people. Dividing them proved to be no problem. How might that have been done? Fran drew on the paper [see Fig. 1.2]

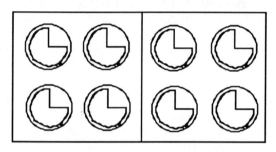

**FIG. 1.2.** Fran's drawing of fractions.

Note: From *Fractions in Realistic Mathematics Education* (p. 71) by L. Streefland, 1991, Dordrecht: Kluwer Academic Publishing. Copyright 1991 by Kluwer Academic Publishing. Reprinted by permission.

and wrote that this was the same as three pancakes for four people, only, "Now it is doubled." Margareet still needed the support of names, and called the woman with the children 1, 2, . . . , 8. She used these symbols to indicate the pieces each person received and drew [on the paper; see Fig. 1.3].

Marja wrote: "First each one gets a half and then a quarter." Kevin used his paper to actually distribute pieces. He relegated the pieces of each pancake systematically and fairly to the eight dishes by drawing connecting lines.

In general, the students' earlier experiences with "divide three pancakes among four children" were called upon here. Five students divided the pancakes exclusively into quarters, and eleven students made halves and quarters. No one divided them into eighths. (Streefland, 1991, pp. 71–72)

FIG. 1.3. Margareet's drawing of fractions.

Note: From *Fractions in Realistic Mathematics Education* (p. 72) by L. Streefland, 1991, Dordrecht: Kluwer Academic Publishing. Copyright 1991 by Kluwer Academic Publishing. Reprinted by permission.

A common feature of the problems used in Streefland's curriculum is that the teacher supported students' approaches to creating representations while they were solving a problem. The same problem context, such as a restaurant visit, was used repeatedly for a variety of different fraction problems.

*Comparison of Constructionist and Realistic Approaches to Building Fractions Representations.* Both Harel's and Streefland's studies emphasized the importance of students' constructing fractions representations as a means of gaining access beyond the algorithmic surface knowledge of fractions. In Harel's study, the basic claim was that students come to a deeper understanding of fractions through programming their own representations, choosing their themes and contexts, and doing all this for the purpose of teaching others; whereas in Streefland's study, students were brought into contact with fractions by designing representations of familiar situations. The connection to everyday situations was important in both studies: In Streefland's study, the "Fractional Family" provided different situations for students to create representations for explanations. In the same context, students' own experiences were integrated as examples and topics of discussion. In Harel's study, the students chose and designed their own representations according to what they thought were the most important and difficult aspects of fractions to learn. In both studies, a particular classroom atmosphere was created that facilitated personal constructions (i.e., students felt free to produce their own representations as valid examples) as well as exchanges among the class members (i.e., the dialogue among class members contributed to the learning experience, directly and indirectly).

There are several differences between these studies. The pedagogical approaches differ mainly in terms of who generates the representations: the teacher or the student? Harel chose the situation of being an instructional software designer to motivate the students' thinking about fractions and perceived difficulties in learning them. Streefland, in contrast, gave students a set of materials and explored different aspects such as seating arrangements, food distributions, different symbolic representations, and notations. The goal in Harel's study was to open the door for the students' own personal and affective connections to fractions; whereas the foremost goal in Streefland's study was to acquire formal propositional aspects (students generating their own rule system based on their experiences with representations and their manipulations).

One of the major and possibly fundamental differences between these two studies relates to the process of building representations. In Streefland's classroom, students used paper and pencil to construct their representations and solve problems. Later on, as they became more sophisticated, they also resorted to diagrammatic representations of the problem. Harel's students, in contrast, used Logo to program procedural representations. Because this aspect is relevant to the context of my study, I explain briefly what it means to create procedural fractions representations in Logo. In order to program, the student has to be aware of certain characteristics of the fraction. For example, to divide a square into fourths, the student needs to know that the division parts have to be equal. Harel claimed that this level of involvement is not attained when the student works with paper and pencil. Instead, in Logo, the child programs and sees the movements of the turtle as it draws the fractional representation on the screen. This is what Harel called a *procedural representation*. In addition, using Logo to program fractional representations allows students many representational modes: Fractions in Logo can be represented by symbols, numbers, words, and real-world representations such as pictures or actions. This avoids the focus to one particular representation. Through this approach, Harel integrated isolated subject domains of programming and mathematics into her research design.

*Constructing Fraction Representations in Games.* The results of this comparison are important for my study. Harel and Streefland both argued that students gain a deeper understanding of fractions through creating and manipulating representations, compared to groups instructed by other pedagogical means. They both showed the relevance of everyday objects and situations for learning. The contexts differed: In Harel's study, students worked on fraction representations for the purpose of creating instructional software. In Streefland's case, students created representations to solve assigned problems in a story context. In my research, I describe a different context for students to construct and program fraction representations—game design. Instructional design proved to be a meaningful avenue for young designers to explore fractions, because they could reexperience the teaching situation from the other side, that is, being the teacher and designer—the person in control. I hypothesize that designing computer games will put the students in the shoes of teachers and that the student game designers will spend many hours working on the fraction representations in the context of their games. In the programming process, students can create procedural representations of fractions. But the open question is whether students will also do this when they have to merge the domains of games and fractions for an instructional purpose. The issue under investigation is whether the combination of designing and programming educational games and creating representations of fractions in Logo, as well as explaining and teaching about the fractions and their representations, will be successful in helping students to overcome their difficulties.

This concludes my overview on the principles of learning through design. In the following chapter, I describe how these principles guided the implementation of the Game Design Project and the methods employed to describe and analyze the interactions that took place among the students, and the learning of Logo programming and fractions that was integrated in the design of the games.

# Chapter 2

# Creating and Researching the Learning Environment

In this chapter, I describe the Game Design Project, a learning and research environment. In this project, students had extensive time, frequent occasions, and freedom of choice to engage in the design of their computer games. My intention was to investigate this project as a complex learning environment as well as a pedagogical intervention. I employed an integrative research methodology to capture and evaluate the students' learning and cognitive processes. The evaluation objectives and methods used are described in more detail in the last section of this chapter.

## CREATING THE LEARNING ENVIRONMENT: GAME DESIGN PROJECT

The Game Design Project provides one example of how to implement the principles of learning through design with a class of fourth graders and their teacher. I created a learning environment that emphasizes time, diversity, integration, choice, and conviviality as its main principles (Falbel, 1991; Harel & Papert, 1990; Resnick, 1991).

The project addressed the time issue in learning and broke the traditional concept of a curriculum unit (used in the school sense of focusing on one topic for three to four weeks). Students worked on the design and implementation of their games and related materials during a period of six months. In this project, diversity was emphasized because individuals with diverse styles of thinking and learning had the opportunity to build their own connections with the subject matters at hand and to experience themselves as competent learners and thinkers. Several subject matters, such as programming, language arts, mathematics and arts, were integrated in one larger project enterprise over a long period of time.  Different media and activities, such as computer work (documentation, game), drawing and graphical design (advertisement, cover design), audio and video (advertisement), and personal presentations (to class members and visitors), were combined to give students multiple opportunities to express their ideas.  As we see later in the description of the various activities, students could choose different themes for their games and engage them in their own personal ways.  The extended time frame of the project allowed students to investigate a variety of avenues.  Many aspects of this project were convivial as the environment, and the activities were open and welcoming to the ideas and interests of the students.

## The Learning Environment: Game Design Project

The following descriptions of the Game Design Project are meant to provide a sense of the project evolution and its major aspects throughout the school year.

*A class of 16 fourth-grade students were engaged during an extended period of time in the design and production of educational games to teach fractions.*

The project started in the beginning of March 1991 and continued after the summer in a second phase until mid-November.  The class turned into a design studio for one hour a day, when students worked on their projects.  In general, students spent the first five minutes writing their plans and ideas in Game Design Notebooks before they went to work on their own computers for 45 minutes.  These notebooks contained sheets that included a number of prompts to stimulate the students' ideas and plans.  As students worked on their games, they were allowed to walk around to see and discuss each others' projects.  Students then returned to their classroom and wrote again about their experiences.  During the six months of the project, students spent approximately 92 hours on programming and 20 hours on other activities and school materials related to the project.

*Students were involved in designing a finished product: an educational software game with packaging, advertisement, and documentation.  The project emphasized the highly integrative nature of design enterprises*

*consisting of a series of parallel, interconnected activities in different*
*subjects on and off the computer.*

Because the purpose of this project was to create a finished
product, students also worked concurrently in their art classes on
cover designs for packaging their games. In May, two months after the beginning of the project, students began the art activities;
this work continued over seven sessions until October, when the
last designs were finalized. In their language arts class they
worked on advertising aspects of their product and writing the
documentation for it. In October, students concluded their advertisement unit with a homework assignment to produce the advertisement of their game via any media of their choice. The students
had covered the basics of propaganda and advertisement by
reading books and looking at different examples. Students had a
few days to complete this assignment. They had to include one or
two means of advertisement but were free to choose whatever
medium or approach. Toward the end of the project, students
started working on their documentation.

*Focus sessions presented opportunities for the teacher and researcher to*
*initiate discussions around issues and ideas relevant to all game*
*designers. These sessions were examples of the general discourse in the*
*project initiated by the teacher and researcher.*

The daily sessions on the computer and in the classroom were
complemented by 10 focus sessions in which students discussed
issues related to games, their projects, their ideas or difficulties
about fractions, and how to represent them. The focus sessions
were designed for brainstorming and discussing issues of interest
for all students. Several of these focus sessions were dedicated to
discussing issues around games. In these sessions, students gave
different examples of games where one could learn something and
brainstormed together about how to create educational games
around fractions. Other focus sessions concentrated on design issues, such as creating opening pages and giving credits. For example, students looked at TETRIS and LogoWriter as two examples of credit designs. Further focus sessions were conducted
around the theme of fractions: discussing the questions of what
was difficult about them and how one could represent fractions
for other students. The content and sequence of focus sessions

were not planned in advance. Instead, these sessions were arranged through discussions with the students.

*The project provided opportunities for the game designers to discuss their project with their classmates, and to show it to their potential users and a wider public. These interactions were examples of the discourse initiated by the students.*

The Game Design Project created a culture of presentations and exchanges on its own. All these sessions were arranged in discussions with the students. For the evaluation sessions, the third graders visited the classroom every month to evaluate and discuss the older students' game projects. While the game designers were working on their games at the computers, the younger students would walk around, look at different games, try them out, and answer questions. In addition, in May, students began presenting their games in "show and tell" sessions to their classmates. In these sessions, a student other than the game designer would play the game. Students discussed all kinds of issues related to fractions, color, interface design, and program speed. The game fair was the last of these presentations where all students presented their games and related products to other students of the school, to parents, and to other visitors.

Of further importance was the research site at which the Game Design Project took place. Many features would have been difficult to implement in a school that did not have daily guaranteed access to computers. My description of the project's features and activities have to be seen in context within the particular arrangements of Project Headlight.

**The Research Site: Project Headlight**

The study took place at Project Headlight, which is located at an inner-city public elementary school in one of Boston's low socioeconomic neighborhoods. To the outside, the school presents a gray concrete facade with small windows that give limited views of the neighborhood. The section of the school devoted to Project Headlight has a narrow and windowless entrance that leads into an open space, lit by natural light and surrounded by classrooms. Project Headlight operates as a "school within a school" with approximately 220 students from first through fifth grades, including advanced, regular, bilingual, and special education classes. As well as Project Headlight, the school has an ethnically mixed population of students: approximately 49% Hispanic, 20% African-American, 11% Caucasian, and 20% of mixed backgrounds.

Project Headlight was started during the 1985–86 academic year, when a collaborative project involving the Boston Public Schools, the Media Laboratory at the Massachusetts Institute of Technology (MIT), and the International Business Machines (IBM) Corporation began laying the foundation for a model school of the future. A committee of MIT scholars and Boston School Department officials selected the school after inviting proposals from all of Boston's public elementary schools. The design of Project Headlight, which was mainly inspired by Seymour Papert (1986), anticipated a near future in which technology would be used far more extensively than anything currently used in schools. Although Project Headlight uses technology extensively, it is not defined as a technology project. Instead, it is an education project. It explores new approaches to learning and teaching in the context of a technology-rich school environment.

The project uses more than 100 computers in classrooms, in open areas at the school, and in teachers' homes (see Fig. 2.1). All of the computers in the school are connected to each other in a local area network. One special feature of this elementary school is its open architectural structure. Before the project started, this feature was virtually unused by the school. The most prominent view of the two-story central space is the arrangement of four clusters of computers. Each cluster has 17 computers arranged in a circle, with screens facing out. The clusters of computers are called *pods*. The arrangement of the computers in groups emphasizes further the cooperative and communal aspects of learning: As students come and go from their classrooms, they have a chance to walk along the computer pods and see the projects of other students. Another particular feature of Project Headlight is that all students have access to the computer pods for at least one hour per day. In contrast to most other computer labs, Project Headlight students rarely use educational software packages. Instead, they work with LogoWriter, a programming environment with multimedia features, to create their own software.

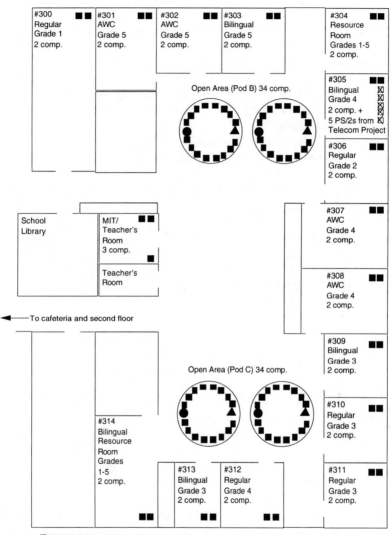

**FIG. 2.1.** Floor plan of Project Headlight.

During the first years of Project Headlight, MIT personnel were in continuous contact and exchange with the Headlight teaching faculty and participated in several ways in school-related activities. They supported the teachers responsible for instruction in computer skills such as Logo, word processing, and integration of the computer into the basic curriculum. They gave some special courses including music, animation, and technical design and invention using Logo. The Fractions Project provides a good example of the kind of interactions between Project Headlight and MIT. It presented an unusual approach to learning and problem solving in the domain of mathematics using rational numbers as its focus. From December 1985 to April 1986, Sylvia Weir, Seymour Papert, and others from MIT had weekly meetings with the 15 teachers during which they discussed new ideas for integrating Logo into the study of fractions. The teachers were inspired by those meetings to explore different ways of integrating Logo into their traditional fractions unit. One teacher, Mrs. Minda, expressed this impact on her own learning and teaching when she talked about these lunch meetings:

> But I really find that this year, I was paying much more infor-
> mation, myself, to concepts related to fractions. For instance,
> when you multiply a fraction by another fraction . . . I never re-
> ally concentrated much on that . . . I'd say it is clearer to me this
> year and that's surprising . . . I always felt comfortable with
> math, with numbers but never deeply examined some of that. It
> was wonderful to understand and illustrate through Logo what
> it means to multiply 2/3 by 2/3!! The whole idea of REPEAT ing
> itself, or of itself, is clearer to me now. I could see kids
> understand it better through using Logo. (in Harel, 1986, p. 64)

The special atmosphere created among the teachers and the researchers is important for the later analysis and discussion of my research. The Instructional Software Design Project (Harel, 1988), in which one of my control classes participated, grew out of the discussions and experience of the Fractions Project and was conducted with Mrs. Minda's class of fourth-grade students, who designed software to teach fractions to younger students.

Between the Instructional Software Design Project in 1987 and the year 1991, when my study took place, the major features of Project Headlight remained the same. The physical arrangement of the computers in four circles in the open areas did not change. The ratio of one computer for every two students was also the same. Some more computers had been added to the initial configuration; they contained the LEGO/Logo activities that circulate on a monthly basis around the 15 classrooms of Project Headlight, and the visual telecommunication stations that maintain exchange with a partner school in Costa Rica.

In addition, in 1988, a second initiative called the Science and Whole Learning Workshop (SWL) was started from the MIT Media Lab's Epistemology and Learning Group with teachers of various Boston-area schools to direct attention to teachers' learning and thinking for promoting change in schools. Four teachers from Project Headlight participate in the SWL's monthly meetings and summer workshops. But in the last four years, the Headlight teachers have been for the most part operating the environment and managing the network on their own. As some of the original Headlight teachers left the school for other positions, several new teachers joined. The MIT personnel are mostly involved in research activities with different teachers and classes. Many teachers have created and implemented their own project activities involving Logo (see a collection of teacher reports edited by Harel & Kafai, 1993). The teaching faculty of Project Headlight meets at the beginning of every school year to share the computer access times for their classes. The daily access to and use of the computer time is taken for granted by all Headlight teachers and integrated into everybody's time plan throughout the school year.

## RESEARCHING THE LEARNING ENVIRONMENT

The really interesting problems in education are hard to study. They are long term and too complex for the laboratory and too diverse and non-linear for the comparative method. They require the longitudinal study of individuals (Hawkins, 1973, p. 135, quoted in Streefland, 1991).

What Hawkins called the "really interesting problems in education" are the ones that focus not only on the product, the outcome of the learning, but also on the processes that describe the different paths taken, extended, or abandoned by the learner. Few longitudinal studies investigate children's learning and thinking over extended periods of time. But in addition, other factors such the interaction among students and the surrounding culture need to be considered; the long-term study of individuals is not the only focus.

The Game Design Project represented such a longitudinal study in which students were observed for a long period of time while creating a culture of their own. Sixteen students worked daily on the computer for a period of six months designing a complex piece of software for use by others. In the beginning of the project, it was unclear whether students would be able to design a computer game and, if so, what their personal solutions to this design task would be. The context of design placed students in the mode of thinking simultaneously like planners, problem solvers, designers, and teachers over and over again. Designing a game presented students with a task that was ill-defined and open-ended, in contrast to most school assignments or education research (e.g., Dreher & Oerter, 1987; Kreitler & Kreitler, 1987; Pea & Hawkins, 1987).

To document the ongoing activities, interactions, and cognitive processes of students in such a learning environment requires an adequate methodology. Given the breadth of the learning experience, I used different methods to collect data from the students' learning of programming and fractions during the projects' activities. The purpose of this integrated research methodology was to compensate for the shortcomings of one methodology with the strengths of the other (see also Kidder & Fine, 1987; Light & Pillemer, 1984; Maxwell, Bashook, & Sandlow, 1986; Mischler, 1990):

- The data collection included quantitative and qualitative methods to assess different aspects of the students' learning. This allowed me to place individual students' progress in a larger context and to use the results of case studies to illuminate the general trends.
- The data collection was longitudinal. It documented the students' continuous progress on a daily basis during the six-month period. This method of detailed and prolonged data gathering allowed for a more fine-grained data analysis of development and learning. It was also cross-sectional, because it compared the students' learning with groups instructed by other pedagogical means.

• The data collection integrated multiple instruments of observation and assessment: paper-and-pencil tasks, videotaped interviews with students and teacher, video-taped classroom discussions and computer observations, and impressions from outside sources.

The research objectives of the project's evaluation were twofold: for one, to investigate the Game Design Project itself as a learning environment. The extended time frame of the project presented an opportunity for me as a researcher to observe and investigate individual students' learning and thinking in a meaningful and challenging context. At the same time, I was able to follow the development of a particular project culture as the students' games progressed. The second objective was to investigate the Game Design Project as a pedagogical intervention. I placed the game designers' learning of Logo programming and fractions in relation to that of students instructed by other pedagogical means. In the following two sections, I present the questions and methods employed to evaluate aspects of the Game Design Project: (a) the individual and project evolution and (b) the comparison with groups instructed by other pedagogical means.

**Individual and Project Evolution in the Game Design Project**

In this part of the evaluation, my focus was directed at the individual student and the project culture at the same time, in order to situate and integrate the individual's thoughts, ideas, and actions in a context. Questions that guided the documentation of the students' activities, interactions, and processes in this learning environment included: How is the individual student approaching the game design? How do the students' games change over time? What are the students learning about programming and fractions? How does their knowledge of programming and fractions develop? The evaluation aimed at following the students in the Game Design Project and their development of design styles, of knowledge of Logo programming, and of fractions during the making of their computer games. My experimental class was a fourth-grade class of 16 students, 8 girls and 8 boys of mixed ethnic background. As the students were working every day on their project, they each established a personal portfolio composed of their notebook entries, program log files, interviews, and observations, which I describe next in more detail.

*Notebook Entries.* Students kept designer notebooks and wrote in them about their plans and designs at the beginning and at the end of the computer sessions. The goal was twofold: On one hand, I wanted students to participate in the data collection and the research process; on the other hand, the notebook writing was intended to help students in their game design by documenting and reflecting their plans, thoughts, and ideas. The designer notebook consisted of sheets designed to prompt students to think about their plans, problems, and changes. The section PLANS FOR TODAY asked students to write their ideas and provided place to sketch out designs. The sections PROBLEMS I HAD TODAY and CHANGES I MADE TODAY were reported at the end of the computer session when students also wrote about their PLANS FOR TOMORROW. Students collected these sheets in personal ring binders that they also could take out to the computer pods. In the month of April, students suggested changing and extending the prompt PROBLEMS I HAD TODAY to THINGS I DID AND PROBLEMS I HAD TODAY. Most students complained that they did not have problems every day (at least did not perceive them as such) and therefore could not write about anything. At the students' request, the notebook writing did not continue after the summer break.

*Program Log Files.* Each student saved the LogoWriter pages related to their games at the end of every day. Each file was saved under its current date (e.g., MAR28 for March 28); in the case of multiple files, these were distinguished by letters (e.g., MAR28a for March 28 LogoWriter page GAMES). These daily file savings captured the daily progress of the students' programming and designs and provided backups of program files in case of loss. For example, I collected 57, 65, and 66 program files over 92 total project days for the three case studies (Amy, Albert, and Sid, respectively).

*Video Interviews and Observations.* Every day throughout the project, I videotaped interviews with students and their interactions at the computer and in the classroom. For these purposes, I used the video camera in different modes as described by Harel (1988): (a) as the silent observer to document ongoing events in the classroom or in the computer areas, (b) as a holistic interview recorder to document interviews with students and to capture their verbal as well as physical behavior, and (c) as a note taker to document events or interviews. Students also used the video camera to document interviews or interactions and for the production of their own projects: (a) as a interview recorder to interview each other or the researcher, (b) as a documentation recorder to record on-going events, and (c) as a production tool to create the commercials for their games.  On several occasions I also interviewed the teacher about the project, asking about her impressions  both in general and about particular students.  Very often, these conversations were initiated over lunch as we were working together solving programming problems, or when we were discussing future activities of the project such as focus sessions and the evaluation meetings with the third graders.

*Field Notes.*  In addition, I kept notes about my interactions with the students, which I accumulated in a diary format.  Those notes served multiple purposes: They documented interactions I had with students that were not tape recorded, they kept track of class events and other school-related activities, and they were a repository for my general reflections on the overall progress of the project or a student.

All of these different sources were used in the analysis of the project evolution and the students' thinking and learning.  From each child alone, I experienced and collected not one isolated aspect but many different facets over an extended period of time, all of which influenced my perceptions and conclusions.  In the presentation of the project evolution (chapter 3) and the case studies (chapter 4), I decided to condense certain sections in the game developments and to present summaries of them instead.  My reasons for doing so were particular periods during the project and in each case that I wanted to emphasize.  As a common denominator for the project evolution and the case studies, I used the students' design progress during the months of the project.

## Comparative Evaluation of the Game Design Project

The intention of the comparative evaluation was to understand better the many issues involved in the learning-through-design pedagogy and its possible benefits for learning, schooling, and cognitive development.  Many questions could be raised about what the students learned during or as part of their participation.  For the purpose of this evaluation, I decided to focus my investigation on two areas: Logo programming skills and fractions.  The evaluation was designed to compare the students who participated in the Game Design Project (the experimental class) and their learning of fractions and Logo programming skills with students who learned these skills through other instructional means (the control classes). The four classes that were included in this evaluation came from the same school and the same grade level, and participated in the same mathematics curriculum, but the teachers of each class used a different approach for integrating Logo programming with fractions. From now on, I label the classes who participated in the evaluation according to their different Logo programming instruction to facilitate the distinction between them. Therefore, the experimental class is also called Game Design; control class 1, Instructional Design; control class 2, Integrated Logo; and control class 3, Isolated Logo. Figure 2.2 provides an overview of the differences between the experimental and control classes.

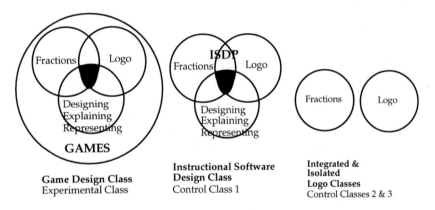

FIG. 2.2. Overview of classes selected for the evaluation.

*Student Characteristics.* The four classes, the experimental and three control classes, were all fourth-grade classes from the same inner-city elementary school. In addition, all classes were Advanced Work Classes (AWC) whose selection criteria had not changed in the previous four years. The selection of students for AWC classes is based on their performance on the Metropolitan School tests given by the end of the third grade, and evaluations written by their homeroom teachers. Furthermore, parents must to be motivated to place their children in these classes, because they usually have to dedicate time to visit different schools and talk with different teachers prior to their decision. The placement in AWC classes also means that many students come from other

schools (public or private), and join this school for the fourth and
fifth grades only.

The number of students per class varied slightly (see Table
2.1). In total, 67 students were included in the evaluation. The
distribution of girls and boys was nearly equal in all classes, except for control class 2, which had more girls than boys.

**TABLE 2.1**
Distribution of Gender in the Participating Classes

| Group | Girls | Boys | Total |
|-------|-------|------|-------|
| Experimental Class<br>**Game Design** | 8 | 8 | 16 |
| Control Class 1<br>**Instructional Design** | 8 | 9 | 17 |
| Control Class 2<br>**Integrated Logo** | 11 | 7 | 18 |
| Control Class 3<br>**Isolated Logo** | 9 | 7 | 16 |

**TABLE 2.2**
Distribution of Ethnicity in the Participating Classes

| Group | Caucasian | Hispanic | Asian | African/<br>American |
|-------|-----------|----------|-------|----------------------|
| Experimental Class<br>**Game Design** | 7 | 4 | 0 | 5 |
| Control Class 1<br>**Instructional Design** | 9 | 0 | 2 | 6 |
| Control Class 2<br>**Integrated Logo** | 6 | 1 | 3 | 8 |
| Control Class 3<br>**Isolated Logo** | 0 | 16 | 0 | 0 |

The distribution of ethnicity reflects the variety of back-grounds (see Table 2.2). Although the AWC classes have, in general, a higher percentage of Caucasians than do other classes in the school, the classes still maintain the features of an inner-city elementary school. The third control class was a bilingual class. I decided to include this class in the comparison because these students were selected based on their performance on the Metropolitan test. Furthermore, their regular mathematics and programming instruction and testing were usually conducted in English only. I assumed that for these reasons this particular feature would not impact the results of the comparison.

*Logo Programming Instructions*. All four classes began learning Logo in September, but they used different approaches. The experimental class and Control Classes 1 and 2 (which were all part of Project Headlight) used the computers daily. In general, they programmed shorter projects in LogoWriter, ranging from one to four weeks. Because most of the students were new to Project Headlight, students were also introduced to Logo commands in these initial projects. In contrast, Control Class 3 met only for one hour per week in a computer lab and worked on short programming assignments. To provide a sense of students' knowledge of the programming language Logo before the evaluation period, I included a copy of a programming project in the introduction of Amy's case (see chapter 4).

The evaluation period started in February, before the character of the Logo programming instruction and integration into the curriculum began to change significantly for some of the classes. I now describe briefly the ways in which the four classes differed in their Logo instruction from March through June (the end of the school year):

• The experimental class (game design) was part of Project Headlight. Students worked 45 to 60 minutes each day on a project over a period of four months. In this class, students integrated the programming of Logo into their design of educational games to teach fractions.
• Control Class 1 (instructional design) was part of Project Headlight. Students worked 45 to 60 minutes every day of the week on projects at the computer. These students designed instructional software to teach fractions to younger students, and spent four months designing software.

• Control Class 2 (integrated Logo) was also part of the Project Headlight. Students worked 45 to 60 minutes every day of the week on the computer. The projects usually incorporated specific curriculum aspects such as science or literature. These students worked on most projects no longer than a month. The major difference between the students in the experimental class and those in Control Classes 2 and 3 was the purpose, structure, and length of projects.

• Control Class 3 (isolated Logo) was located in the same school, but the students used Logo only once a week in the computer lab for 30 to 45 minutes. They worked on pro- gramming exercises assigned by the teacher and were graded based on these. These students did not work on projects nor did they integrate programming into other subjects in their curriculum. They learned programming in the context of a computer literacy program. This class was included because it represented the "standard" approach to learning programming in most schools.

*Mathematics Curriculum.* All classes participated in the regu- lar mathematics instruction. The mathematics instruction for the control classes was divided into low-, medium-, and high-level students and each of the teachers instructed one group throughout the year. In contrast, the students of the experimental class were instructed as a whole group by the same teacher (the teacher of the experimental class was also in Harel's study [1988], where she taught one of the control classes). The fractions unit of the school's mathematics curriculum started for all classes in February and covered the following topics during the following two months (approximately 40 hours): algorithmic operations (such as adding, multiplying and dividing), decimals, mixed fractions, and per- centages. The teaching of the experimental and control classes was handled in the same fashion: Teachers provided introductions to units, then students completed assignments and worksheets. The teachers used a variety of methods and manipulatives, such as Cuisenaire rods, pattern blocks, and fraction machines. All the teachers got their training in the United States and had been part of the Boston Public School system for at least 10 years.

The students of both design projects did not receive any addi- tional formal instruction compared to the students of Control Classes 2 and 3. However, during the design project time at the computer pods, there were many occasions for discussing issues related to fractions. These interactions and conversations were initiated either through the questions of the students themselves, instructional screens that they had designed, remarks that class-mates made, or questions from the teacher or researcher. For ex-ample, Jero, one of the game designers, created a screen with the question of $2/3 + 2/3$ and gave as the right answer choice $4/6$. As Trevor, one of his classmates, pointed out the mistake in his answer, we discussed together with Jero how he could figure out the right answer, how he could create representations for it, and what explanations he could provide for the third graders. Sometimes, I asked more general questions, such as whether the students thought a third grader could understand a specific prob-lem. Ideally, the mathematics curriculum could have been inte-grated within the Game Design Project. This would have meant that the whole mathematics curriculum would have had to be reconceptualized. I decided against this solution, because I felt that the documentation of the project alone placed high demands on me as a single researcher.

*Evaluation Procedures.* In order to establish a baseline, the Game Design class started in February with the pretests and in-dividual interviews. Their regular fractions unit began in March, and lasted two months. The posttests and individual interviews were given in June, four months after the pretests. The Game Design Project continued after the summer break until November. The time frame of the evaluation and the tests was chosen to en-sure compatibility with the selected control classes from Harel's previous study (1988) that I included in my analysis. Both data sets shared important features. First, the goal in both studies was the same: to assess the students' knowledge before and at the end of the experimental project. Second, I had been introduced to the methods of data collection and test administration by Harel, the researcher who collected the data of my three control classes. The same tests were given to the students of the experimental and con-trol classes during their regular class time. For all classes, experi-mental and control, the teachers introduced the test activities to-gether with the researcher, and was present during the test admin-istration. Figure 2.3 summarizes the time frame and evaluation procedure used in the selected classes.

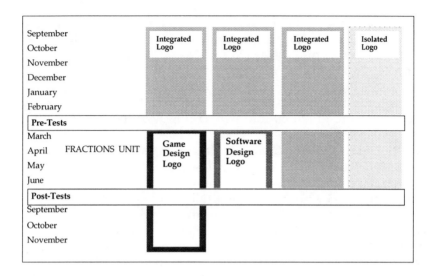

FIG. 2.3. Overview on Evaluation Procedure of the Participating Classes.

*Evaluation Instruments.* The students' knowledge and skills of Logo programming and fractions were evaluated with different instruments. Table 2.3 gives an overview of the tests and interviews that were used for the pre- and posttests. Each test is described next in more detail.

TABLE 2.3

Overview on Pre- and Posttests and Interviews Used in the Evaluation

| | | | | |
|---|---|---|---|---|
| Pretest | Fractions | • Rational Number Test | 50 minutes | 43 questions |
| | | • Boston Public School Test | 10 minutes | 12 questions |
| | | • What Is a Fraction? Interview | 20 minutes | n/a |
| | Logo | • Logo Test | 50 minutes | 6 questions |
| Posttest | Fractions | • Rational Number Test | 60 minutes | 60 questions |
| | | • Boston Public School Test | 45 minutes | 40 questions |
| | | • What Is a Fraction? Interview | 20 minutes | n/a |
| | Logo | • Logo Test | 50 minutes | 7 questions |

*Logo Test.* For the assessment of the Logo programming skills, I adopted a paper-and-pencil test developed by Harel (1988) for her study, to ensure compatibility with the control classes that had taken the same test. This test assessed a number of different components of Logo programming knowledge: listing of Logo commands and quality of explanations, categorization of Logo commands, execution of Logo code, simplification of Logo code, and input parameters in Logo. Most of these questions were open, and students were asked to generate lists on their own. Students were given 60 minutes to complete the test in both the pre- and posttest versions.

*Rational-Number Concepts Test.* For the assessment of the students' fractions knowledge I selected a subsection of the Rational Number Test as developed by Lesh, Landau, and Hamilton (1983; Cronbach-alpha reliability is 0.881, p. 289). This paper-and-pencil test dealt specifically with the students' ability to translate between different modes of fraction representations. The pretest version included 43 items in multiple-choice format, whereas the posttest version had the complete set of 60 questions, including the pretest questions. Students were given between 45 and 60 minutes to complete this test.

*Boston Public School Mathematics Test.* I also chose questions from the Boston Public School curriculum reference test, which focuses on students' computational skills with fractions (no reliability score available). The Math Level 4 curriculum reference test is given to all fourth graders at Boston public schools at the end of the school year. This test has 40 questions in multiple-choice format, covering curriculum units such as multiplication, division, and rational numbers in various formats (calculations, word problems, interpretation of diagrams). In my pretest version I included only 12 items that dealt specifically with rational-number concepts. The posttest version contained all 40 items. The students had up to 60 minutes to complete this test.

*What Is a Fraction?* In this interview, which lasted approximately 45 minutes, I asked students a series of questions. The first set of questions explored students' general knowledge of rational numbers and their abilities to express themselves using this concept. I asked such questions as: What is a fractions? Do you like fractions? Can you give me a good example of a fraction? If you close your eyes and think about fractions, what comes to your mind? My main purpose was to investigate how students thought and felt about fractions. The second set of questions dealt with more specific problems. For example, I asked students to construct a representation of 1/2 or 2/3 using available material on the table, such as Cuisenaire rods, pegs, dough, and fraction bars.

I also showed students a number of different configurations using Cuisenaire rods and pattern blocks. For example, I constructed a rectangle consisting of five small red rods and one large orange rod (where 5 red rods equal 1 orange rod). Then I asked students if they could tell me what fraction of the rectangle the orange part was. After a student gave an answer, I usually asked them to explain to me "how they figured out" the answer and probed their understanding by proposing, "But another student told me that the orange part could be 1/6. What do you think?" These interviews were videotaped.

To ensure the reliability of my results, a research assistant was independently involved in coding the test results. For the Logo test, the research assistant and I used Harel's coding scheme for the pre- and posttests of the experimental class. After the independent coding, the results were compared. Divergences in coding (in eight cases) occurred primarily in the category of evaluating the quality of explanations of Logo commands. This resulted in a total agreement of 92%. To ensure compatibility with the scoring in Harel's study, I also coded the Logo pretest of the instructional software designer class (which is Control Class 1 in my study) and compared the results of my coding with her results. Both the Rational Number Concept and the Boston Public School Math Curriculum tests had multiple-choice formats.

## Summary of Research Objectives Pursued in the Game Design Project

The Game Design Project presented a rich and multifaceted learning and research environment. I used and integrated various research methods to capture the complexity of this environment. Two objectives were pursued in the project's evaluation. The first objective was to describe the Game Design Project itself, from the perspective of the class as well as of individuals. My goal was not to provide precise models of the students' conceptual development of fraction knowledge or Logo programming; rather, I wanted to provide rich descriptions and interpretations of what students were doing. On one hand, I documented the project development as a whole, which allowed me to study students' thinking and learning over long periods of time. On the other hand, I analyzed the development of all students and build case studies for in-depth views. The daily log files of the programs and the notebook entries paired with interviews and observations provided the backbone for each case construction, because those were the most continuous data available from each student.

My second objective was to analyze the Game Design Project as an pedagogical intervention. For that purpose, I collected data from the assessments conducted before and after the project participation. The design of this evaluation was influenced by the existence of a larger set of data from a previous study (Harel, 1988). This allowed me to investigate how the design task situated students' thinking and learning of Logo and fractions in a more systematic fashion and to relate my results to existing research. I compared in which ways students changed their understanding of the Logo programming language and fractions. One of the claims to investigate was whether programming and designing fraction representations would provide a different entrance for students to build a connection to their fraction knowledge.

In the following chapters, I report the results of the evaluation. In chapter 3, I present the results of evaluating the whole class of game designers in respect to the development of their game ideas and design styles. Chapter 4, is an extension of the previous chapter and reports in more detail the individual development of three students—Amy, Albert, and Sid. The comparative aspect of the evaluation is covered in chapter 5.

# Chapter 3

# Project Evolution

During the 92 days of thinking, designing, programming, modifying, and playing their computer games, the students were
involved in many activities and touched on many issues. The
extended time frame allowed for a closer investigation of the
project trends and development. As the students started
implementing their game ideas, they tested their programming
skills and they learned about the feasibility of their game ideas
and different aspects of the design process. It is worthwhile
investigating transitions or shifts  and whether they occurred
throughout the class or whether they were only experienced by
individual students. Over time, two kinds of developments could
be observed: One kind was of incremental nature as reflected in
the daily growth of the game designers' programs of a few lines of
Logo code; the other kind represented shifts in the nature of the
games as well as the approach chosen by the designers. I chose
two areas for my analysis of the project development: the
students' game ideas and their design styles. These are of
particular interest because little is known about what ideas
students have about games and about the process of making
games.

My first choice focused on what kind of game ideas students
generated and implemented. In the beginning, most students concentrated on creating a context, or a world, in their games in
which to ask the fraction questions. Some students also created
microworlds in which fractions were central to the game idea. As
the game implementation moved along, many game designers
shifted to a more story-oriented format in their games. The narrative theme underlying most computer games was one of the unexpected findings in this study.

My second choice focused on how students approached the challenge of designing a game. Here, I examined the beginning phase when students formulated their game ideas and what difficulties they expected or perceived. Because not all the students shared the same game ideas (in fact, there were 16 different game ideas—as many as there were designers), they also chose different approaches to handle this task. A further important point in the development was when students "got stuck" for the first time and examined the possibilities of changing designs. A look along the time lines provides a better sense of how students came to handle the complexities of this task and find a solution they might not have anticipated in the beginning.

## THE EVOLUTION OF GAME IDEAS

My analysis of game ideas must be preceded by the recognition that we do not know very much about children making games. A search through the psychological and educational databases of the last 10 years showed not one entry of learning through making games instead of playing games. Incidentally, game design has also not been discussed by the few projects that use games in an educational context. We know more about different aspects of children playing games. The increasing presence of computer and video games in homes has initiated many discussions in the media and educational circles about their value and influence on children's affective, social, and cognitive well-being (Provenzo, 1991). Most of the research efforts have focused on identifying the psychological processes involved when playing video games (Dominick, 1984; Morlock, Yando, & Nigolean, 1985; Silvern & Williamson, 1987) and discussing the pros and cons of game playing (Harris & Williams, 1984; Selnow, 1984). It is, however, unclear to what extent the results of these studies (which investigated video games as they were available on the market 10 years ago) apply to the new generation of video games currently available. The primary difference between the "old" and "new" generation types of games is the complexity of interactions as well as their thematic embedding.

Notwithstanding the absence of updated research, children's attraction to video and computer games has not changed (Baugham & Clagett, 1983; Greenfield, 1984, 1990; Loftus & Loftus, 1983; Provenzo, 1991). Children love playing these games. Lepper and Malone investigated the intrinsic motivational value of computer games (Lepper & Malone, 1987; Malone, 1981; Malone & Lepper, 1987). They asked students to play a number of different computer games, then to rate the games according to attractiveness and to name their outstanding features. In the presentations of their results, these investigators distinguished between the following factors: individual motivations (e.g., challenge, fantasy, curiosity, and control) and interpersonal motivations (e.g., cooperation, competition, and recognition) as the main attracting features of games.

A different view was provided by Turkle (1984), who not only analyzed several video game players and their interests in games but also investigated the attractions of programming. Pertinent in her interpretations of the players' motivation is what she called the "holding power" of video games. Part of the holding power comes from the role-playing and fantasy aspects included in video games. Turkle characterized video games as a

> window onto a new kind of intimacy with machines that is characteristic of the nascent computer culture. The special relationship that players form with video games has elements that are common to interactions with other kinds of computers. The holding power of video games, their almost hypnotic fascination, is computer holding power and something else as well. At the heart of the computer culture is the idea of constructed, "rule-governed" worlds. (1984, p. 66)

This holding power is not the same for all players. One of Turkle's cases, Marty, played video games to be in control. In contrast, David liked to play video games because it allowed him to concentrate fully in a relaxed way and to be in the "perfect contest." One can conclude from these observations that playing video games resonated with different aspects of the players' personalities. Turkle saw also a parallel between the attractions of playing games and of programming computers:

> When you play a video game, you are a player in a game programmed by someone else. When children begin to do their own programming, they are not deciphering someone else's mystery. They become players in their own game, makers of their own mysteries, and enter in a new relationship with the computer, one in which they begin to experience it as a kind of second self. (1984, p. 92)

There seems to be a common denominator between why people love to play video games and what gets them involved in programming. Making games could combine attractions from both playing games and programming in that players not only explore worlds but also build them. The "holding power" of playing games (i.e., moving in rule-governed worlds with determined boundaries) may also apply to the "holding power" of making games, in which the rules and boundaries governing the world are determined by the designer.

This short overview on the attractions of game playing provides us with the following important features of games: rule-governed worlds, fantasy, and control. In the analysis of the games designed by the students, I explore these aspects and provide an overview of their different game ideas, their potential origins, and on the games' educational content: fractions.

**First Game Ideas: Game Worlds and Fraction Microworlds**

The student designers came up with a variety of game ideas. The following list is a collection of the game ideas as they were formulated by the students in their own words or in their notebook writings during the first days of the project (see Fig. 3.1).

> *Albert:* "Ok, I'm gonna make a haunted house . . . ahm . . . in the beginning, I'm making the front right now and it's gonna say "Your friends dare you to explore the haunted house. You have to . . . and so it's gonna give you a choice to say "If you want to be here or if you want to go back and check it out." And if so, your object is to explore the whole house and without getting killed or murdered or

kidnapped . . . There is a number of rooms and I am not sure what fractions, how many rooms, I am going to make. So, it's going to explore, you have to explore this fraction of the house without getting killed. And . . . well, you can collect stuff, like you got a map as to where stuff is and what rooms are and if there is any secret rooms. Because there are going to be a few secret rooms that you can go in. You have to find those to explore the whole house. So, then I haven't figured out what I am going to do. Well, I am going to make something like . . . I am not sure I am just going to have murder in it . . . One thing, fractions come in as, or, I can have some game a murderer is in the house and it could say "One third of the game is coming at you."

Amy: "Well, I am going to do a whole bunch of shapes, like this, they got part of it filled in, and which fraction is, you know, you know this kind of thing Miss Gwenson's class did."

Barney: "Yeah I am just going to do like . . . you have to go on an adventure or something like this and people have to ask you all these fractions questions and if you get them right, you go on and if you get them wrong you . . . see it's going to be hard, if you get it wrong, once, then you are out . . . The questions will be pretty easy but it's just if you get it wrong once, you are out."

Darvin: "To make a game called 'Run' and make it with bonus games. With fractions. I will make a game that you have to go through. I will also make a title and some rules."

Gaby: "I am going to make a spider web, right. I need to make some blocks up here, but I don't know how to make them....You see a square, like here, and it has a little space so the fly can get over here and then, you see, the spider, the web is going to be right over here and if it gets closer to the web, the spider is sitting there and it is going to eat it. But if not, this is going to be the safe place and if it gets the right answer it's going to get a little bit closer and closer until it gets to the safe place, and then like a smiling face."

Gloria: "The teacher screams and a fraction comes out of her mouth. Then she asks you what is this fraction.

Jero: "I am going to make a magician . . .and then I am going to do my map .... There will be worlds on it like this with stages . . . The second stage is, ahmmm, a little bit harder than the first one. And then the third one gets more and more harder and when you get to the ninths, it gets really hard. That's where you have twenty fractions and you have to answer them and if you get them right you get a prize."

Miriam: "You know what I am going to do? I am going to have a person in a game like Mr. Fraction. There is going be a fraction, and he is going to teach kids about fractions and how to do them, like about the numerator and denominator . . . there is going to be, he is going to ask at the end of the lesson, he is going to ask you some fractions, and if you get them right, a picture, a piece of a monster will appear . . . It disappears at the end. So when you get a fraction right, then you see half, then the bottom shows, then . . . "

*Oscar:* "The pacman who is eating fractions."

*Rosy:* "I will work on my game. My man will go around the world. He will ask how far around the world he is. If you get a prize, if you get it wrong then you have to answer a fraction."

*Shaun:* "I will make a guy who is walking in the street and he will see a fraction coming at him. And if they touch him, he will die. And he has five lives. He can kill the fractions by shooting the right answer at them. He has to shoot the right answer at them, before he hits them. So he has a certain amount of time. Once he shoots all hundred fractions it's going to be over."

*Sid:* "Personally, what I am trying to do here is to make a basketball court and I'll have players going back and forth, back and forth. And then I make the player, the guy, with the ball go back and forth, back and forth. And I will have him insert a letter like A, to press A and that gives you a fraction. And I have him answer this and you will dunk the ball if you get it right. So, if you get the right answer, then the guy is going to come up and dunk the ball."

*Shanice:* "I will make a cloud and a helicopter for my game."

*Sina:* "A game that's about fractions."

*Trevor:* "I am going to make a grid and there are coins and when you move the guy around, and when you press a button, it makes it so

. . . you have to do a fraction and that's it."

*Tyree:* "Welcome to Space City" (notebook design)

**FIG. 3.1.** Students' descriptions of their first game ideas (verbally or written) during the first days of the Game Design Project.

These ideas all share the common feature of describing different worlds in which the player interacts with fractions. The worlds described in the games include, besides adventures and travels the following:

| | | |
|---|---|---|
| airport | basketball court | map |
| mazes | space city | classrooms |
| haunted house | coin grid | fraction world |
| town | spider web | street |

This list of worlds can be broken up into two different kinds: One puts the game itself in the center, whereas the other puts fractions in the foreground. In the following sections, I describe the game worlds and fractions microworlds in more detail.

## Game Worlds

In the first days of the project, the students described a wide range of contexts in which their games would teach fractions. Many students also had quite original ideas for their games: Trevor's coin grid, Shanice's helicopter madness, and Jero's map game. Figs. 3.2, 3.3, and 3.4 show some initial notebook designs of game worlds.

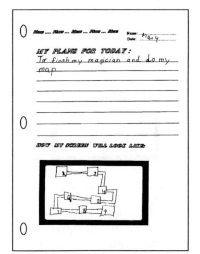
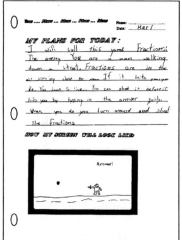

**FIG. 3.2.** Designer notebook entries: Jero and Shaun's game designs. Jero's map shows the different stations or levels of the world that the player has to pass. Shaun's street scene is the context in which the fraction questions will be posed.

Many games in the Game Design Project make reference to commercially available games such as Nintendo. For example, Jero's different warp zones are reminiscent of Mario Brothers tunnel system. Oscar made explicit reference to the PacMan game, with the creature eating fractions instead of points. Sid's basketball game was available in various video game versions. Gaby took an educational game she had used in her previous school, the spider web, and adapted it to fractions. Some of the students used the educational situation when choosing a game theme. For example, Sina's outline of her teacher game shows a teacher asking (rather screaming) a fraction (see Fig. 3.4). Gloria came up with a similar idea.

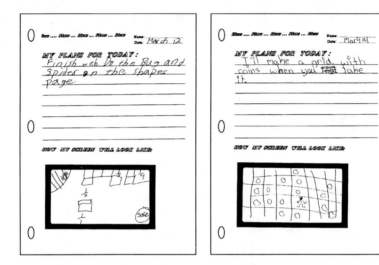

**FIG. 3.3.** Designer notebook entries: Gaby's and Trevor's game designs. Gaby's game describes a spider web in which the player moves around as a fly, away from the spider, and turns on fraction blocks where questions are posed. Trevor shows the coin grid and a figure that represents the player.

What pertains to all the ideas of game worlds is that the rules are bound to the fraction questions and the player's success depends on figuring out the correct answer in order to continue or finish the game. Fractions have become the obstacle to be overcome. This emphasizes an interesting relation with fractions. It might express the negative feelings many game designers have toward fractions, unlike the Instructional Software Design Project, where much of the students' energy was dedicated to making fractions favorable to their prospective users. One could say that, at least in the beginning, the game designers were not able to detach from and to develop positive feelings about fractions.

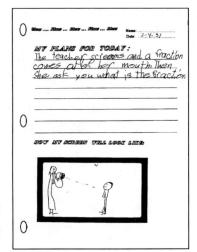

FIG. 3.4. Designer notebook entries: Barney and Sina's game designs. Barney draws the underwater scene. Sina shows the two protagonists of the game, the teacher and the player.

## Fraction Microworlds

A second kind of game can be described as a microworld in which fractions are situated. Initially, the term microworld was reserved for the creation of software tools that allow the learner to explore their knowledge. Papert described the microworld as "a computer based interactive learning environment in which the prerequisites are built into the system and where learners can become the active, constructing architects of their own learning" (1980, p. 122). One example of a microworld is the Turtle geometry in Logo, the programming language that the students used to design their games. Here, children can access a different kind of geometry based on their own body experiences. Geometric objects such as circles or rectangles can be drawn with turtle steps in a way similar to the steps that children would make with their own bodies to produce a circle or a rectangle. Turtle geometry is body syntonic, because it is firmly related to with their own bodies to produce a circle or a rectangle. Turtle geometry is body syntonic, because it is firmly related to children's sense and knowledge about their own bodies. Based on these interactions, objects in the microworld, such as the turtle, can become objects-to-think-with and can initiate thoughts about formalisms. Papert's idea of microworlds has been mostly translated into the creation of software tools (diSessa, 1985; diSessa & Abelson, 1986; Feurzeig, 1988; Hoyles & Noss, 1992; White, 1984).

**FIG. 3.5.** Designer notebook entries: Miriam and Rosy's fraction worlds. Miriam's text to the graphic of Mr. Fractions says: "Hello, my name is Mr. Fraction and I am going to teach you about fractions." Rosy described her first game idea as: "I will work on my Game. My man will go around the world. He will ask how far around the world he is. If you get a prize if you get it wrong then you have to answer a fraction."

In the context of the Game Design Project, the term *microworld* is used when the idea of fractions was inherent in the game concept. Here, the students became the designers of software tools for other children. Students used Logo to design their games as as Amy's fraction thing, Miriam's Mr. Fraction, or Rosy's World Map (see Fig. 3.5).

One issue of immediate concern is why so few students considered the design of fraction microworlds. I have two possible explanations. One addresses the very nature of educational games. Educational games lie between learning and playing. They are a particular breed of games, because the rules necessary to play the game demand the use of valuable educational skills. Game playing is placed in an unplaylike situation, because the social structure of students in school does not allow them to participate or to decline participation of their own will. The consensus is that educational games are unplayful because they are structured.

The students obviously felt the tension between the demands of playing and learning. Darvin saw the two poles clearly as he expressed in his notebook entries on March 1: "I want to make it [the game] as fun and educational as possible but especially fun." Another example is Shaun's reflections toward the end of the project:

> "Mine was educational because you had to type in fractions but it is not educational if fractions just start falling down and you go dit, dit, dit [imitating the sound] and you just shoot them. See, I don't like that. You know, they have those games where Alien Martians come down and you have to shoot them and the space ship by pressing the space bar. That's what I meant."

Students were obviously conscious about the particular nature of their games. They drew a fine line between what they considered educational versus fun.

My second explanation comes from observations of educational games designed by researchers and educators. Educational games on and off the computer have been used for a long time by teachers to keep students motivated (Avedon & Sutton-Smith, 1966; Block & King, 1987; Lepper & Malone, 1987). Teachers and software designers obviously put a great deal of time and thought into creating educational games. My survey of teacher mathematics journals indicated that teachers have created many games involving fractions, both on and off the computer, to use in their classroom teaching (Bride & Lamb, 1991; Fennell, Houser, McPartland, & Parker, 1984; Priester, 1984).

These teacher-designed games shared some common aspects: The game idea, content, or form was external to the game. In all cases, the game idea and format could also be used for other subject areas. By this I mean that the content—fractions—did not matter. The game context was used to keep the students' attention alive and to keep them motivated and accomplishing the tasks. Many of the students' games shared this quality. Another feature of most games was their emphasis on drill and practice of computational skills, manipulating fractions of all kinds. Very few games used multiple representations of fractions. The training of a particular concept seems to concentrate on one particular representation. A third and last feature was that games on and off the computer orient themselves on commercially available forms such as arcade games, board games, and card games.

My conclusion is that the students' game designs dealt with the same issues as did most of the teachers' games. This might be one explanation of why so few game designers made the ideas of fractions central to their games and why some of the good ideas were quickly abandoned. Furthermore, it might be that microworlds are harder to invent. A situation where answering fraction problems allows you to advance is conceptually simpler: The fraction challenges are fully factored out of the game context. Microworlds may also be harder to implement because the intertwining of fractions and game context creates interactions between the two that may pose complex programming challenges.

Miriam and Rosy decided to switch to a game context in which fractions were not central. Amy's new game was the only one that still put fractions in the foreground of the game (Fig. 3.6). In constructing their games, students integrated aspects that resonated with their personal interests. Miriam liked skiing, so the choice of a ski slope as the main theme of her game was a personal one. Sid was interested in basketball. Rosy liked cats, so a cat played the major role in her game. One could say that the game ideas were ego syntonic in many instances: The game ideas integrated the designers' sense of themselves as people with intentions, goals, desires, likes, and dislikes (Papert, 1980). In that sense, the design of the game world was also a reflective conversation between the designer and the situation on different levels, as Schön (1988) would say. In the course of this dialogue, many game designers opened a second line of inquiry: They integrated story elements in their games. I explore this aspect further in the next section.

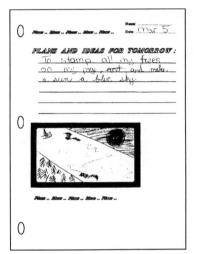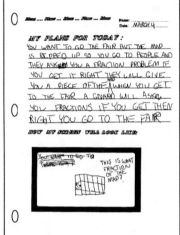

FIG. 3.6. Designer notebook entries: Miriam's new design and Amy's fraction map design.

## Changes of Game Format: The Emergence of the Narrative

If the interpretation of microworlds offered a view of why children are drawn into designing games, an even more powerful theme emerged as the project moved along—the development of the narrative. As students continued developing their games, defined their characters, and outlined the scenes in the subsequent weeks of the Game Design Project, they also created a story that situated the actors in a fantasy yet meaningful context.

One of the most prominent examples for the development of the story or narrative in games can be found in Barney's game. I could see his impact on many other students as they were playing his game or talking about it. To emphasize the narrative stream in his game, I extracted the text from his Logo program code and excluded the fractions exchanges (see Fig. 3.7). Barney's game started with the story of Jose, who gets lost and experiences a series of adventures that stretch over a several days and nights. His story was driven by the plot that Jose tries to find his way home. The story had a number of dialogues accompanying the graphics: Sometimes his text was direct speech, other times it had the function of introduction, and still other times, the text became the inner thoughts of Jose or other characters in the game. The text essentially has an explanatory function as it set the mood and annotated the events on the screen for the player.

The rules are fairly simple. You are Jose, a third grade kid who gets lost and must find his way home. You will go on many different adventures. Along the way, people (or beasts, creatures, etc.) will ask you questions about fractions, (you will type A, B or C, remember to press enter.) If you get the question right, you will go on safely, but beware! Danger lurks if you get the question wrong. Have fun if you dare! Type play and press enter.

"Where am I?" "I have to get home!"

A mysterious man approaches you. "Hey kid, I'm Marley the Magician and I'm going to make you disappear if you don't tell me how much of this square is colored!, says the man.

YES! Go free says the man.

A man comes out of a hot air balloon and approaches you. "I'm going to take you prisoner in my balloon if you don't tell me which one of these fractions is equal to one-thirds." says the man.

Yes! See Ya'

I'm tired," you say "I'll look for home in the morning."

While you are sleeping, a rober comes and takes the $33 dollars you have in your pocket. "MONEY!"

Morning comes. You get up and realize you have no money in your pocket. "OH NO!" "I'll just have to do without it."

You see a man coming toward you. You need some money so you kindly say "Excuse me sir, could you please give me a few dollars, a robber robbed me broke! It doesn't look hopeful. After a minute the man says "I'll give you $30 dollars if you tell me what one-half of $30 dollars is, otherwise I kick you to the moon!

"Here kid, 30 dollars, don't spend it all in one place.

It get's a bit darker. You thought you would take a walk on the beach.

"I'll take a swim," you say.

Onder the water .....

A fish swims with you. You see a shark. You are too terrified to move but the fish swims away.

"You'll be makin' me a fine meal, lil' one."

Who said that?

It was you the shark! You can talk!

"Boy, kid, you're a regular Einstein!"

You are very scared.

"I'll just want to leave, please don't eat me!" you say.

"I'm hungry! But if you tell me what four-twenty-fourths is in lowest terms you can go."

I guess I'll go and eat that dumb old fish.

You get out.

Meanwhile at home ..... "Where's Jose, I'm so worried!"

It's getting late again. You walk around for a place to sleep. You walk into a jungle. You see a lion.

The lion is looking for supper when he comes upon you. Just as the lion is about to lunge forward and eat you, you dodge him.

"You look like a nice little kid, I'll let you free if ....

A talking shark, a talking lion! This is getting wiered!

The lion says "As I was about to say, you can go free if you tell me which one of these decimals is equal to one-tenth."

Well, you're aright, see ya' later.

You go to sleep. When you wake up you walk back into the city.    AIRPORT

I don't even know where I am, I'll go into the airport to find out.

INSIDE THE AIRPORT  TICKET BOOTH

FIG. 3.7. Barney's game Jose in the Fraction World. Barney's game was never finished because he left class after the summer and moved to another school.

To document the shifts toward the narrative in the students' game formats, I analyzed the game development of all 16 students and compiled the results in one figure (see Fig. 3.8). Some students, such as Barney, Albert, Gloria, Rosy, and Sina, started early on incorporating narrative elements in their game design. Several students stayed with their game format: Gaby's Spider Web, Shaun's Fraction Killer, Darvin's Maze, Gloria's Teacher, Sina's Teacher, and Shanice's Helicopter Madness.

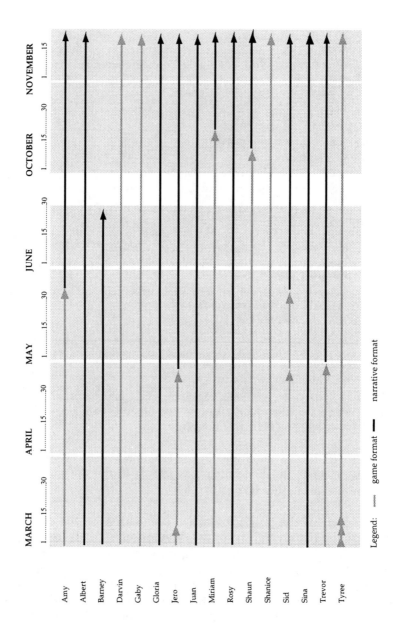

**FIG 3.8.** The development of narrative.

But the number of students who used the narrative format doubled (from 6 to 12) in the course of the game development. This change had different forms. Some of the students changed their game on the surface without having to redo a lot of previous programming: Amy retained her map idea but changed the content of the game to Greek myths; Albert's haunted house turned into a game called Mission Town; Rosy's game first took place around the world and then changed to an adventure story. In all these cases, the change of the story plot, as some students called it, did not affect the programming done prior to the change, but for another group of students, it meant that they started a new game. For example, Sid's new game was a fractions journey of two characters, Gemini and Swartz. Trevor's second game, after he finished his first, involved adventures on the Island of the Goon.

The characteristic of this conversion to the narrative is that students designed scenes not solely for instructional purposes. They included additional scenes in which the different actors spoke to each other. The graphics were accompanied by text and the fraction questions were asked in the context of dialogue. The narrative development in the game design is also an example of what Perkins (1986) called *writing by design*. The context of the game provided a framework that allowed students to address the essential design questions. The purpose of the story was to situate the player in a fictional environment.

The story structure was based on other commercially available games, which meant that students had to create an environment and characters, all specific features that made the player feel excited and comfortable. The model cases were based on adaptations of role playing games. The argument concerned the coherence of the story: Did it make sense to have the player free the kidnapped princess? The logic or soundness of the narrative was not necessarily abstract and formal. It followed the convention of making sense and constructing meaning.

Students used different composition techniques to enhance their stories. One example of the use of composition techniques was found in Albert's game. Albert used the tool of prolongation or a false ending when he stated "It ain't over yet!!!" This composition technique is commonly used in other media, such as movies, literature, or music (Fig. 3.9; I refer the reader for a more detailed description to Albert's Case Study in chapter 4).

```
I can't belive it!!! You got it right!!!!!
AAAAARRRRGGGGGHHHHHH!!!! You have killed the evil frac-
tion aliens. You have won the game so you get in your
spaceship and blast home      (warp speed)

You have landed in your backyard. Your ship blasts off.
You've globed ghosts, defeated demons and mashed
Martians. Basically you've won the game!!!!!! YOU'VE WON
!!!!!!!

This isn't over yet!!!! HA HA HA HA HA HA!!!!!!!! THAT'S
WHAT YOU THINK!!!

THE END
```

**FIG 3.9.** Albert's game MISSION :TOWN.

Amy provided two endings in her game (Fig. 3.10).

```
"Hello, my name is Zeus" said Zeus.

"Hello" you say.

"Congratulations, you may stay here with me and be King
of all fractions or you may go home" says Zeus.

If you want to go home type home but if you want to stay
and be King type King.

[In case the user typed KING:]

"I'm glad you decided to stay with me.  Now you will live
forever!"
```

**FIG. 3.10.** Amy's two endings in her game Greek Myths.

A possible explanation for the popularity of the narrative game format is that it allowed students to incorporate fantasy and to decorate their worlds in a more appealing way. This was also one of the features that the children in Malone and Lepper's study (1987) identified as appealing in playing games. Furthermore, it made the role-playing aspects of most games more realistic. Role-playing fantasy games allow a number of players to assume the roles of imaginary characters and operate with some degree of freedom in an imaginary environment. One of the students, Shaun, characterized the students' games as role-playing games.

> *Yasmin:* You call them role-playing games. That's an interesting distinction. Why role-playing?
>
> *Shaun:* Because you are playing the role of the character and you want to type in your things. Everything is you. And if you are, say, role playing for, I mean, in arcades it is someone else and in arcade games, you don't role playing isn't like, you don't play the role, you just like someone, like the space ship or the gun plays the role. . . . Role playing is when . . . actually Dungeons and Dragons is kind of role playing for, that is kind of, a play on words because you roll with dice to see if you shoot something, and you're also playing the role of the character. You see, in role playing in Dungeons and Dragons you have the character sheet. You write down your name, what you want your character to be, write down all his abilities and all his strengths. See you are playing his role, you try to kill monsters and get treasures. You are playing his role.

Furthermore, the narrative could be considered as a form of problem solving. It reconciled two seemingly adverse domains in a more coherent framework. If the narrative was the most prominent and unexpected feature of the designers' games, then another difference from the Instructional Software Design Project became clear: their software consisted mostly of isolated scenes whose common denominator was that they all had the instructional content of fractions. In the games, the narrative provided the glue or sugar coating that connected the different scenes or places and the instructional content. It made clear that designing a game was a different task for the students than designing instructional software. Students in the Instructional Software Design Project referred to gamelike contents such as Naomi's Sesame Street screen, where four objects were placed on the screen and one did not belong. But again, this constituted one screen among many others that did not necessarily have a narrative as the common denominator. The common denominator for all of the instructional screens is that they dealt with fractions. This was not true for the games.

## DESIGN STYLES

In designing and implementing their games, students choose different approaches to handling this task. Previous efforts to label methods of handling complex tasks mostly used bipolar descriptions such as "top-down" versus "bottom-up" (Jeffries, Turner, Polson, & Atwood, 1981; Newell & Simon, 1972) or "planning" versus "bricolage" (Turkle & Papert, 1990). The view that has been called *planning* or *top-down* tends to see the process of problem solving as one of breaking down the problem into more meaningful subproblems. The opposing view, called *bricolage* or *bottom-up*, describes problem solving rather as a conversation with the situation, in which the final solution emerges in the end. The traditions of school and academia have favored the formal and abstract approaches, as represented by planners, to the neglect of other approaches (see also, Gilligan, 1982; Keller, 1985; Turkle & Papert, 1990). The observations in the Game Design Project are of particular interest, because they touch on two important issues. One, they allow us to observe students' styles of thinking and problem solving over a long period of time in a school context and to explore whether the distinctions between bricolage and planning apply as clearly as claimed. An alternative view might postulate that a mix of both planning and bricolage can be observed in the students' approaches. Second, the limitations of young students' abilities to plan and deal with complex tasks have been documented in the research literature (for an overview, see Friedman, Scholnick, & Cocking, 1987). It was, therefore, important to see whether they would be able to handle this complex task and, if so, in which manner.

Hence, in the following analysis, I examine this distinction between planning and bricolage more closely by looking at the design process at large and how different students chose to implement their games. This section does not attempt a day-by-day analysis of the process. Rather it focuses on particular periods in the context of the extended time frame. In particular, I pay attention to the beginning phase, when students began formulating their first game ideas and what expectations they had about upcoming difficulties, and the period of first transition, three to four weeks into the project, when students had accomplished part of their implementations and had already handled design and programming problems. (For a more detailed description, I refer the reader to the case studies in chapter 4, where all the aspects discussed here are presented in the context of daily progress.)

### Beginning Phase: Formulating Game Ideas

In the first days of the Game Design Project, students formulated their game ideas and began to implement them. My observations of the students' work in this beginning phase captured a variety of activities, but two different approaches stood out. Many students did not start working and implementing their game ideas right away. whereas others started with one idea, abandoned it quickly, and moved on to a new one. Those who did not immediately start programming their games explored or played around with other aspects seemingly unrelated to their assignment. For example, Albert and Shanice both experimented with some new Logo commands to which they had been introduced a few days before. Barney refused to start the project at all because, as he told me, he did not have any game ideas that involved fractions. Shanice, Sina, and Rosy wrote for several days in their notebooks "I am going to start my fractions project."
A different approach was taken by several other students. They started with one idea, worked on it for a few days, and then moved over to a new game idea. In this category, we find Amy with her "fraction thing" that she later turned into a map design, Miriam with her "Mr. Fraction" that turned into the skiing game, Jero's magician that turned into a map with different levels, and Tyree's fraction screen that turned into a space game. In this approach, students outlined a few features of their first games in their notebooks or programmed a few lines before they came up with a new idea. This change in the beginning phase was rather abrupt, because most students did not indicate that they were not

confident about their first choice. Instead, their games seemed to take a new turn from one day to the next.

The students used both approaches to the design task and to enter the new domain of game design. I do not interpret either approach as unproductive or inactive. In both cases, it provided a time when students grappled with the issue of bringing together the two domains of fractions and games in one design. In Harel's Instructional Software Design Project, Debbie actually took several days before she started with the design of her instructional screens. Very much in the same way that professional designers would start out, the students in the Game Design Project either tried out alternative ideas and designs or decided to postpone the beginning of their game until they had formulated a more coherent game idea and knew what they wanted to do.

A further look at the content of the students' first designs repeats this impression of diversity. Some students, such as Barney, Tyree, Shaun, Juan, and Rosy, started with their welcoming screen or introductions (the first screens that the player usually saw when starting the game). Other students immediately started working on their first game scene, designing shapes or the environment, and did not implement the welcoming screen and the introductions until midway through or toward the end of the project. These observations of approach and content in the game design process indicate that there was no uniform way in which students handled the beginning of creating their games. These observations furthermore reinforce the impression that there is no one "right way" to start a design task, and that many of the students' choices in approach and content were related to their personal preferences. The entrance point of forging a relationship with the task is not necessarily the same for everyone. A planner might consider it a bad strategy to start the game with the most important scene instead of designing the first screen. Yet, for a bricoleur, this might be the only possible and reasonable way to begin.

### Transitions in the Game Design Process

Three to four weeks into the Game Design Project, students had implemented different aspects of their game. Some had designed an opening screen and started the programming on their game contexts; others had just finished their first game scene and created a first fraction quiz. Students were thinking about how to combine both fractions and game ideas in a meaningful and appealing way. At this point, students asked themselves: Is my game idea interesting? Is what I implement producing the right effects? Will I have enough time to implement all the features of my game? Do I like what I see? How do I integrate fractions in the best way? However, the observations indicate that most students were dealing with implementations of game aspects and less with those aspects related to the content to be taught—fractions. From a design perspective, many students were confronted with the feasibility of implementing their game idea. For example, many students were still in the process of learning to understand programming commands such as SETHEADING and SETPOSITION (which address the direction in which the Turtle looks and the position from which it starts). In order to understand the problems that students confronted after having started their games, I take a closer look at their expectations about the size of the project and upcoming problems.

*Students' Expectations*. One example is the number of fraction problems that students intended to design. In the first days, Amy projected doing 21 fraction questions (taken from the parts of her map), Jero planned to do 20 questions on 9 different levels, and Shaun was thinking about 100 fraction problems. The students' projections were probably influenced by worksheets, textbooks, or educational software that contained a large number of problems. These models might have influenced the students in their initial projections of how many questions they could or should incorporate in their games. This also replicated the experiences of Debbie in the Instructional Software Design Project (Harel, 1988, p. 192), who wanted to show all the fractions in the world. In the course of the project, all students reduced their expectations and the average number of instructional situations was approximately five.

Students also had varied expectations about upcoming difficulties in their project. Some students were not concerned, whereas others considered the feasibility of their game ideas in the light of implementation difficulties. In interviews during the first days of the project (March 5), both Amy and Sid were not concerned with any problems.

> *Yasmin:* What do you think is the biggest problem right now?
> *Sid:* I don't know. Actually I don't have a problem right now.
> *Yasmin:* What do you think could become a problem?
> *Sid:* Nothing.

> *Yasmin:* Let me ask you something: What do you think right now will be your biggest problem with this project?
> *Amy:* I have no idea right now. [waves her hand] Beats me.

In contrast, other students thought of some problems in relation to their game ideas or upcoming implementations.

> *Yasmin:* That sounds like a neat idea. The PacMan who is eating fractions?
> *Oscar:* That's what I wanted to do.
> *Yasmin:* So work on that.
> *Oscar:* It's a little bit too hard.
> *Yasmin:* So can you think of a simpler version?
> *Oscar:* I am trying . . . but I am going to think of something different.

> *Yasmin:* If you think about your project now, what do you think might be the biggest challenge for you?
> *Albert:* Ahm . . . right now . . . I think the biggest challenge that I am gonna make here, is making the robbers come at you or something. When you open a door, something, the guys come at you and making all that happen.
> *Yasmin:* So, it has to do with Logo programming?
> *Albert* [nods yes]: I can also have, once you type in you want to open the door, it shows you and the guy will step out with

the knife and the guy will go like this. [he indicates a cutting movement with his arms and he is laughing]

*Yasmin*: Are there any challenges related to fractions for you?

*Albert*: I don't think I will have any problems, but I might come across some of them that might be kind of difficult.

Oscar was concerned about the difficulties in his idea of adapting a PacMan game to eat fractions instead of points. Albert thought about the difficulties related to programming future animations. In the following interview, Gaby discussed the number of different parts in her game Spider Web that she will have to implement.

*Yasmin*: OK, so you are going to make a spider web, there is going to be a safe place and some fractions? These are many things you are thinking about for your game. So what do you want to start with now?

*Gaby*: Well, I am starting a web because I am thinking it is going to be a little bit hard plus making the spider, and the fly, and the blocks and the fractions, and things and the smiling face, would be hard for me, you know, to get it all started. It will take me more than . . . it wouldn't take me less than a week. But it would take me more than a week trying to plan all these things. We have a short amount of time.

The variations in expectations might be related to the students' lack of experience in working on such a complex and time-consuming project. The students' own evaluations written at the end of the project were good indicators of this. For example, Gaby wrote: "I disliked it because sometimes I kept working on the same thing over and over again. I liked it because I finally finished it and I made everything move." Amy wrote: "I disliked working on the fractions software project because sometimes it got boring because you had to work on it day after day, week after week, month after month but at the end I felt like I had accomplished something." In the past, students usually had worked three to four weeks on one assignment and then moved on to the next one. Their planning skills and estimations in regard to the game design were based on their previous experiences. One should not forget that these issues were hard to express as students began to formulate what their games would be about. Even if we expected students to map out from the beginning their plans and ideas for implementations, it would be unrealistic to think that they could take into consideration all the aspects that would be involved in planning and designing a game. Related to this might be that few students realized the complexities of the programming behind commercially available video and computer games. Many students might have felt comfortable with the implementations of the graphical aspects, but the animations and interactions required a level of programming sophistication that most students had not achieved.

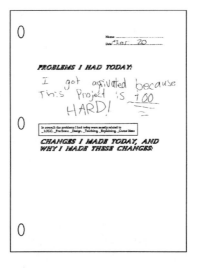

FIG. 3.11. Shaun's designer notebook entry from March 20.

As students progressed in their game design, they implemented features of the game, such as a fraction question or a game scene. At this point in time students were able to speak more clearly about the different scenes and features they would implement. Their games started to take shape. But at the same time, they were now realizing the constraints of their programming skills and the remaining time. In the final evaluation, many students expressed their frustrations with the game design when they met problems. Trevor, one of the most proficient programmers, said in the end that "I disliked working on the fractions software project because if I made a mistake it sometimes affected the whole game." Tyree, another student, wrote that "I disliked it because they sometimes didn't work and you couldn't save on the disk. I disliked it. Sometimes I got real frustrated 'cause something goes wrong in the computer." Shaun, for example, wrote on March 20 in his notebook: "I got agrivated because this project is too HARD!" (see Fig. 3.11). Shaun wanted to program a scene that involved the parallel animation of two figures, a player and flying fractions, with the possibility of the player to interact. In the process of trying to coordinate the movements and interaction of the player, Shaun got stuck and needed to reconceptualize his game idea.

To gain a better understanding of the dynamics in students' game development, I compiled information about major changes that students made during the project (see Fig. 3.12). In this figure, I documented the changes of game ideas and titles or when students just thought about starting a new game. The information is based on evidence from their notebook writings, program implementations, or interviews. Some students, such as Darvin, Gaby, Gloria, Miriam, Shanice, and Sina, implemented their project and pursued the same idea from the beginning. Other students changed some features of the game (what I called *surface changes*) such as the title or the introduction and directions, but did not require any new programming. This happened mostly in April, when many students changed the plot of their story. Amy, Albert, Juan, Rosy, Shaun, and Tyree fall into this category. A few students, such as Jero, Sid, and Trevor, started new games in the middle of the project. Most of the changes occurred either in the first days of the project or three to four weeks into the project. I see these changes (the real as well as the intended ones) as indicators of a critical phase in the project, even though they occurred at different times in the project for each student, depending on the individual's game design development.

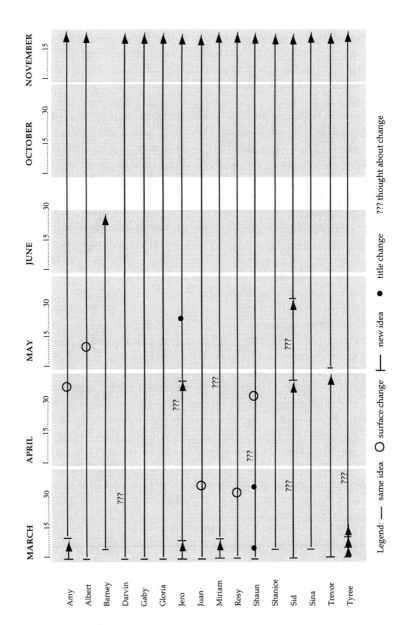

**FIG. 3.12.** Changes in game development.

In this time period, the students were in close dialogue with the situation (Schön, 1983), or investigated whether their design was a structure adapted to the game's purpose of being fun and educational (Perkins, 1986) or whether their game ideas and implementations resonated with their personal interests (Papert, 1980). When students thought about these changes, they thought about what this project meant to them and whether or not they liked it.

## Design at Large

The investigation of students' approaches in the beginning and as they met their first problems showed diversity in the ways students handled them. A different perspective opens by looking at the development of the students' games as a whole, from the beginning to the end, and how students outlined features of their games and also set out to implement them. We could expect that "planners" would carefully lay out what they want to do in advance. We would expect "bricoleurs" to develop their game as they go along. To make this point clearer, I look at Barney's and Gaby's games as two extreme examples of game development (see Fig. 3.13).

In her first interview, Gaby described the different parts that she will implement for her spider web game. She had already segmented her descriptions of the different game components into the blocks, the web, and the fractions. When Gaby started implementing her game, she first did the spider web, and then the blocks on the screen, then the colored blocks, before she began working on the fraction questions one after the other. In her programming, each unit was assigned a procedure. For example, the five colored blocks all had the name BLOCK but each different color had a different prefix (LBLOCK, MBLOCK, and so on). One could say that Gaby laid out from day one of the project the implementation of her game, and followed through even though she did not implement some aspects of her initial plans. In that respect, Gaby fell most clearly into the category of the planner. In the second part of the project (which was not represented in the diagram), Gaby wrote the introduction and directions, and programmed the spider's movements as it followed the fly.

*Gaby* : I am going to make a **spider web**, right. I need to make some **blocks** up here, but I don't know how to make them . . . You see a square, like here, and it has a little space so the fly can get over here and then, you see, the spider, the web is going to be right over here and if it gets closer to the web, the spider is sitting there and it is going it eat. But if not, this is going to be the safe place and if it gets the right answer it's going to get a little bit closer and closer until it gets to the safe place and then like a smiling face.

*Barney* : Yeah I am just going to do like . . . you have to go on an adventure or something like this and people have to ask you all these fractions questions and if you get them right, you go on and if you get them wrong you . . . see it's going to be hard, if you get it wrong, once, then you are out . . . The questions will be pretty easy but it's just if you get it wrong once, you are out.

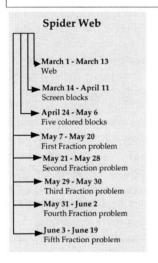

**Spider Web**

March 1 - March 13
Web

March 14 - April 11
Screen blocks

April 24 - May 6
Five colored blocks

May 7 - May 20
First Fraction problem

May 21 - May 28
Second Fraction problem

May 29 - May 30
Third Fraction problem

May 31 - June 2
Fourth Fraction problem

June 3 - June 19
Fifth Fraction problem

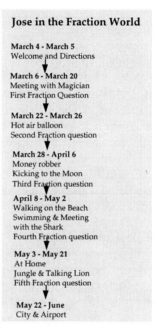

**Jose in the Fraction World**

March 4 - March 5
Welcome and Directions

March 6 - March 20
Meeting with Magician
First Fraction Question

March 22 - March 26
Hot air balloon
Second Fraction question

March 28 - April 6
Money robber
Kicking to the Moon
Third Fraction question

April 8 - May 2
Walking on the Beach
Swimming & Meeting
with the Shark
Fourth Fraction question

May 3 - May 21
At Home
Jungle & Talking Lion
Fifth Fraction question

May 22 - June
City & Airport

**FIG. 3.13.** Comparison between Gaby's and Barney's design approaches, from March to June.

In contrast, Barney described the idea of an adventure story in the interview and his notebook designs. He initially provided only one screen display: that of a fish speaking. As Barney set out to implement his game, he started with a welcome screen, introduction, and directions. From then on, he developed scene after scene. Even though most of his scene units, such as the magician or the money robber, were centered around a fraction quiz, they were composed of a series of connected animations that led to the fraction question and then away from it to the next adventure. His game was a series of connected adventures that were created one after the other. In that sense, Barney was very much like a bricoleur.

I would categorize both Barney and Gaby as extreme cases for each approach. Other students (e.g., Darvin, Albert, Miriam, Trevor, Sina, Shanice, Amy, and Jero) also exhibited the same planning behavior but to a lesser extent. Their planning seemed to be more localized and dealt with particular sequences. In particular, I refer the reader here to Amy's blueprint for the instructional quiz that she clearly planned ahead (see chapter 5), or to Miriam's design of the ski slope, which was implemented to the smallest detail from her notebook design. Other students could also be described as working without a preformed plan. Sid, Juan, Tyree, and Rosy were engaged in a continuous dialogue with their game as they designed various scenes or fraction questions. A combination of both planning and bricolage seems to be a more accurate way of describing the game design process. My first support for this statement is that in most cases, students' transition to the narrative was not planned for. It grew out of the situation, which was a complex mix of what students saw around them, what they could efficiently program, and what they liked.

It is also meaningful to ask in this context whether it would make sense for the students to outline all the features of the task. Several studies asked programmers of varying degrees, from novices to experts, to solve a well-defined problem in a limited amount of time (several hours) (Guindon, Krasner, & Curtis, 1987; Jeffries et al, 1981). A general software design strategy used by most experts was to decompose a problem into smaller units. One result of these studies indicated that novices or inexperienced programmers do not have a model that guides their problem-solving processes. One could then argue that the design and programming style chosen by the students reflected their lack of experience. But in this particular task, the students' model or image of their game guided their programming. In Barney's case, it was an unspecified adventure scheme that was defined through the characteristics of the narrative. In Gaby's case, it was the model of a computer game that she had played previously and that she planned to adapt to its new teaching purpose—fractions.

A further point could be made in regard to the students' use of modularization. Usually, the degree to which different scenes are decomposed is reflected in the use of procedures and superprocedures. A planning style would make more use of procedures. However, analysis of the game designers' programs indicates that both planners and bricoleurs used superprocedures or no procedures according to their personal preferences. The main problem encountered by the designers was the scarcity of their own design and programming experience. One example here is Sid; when interviewed in October, he reflected on his own approaches to dealing with problems:

> *Cora*: You got a good idea. What is the first thing you do?
>
> *Sid*: First, I start from the hard thing then I just go through the small ones so I can work my way down. Like if, I want to have a major thing, I would do that right away, so I can get it out of my face. You know, just keep on doing it. So I feel that the game should end.
>
> *Cora*: Also, if you have a good idea, you work on it immediately?
>
> *Sid*: Also, I have different ideas. So I have to think for a while, then make my decision which I am going to do.
>
> *Cora*: Where do you get most your idea?
>
> *Sid*: I get my ideas like . . . first, when I started the game, well I am just typing that stuff. I get ideas. So I just keep on doing.

Sid made two points in his answers. The first point concerned his strategy for dealing with the different design components. He said about himself, "I start from the hard thing then I just go through the small ones so I can work my way down." This description is more accurate of Sid's implementations of his first two games, where he started programming the interactions and animations first. For his third and final game, however, Sid changed his strategy and designed his games as he went along. He said, "I get my ideas like . . . first, when I started the game, well I am just typing that stuff. I get ideas. So I just keep on doing." Sid's case emphasizes how both planning and bricolage can co-exist in one person. For a more detailed description and interpretation of this process, I refer the reader to Sid's case study in chapter 4.

## DISCUSSION OF PROJECT EVOLUTION

I explored the project's evolution from two aspects: game ideas and design styles. The investigation confirmed the diversity within students' approaches on many levels. From the very beginning, students developed different strategies for dealing with the demands of the design situation. Some students started quickly with one idea, abandoned it, and came up with a new one, whereas others preferred to explore new programming commands before beginning their game. In the course of the project, students learned about design principles, such as how to adjust their design expectations about what they wanted to accomplish in relation to their programming skills and time constraints. Students dealt with this particular situation in different ways: Some considered starting a new game but continued with their originals, some implemented several superficial changes, whereas others went about making a new game. Some students, like Gaby, approached the task of designing a computer game by deciding the content of their games at the beginning and implementing one feature after the other; whereas others, like Barney, designed their games as they went along. Students designed game worlds in which the rules were set through answering the fraction questions. A general shift toward the narrative could be observed in the majority of games. This shift might be explained again as an effort to solve the problem of programming complex interactions.

The diversity in the students' game themes and in their design and programming practices show how the students chose different avenues for building relationships with and within this project. The design style, narrative development, and choice of game themes need to be seen in this context.

## Design Styles

In the analysis of the students' games, I looked closely at their individual approaches in dealing with the game design task, ad-
dressing both programming and design issues. My starting point
was that people tend to organize their work in different ways, and
these have been labeled as *planning* and *bricolage* (Turkle & Papert,
1990). Analysis of the students' game development seems to
confirm this distinction. There were clear differences, for example, in the way Gaby approached the design task compared to
Barney, to name the two extreme cases. But, also, Gaby could not
implement straightforwardly all the features she had planned. On
many occasions she had to converse with the situation in regard to
her programming skills, game concept, and personal aesthetics to
decide on the next step. Most students, in fact, chose to walk a
middle line between bricolage and planning. At specific stages in
their game design process, for example when programming the
first fraction questions, they tinkered around with different aspects: They designed different shapes and dialogues before deciding on one solution. In later stages, they switched over to reusing
in a purposeful way program segments that they had written before (e.g., for the instructional dialogue).
    The point of this discussion is that the clear distinction be-
tween planners and bricoleurs seems to fall apart when looking
over a long period of time and the construction of a complex
product. As I show in the case studies in more detail, students
oscillated between the different styles at various points in time.
An important aspect to remember is that students are in the
learning phase of doing design. But because every design
problem presents a new challenge, designers are in this situation
all the time.

## Narrative Development

The stories developed by students match what Bruner (1987, 1990)
called the *narrative mode of thinking*. Bruner claimed that this is a
second, different form of reasoning whose efficacy is not
measured against the laws of logic and induction: "The reality
that is constructed under the sway of narrative modes of organiz-

ing experience is fundamentally different from what prevails in logical/scientific thinking." Bruner used autobiographies as one example of narrative thought: The telling of a life story is a personal construction in which the narrator and the main character happen to be the same person. The fact that life stories change according to whom they are told and in which culture they evolve indicates that the process of story telling is one of construction and not something that is given. One of the possible interpretations is that students chose the narrative format for their games because it gave them an easy and efficient way to construct a meaningful context for integrating fractions. In the design of their games, the students interlaced in a paradoxical way the formal and logical aspects of the computational mode (in their Logo programs) with the fantastical and personal aspects of the narrative mode (in their stories). Schön (1983) spoke about the rules and notations that designers use to describe their worlds. These rules are not necessarily rooted in logic. There is no logic for fractions learning to take place in Greek myths, spaceships, and mazes that the students created except that it made sense to the students themselves.

One could conclude, then, that narrative and constructive thought are at the intersection of constructing meaning and establishing personal relationships. Contructionist learning sees learners as the active builders of their own knowledge structures (Papert, 1980). They do so particularly well when they are engaged in building something external, such as a computer program or a story. In this process, learners establish relationships with the object to be constructed and make it their own. This process of building relationships has also been called *concretizing* (Wilensky, 1991), through which objects become personally relevant. By constructing a narrative, the students could "concretize" the game design task and the integration of fractions.

But the narrative also offers another appeal for children. Kinder (1991) argued that narrative media such as television and video games allow for the integration of the "affective, cognitive, and social" (p. 20). The narrative of these different media formulates and highlights the children's understanding of their own position and place in the social context, and provides examples from which children can draw. The constructions of the game designers showed how they were influenced by commercially available games. In their choices of game themes and their propensity for programming animations and interactions, the students offered a mirror into what they found appealing in the games and stories they experienced through other media. Making a game and the rules allowed the game designers to be in charge and to determine the player's place and role in the world, with all the consequences.

**Gender Differences**

The students' game choices also reflected gender differences. Many of the boys in the Game Design Project chose a game theme and features that resembled commercially available games, such as Nintendo. One of the most prominent features included by most boys was the feedback provided to the player. In case of a wrong answer, the figures on the screen were "kicked to the moon" (Barney's game), "turned into an ice cube" (Shaun's game), "sent frying to the underworld" (Albert's game), or "mentally transformed" (Trevor's game). Many of the boys' game themes were adventure hunts and explorations, in which players rescued "stolen fraction wands, golden snow, or princesses." Other games incorporated some of these action features without necessarily adopting all of them. For example, the aspect of "dying" if the player does not succeed is not present in all games.

In contrast, most girls programmed a different kind of feedback for a wrong answer. In case of a wrong answer, the player continued but did not receive a piece of the map (Amy's game), the player started from the top of the ski slope again (Miriam's game), the player had to take French (Sina's game), or the player did not receive a fraction of the magic power (Tyree's game). Most of the girls' games included themes of teaching, skiing, collecting pieces of the map, moving around a spider web, or landing in an airport.

The differences in terms of feedback are most pronounced. Whereas girls preferred to hold back something or to have the player start over again, the boys provided more violent feedback: In most cases the player got transformed and the game was over.

The boys games were also, for the most part, about "getting something," whereas the girls' games seemed to center more around activities as their main attraction.

Students then replicated many of the gender differences and preferences found in the literature about playing video games (e.g., Provenzo, 1991). But despite this difference in theme and features, both the boys' and girls' games included sophisticated graphics, animations, and interactions in their programming. It was obvious that all groups and all students chose a theme that facilitated their entry into the design task and allowed them to personalize their game design. Girls created their own worlds when making their games, compensating for the sexism and violence found in many video games (Gailey, 1992).

The purpose of studying the project evolution was to focus on the class as a whole and to observe and analyze general patterns in the students' development of game ideas and design styles. The analysis made a strong point for the diversity in the game designers' style of programming and design, choice of game themes, and involvement with fractions. Furthermore, it offered support for the claim that game design is an activity that is open and accessible to students with different preferences and styles.

# Chapter 4

## Case Studies of Game Designers

The case studies of three students presented in this chapter were chosen for various reasons. The individuals showed differences in the following aspects: choice of game theme, conceptual development of fractions, understanding of Logo programming, and changes in their attitudes. Each individual created a computer game to teach fractions that shared some common features, such as a narrative game format. In selecting the cases of Amy, Sid, and Albert I wanted to offer a spectrum of the differences and convergences.

Amy was chosen because her game design reflected most clearly an involvement with fractions: Her game idea of having the player collect "fractions of a map" integrated the content matter to be taught—fractions—into her game. Her game idea underwent considerable changes during the design period: Amy not only integrated Greek mythology into her game, but she also changed the narrative of her game.

Sid was a student who would typically not be chosen for a case study: His initial difficulties in establishing relationships with the project in particular and school subjects in general; his reluctance to follow through on his ideas, of which he had many; and his reluctance to engage in conversations about the game project made him a difficult interview partner. Sid started out with a series of game projects that he abandoned midway. But because Sid succeeded in the end in creating a game, his struggles in the earlier phases of the project are of interest to us.

Albert's game project provided a good example how his personal style of design influenced his style of programming. His personal interests in drawing and graphics found a clear reflection in his investment with particular features of the game design project. Furthermore, he showed persistence in pursuing his ideas and creating his own structures as the complexity of his game grew.

Taken together, these three cases provide an overview of the diversity of styles, themes, and approaches encountered in the Game Design Project. The case studies are based on a combination of data that I collected during the six months (or 92 project days) of the Game Design Project. (I described the rationale, methods, and sources in chapter 2). In the presentation of the case studies, I decided to condense certain sections in their game developments and to present summaries of them instead. My reasons for doing so were particular periods in each case that I wanted to emphasize. As a common denominator for all three cases, I used the students' design progress during the months of the project. Inside these constraints, each case is divided into segments that I felt best represented the student's individual development. The following three case studies are presented in no particular order: Amy, Sid, and Albert.

# AMY AS A GAME DESIGNER

If the computers disappeared I would feel unhappy because I like doing projects at the computer. We get to create and design our own projects. I would feel sad because now I could not relax at the computers. My body is relaxed because I can sit and do my work quietly. Even though my brain is working, my body is relaxed. I would feel gloomy because now I could not feel rewarded when I finish a project on the computer. It is rewarding because I feel that I have accomplished something.

Amy, after the project, in October 1992

## Introduction

Amy was one of two students who has been part of Project Headlight since the first grade. Most students stay in Project Headlight only for one or two years, due to administrative reasons. Amy was one of the very few students who started Project Headlight from the beginning and, hence, could benefit fully over the years from the daily exposure with computer work. In the pre-interview in February, I asked Amy who she considered to be a good programmer in her class. She responded right away: "Well, me and Trevor [the only other longtime Project Headlight student] have been on the computer, this has been my third year, I think. So, I mean, everybody knows how to do it but we have more experience." Three years of working with Logo made Amy confident in evaluating her own programming abilities. Her confidence and knowledge also applied to other school subjects. But the previous statement "even though my brain is working, my body is relaxed" summarizes succinctly another aspect of her experience: the ease Amy felt toward programming and working with computers.

There are several reasons why I chose Amy for a case study. The most prominent reason is her integration of fractions into the design of her game; the two other reasons concern her particular style of programming and the development of her game during the project.

*Fractions.* Amy was the only game designer in the project whose game integrated a fraction concept. Fractions were central to her game design and development (which involved a map ripped into pieces that needed to be reassembled by the player). Most of the representations of fractions that Amy created involved part–whole relations, but she also broke the mold of standard textbook examples with her map design. Amy's further engagement with fractions was reflected in her notebook designs, where she created many more representations of fractions than she implemented in her game. These designs provide further evidence that she explored different representational levels, moving away from the part–whole relationship to the grouping of fractions and equivalent fractions. Amy's case is a good example of a student who appropriated the project's goals into her game.

*Logo Programming.* The second reason speaks more directly about Amy's abilities as a programmer. Being one of the very few long-time Headlight students, she had become a self-assured and competent programmer. To provide a sense of Amy's programming, I included a program that she wrote before starting the Game Design Project. The assignment was to create and design a habitat. Most students concentrated on sea or forest environments. Amy's choice of theme was rather unusual; she choose to show the future of our environment. The program started: "If you would like to look into the future type start," and displays a power plant. It then showed a forest: "If you want to see what will happen to our trees in a thousand years type trees. If you don't type q." It continued: "Our trees won't be green anymore because of the polluted air. If you want to see what will happen to our air type air." The last screen displayed an oil refinery, and the screen comments: "The air will get polluted by oil refineries. Well that concludes our look into the future. I hope you enjoyed my program. If you would like to start over type start."

But I also wanted to show the type of programs Amy and her classmates had designed and implemented before designing computer games. They involved programming the turtle mostly as a drawing tool. There was minimal interaction between the player and the program. The player typed procedure names to continue the program. This program took most students three to four weeks to accomplish. In the Game Design Project, Amy became an efficient programmer and designer and developed a programming strategy for her instructional quizzes about fractions. I include excerpts of Amy's Logo code in Fig. 4.1.

```
to future
cc type se [If you would like to look into the future
type start.] char 13
end

to q
rg cc ct
end

to start                              Draws a power plant.
rg pu setpos [160 -65]
pd rt 90 fd 350 pu setpos [-130 -80]
pd setc 15 fill pu setpos [-120 -65]
lt 90 pd fd 80 rt 90 fd 35 rt 90 fd 45 lt 90 fd 70
lt 90 fd 45 rt 90 fd 35 rt 90 fd 80 ht
pu setpos [-85 -40] pd fill label [Nuclear]
pu setpos [-100 -55] pd label [Power Plant]
fill pu setpos [-140 -55] pd setsh 23 setc 2
stamp pu setpos [-100 85] pd label [Hello]
pu setpos [-100 70] pd label [If you want to see]
pu setpos [-100 55] pd label [what will happen]
pu setpos [-100 45] pd label [to our trees in a]
pu setpos [-100 35] pd label [thousand years ]
pu setpos [-100 25] label [type trees.]
pu setpos [-100 20] label [If you type q.]
pu setpos [120 -55] pd setsh 23 setc stamp
pu setpos [70 -55] pd stamp
end
...
to oil                                Draws an oil refinery.
rg pu setpos [160 -65] pd rt 90 fd 350 pu
setpos [-130 -80] pd setc 15 fill pu
setpos [-120 -65] lt 90 pd fd 80 rt 90 fd 35
rt 90 fd 45 lt 90 fd 70 lt 90 fd 45 rt 90
fd 35 rt 90 fd 80 ht
pu setpos [-85 -40] pd fill label [Oil]
pu setpos [-100 -55] pd label [Refinery] fill
pu setpos [-100 80] pd label [The air will get polluted
by]
pu setpos [-100 65] pd label [oil refineries etc.]
pu setpos [-100 55] pd label [Well, that concludes our
look]
pu setpos [-100 45] pd label [into the future.]
pu setpos [-100 35] pd label [I hope you enjoyed my pro-
gram.] setpos [-100 25] pd label [If you would like to
start over] pu setpos [-100 15] pd label [type start.]
end
```

**FIG. 4.1.** Excerpts from Amy's Habitat program, as of February 5.

*Game Design*. A third reason for choosing Amy was her development of the game theme. For the first two days, Amy was working on a screen displaying a fraction and a question. She then decided to adopt a map ripped into pieces as her new idea for her game. In this game, the player had to reassemble the pieces of the map in order to arrive at the fair. Midway through the project Amy changed the game context to Greek myths. The player arrived now at Zeus' home instead at a fair. In her game design, Amy also reflected the change from focusing on the environment to the telling of a story involving different characters. In this development, Amy was more typical of her co-designers. Her game theme of Greek mythology pointed out another important aspect: the integration of another subject matter. In the context of the Game Design Project, students were already dealing with the two subjects of fractions and Logo programming.

### Structure of Amy's Case

Amy's project development can be divided into three segments. In the first days of the Game Design Project, Amy's idea was to design something similar to what she had seen a year before in the Instructional Software Design Project (Kafai & Harel, 1991a, 1991b). She quickly decided to reject this idea because she felt it would be a boring game. She then started implementing her map idea. The only other change in Amy's game design occurred by the end of April, when the story of the way to the game fair changed to an adventure of traveling to the Greek god Zeus' home. In the context of her game development, we can follow more closely the development of her programming of the instructional quiz and the representation of fractions.

I intentionally did not call these segments different games (as I did in Sid's case, where I divided his game development into three distinct games). Amy's first game idea existed more on the design level and never got implemented. Amy's [Map Game] was the first game idea that she decided to implement. The plot of the story is the only feature that changed when she started "Greek Myths." The animations or fraction questions that she had previously designed for her [Map Game] were not concerned by this change. (See Fig. 4.2.)

The first phase (March–June):

| March | [*Fractions Game*] |
|---|---|
| March–April | [*Map Game*] |
|    March | Creating the people: Blueprint for the instructional quiz |
|    March–June | Collecting pieces of the map: Consideration of fraction problems |
| April–November | *Greek Myths* |
|    May | Arriving at Mount Olympus: Zeus' home |
|    June | Changing to narrative: Meeting the snake |

The second phase (September–November):

| September–October | Combining myth with math: Becoming the god of fractions |
|---|---|
| October–November | Finishing touches |

FIG. 4.2. Overview of Amy's project development. The game names that are put into brackets indicate that Amy had not given a name to this game.

The following case presents an overview of the game that Amy developed in this project from March until November. I concentrate on her development during the first phase, from March to June. Amy completed most of her game during this time, in contrast to most of the other game designers. She added one scene and a fraction question in the second phase. This last phase is only presented in summary form.

## March: The Fractions Game

On the first day of the project, February 28, the teacher and I introduced the idea of becoming game designers to the students. The introduction included the distribution and explanation of designer notebooks. At the end of the session, students did not have time to go to the computers, but we asked them to write down their very first ideas and designs. Amy's first design, in contrast to all other students, was a fraction representation (see Fig. 4.3).

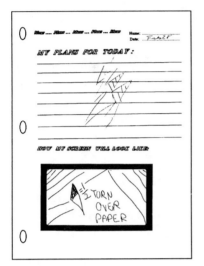 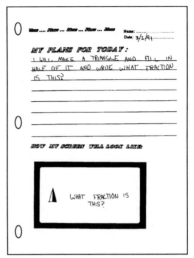

**FIG. 4.3.** Amy's designer notebook entries from February 28 and March 1.

Amy's fraction representation was a tilted triangle cut into halves. The right-side of the triangle was shaded in and next to it she wrote "1/2" and "Turn Over Paper." This is a very typical representation for a fraction: Amy chose one half, represented it in an area, and shaded the right side. As has been noted in the research literature (see Harel, 1991; Lesh, Landau, & Hamilton, 1983), most examples of fractions provided in textbooks and on worksheets show the right side shaded in when using area. On the next day, March 1, she continued working on her idea. In her PLANS FOR TODAY, she wrote, "I will make a triangle and fill in half of it and write: What Fraction is this?" and she announced at the end in PLANS FOR TOMORROW that "I will continue with my triangle fraction." For implementing her first design, she wrote the code shown in Fig. 4.4.

```
to games
pu setpos [-105 0]        Places turtle on the left side of screen.
pd                         Pen down.
rt 30 fd 50 rt 30 fd 50   Starts drawing lines.
end
```

**FIG. 4.4.** Amy'Logo code on March 1.

She gave her procedure, which drew part of her tilted triangle, the generic name of GAMES. While Amy was sitting at the computer and programming, I asked her what she was working on.

*Yasmin*: So what are you working on, Amy?

*Amy*: What? [After a pause, again looking at me] What?

*Yasmin*: What are you working on?

*Amy*: Well, I am going to do a whole bunch of shapes, like this, they got part of it filled in, and which fraction is, you know [she turns to the computer and then back to me] you know this kind of thing Miss Gwenson's class did.

In this short conversation, Amy explained the origin of her idea for the first fraction screen. In third grade, Amy was part of the target users for a class of students participating in an Instructional Software Design Project (Kafai & Harel, 1991b). Amy and her classmates twice visited the fourth graders to evaluate their instructional software. In this context, she saw the screens displaying fractions representations and quizzes. She clearly remembers the instructional screens, which she calls "this kind of thing Mrs. Gwenson's class did."

Amy's friend Miriam had a game idea also rooted in fractions. Miriam's notebook design depicted a "Mr. Fraction" (Fig. 4.5). Miriam, who was sitting right next to her friend Amy, held her notebook on her lap while I interviewed her.

*Miriam* [addressing me]: Do you know what I am going to do? I am going to have a person in a game like, he is going to be Mr. Fraction. There is going be a fraction and he is going teach kids about fractions [pointing toward the screen] and how to do them, like about the numerator and denominator. He is going to ask at the end of the lesson, he is going to ask you some fractions, and if you don't get them right, a picture, a piece of a monster will appear.

*Amy* joined the discussion: A piece of the monster?

*Yasmin*: If you get it wrong, you get punished with a monster?

*Miriam*: No, you get a piece of the monster, a third.

*Yasmin*: Why only a piece?

*Miriam*: So, so so . . .

*Amy*: So if a piece of it shows up and then, like a knife? [while gesturing with her hands]

*Miriam*: A piece of Mr. Fraction shows.

*Amy*: No, no, a piece of . . .

*Miriam*: It disappears at the end. So when you get a fraction right, then you see half, then the bottom shows, then . . .

*Yasmin*: So, when you have all [the fractions] right, you will see his whole body.

Miriam nodded her head in agreement.

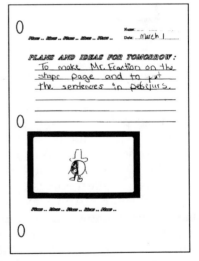

**FIG. 4.5.** Miriam's designer notebook entries from March 1.

Amy and Miriam were both engaged in defining Miriam's game idea during the discussion. Both their game ideas were rooted in fractions. Amy's game idea was strongly influenced by what she

had seen as a third grader while playing and discussing the instructional software designers' projects. Miriam's idea was another example of a game in which fractions were central.

In the next two days, both girls abandoned their initial game
ideas and started with a different game setting. On March 4,
Amy decided to switch her game idea (see Fig. 4.6).

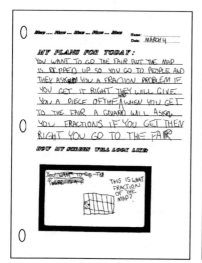 

**FIG. 4.6.** Amy's designer notebook entries from March 4.

Amy outlined the introduction and directions for her new
game in her plans and elaborated on them in the program later:
"You want to go to the fair but the map is ripped up so you go to
the people and they ask you a fraction problem. If you get it right
they will give you a piece of the [inserted in red] map. When you
get to the fair a guard will ask you fractions. If you get them right
you go to the fair." Amy's explanation in the notebook on March
4 was "I am doing a different game because mine was boring."
Another possible explanation of Amy's change is that she felt that
her first idea was not really a game. This reflects a rather fine-
grained insight from Amy's side that instructional software is unlike instructional games.

One day later, on March 5, Miriam announced that she would
change her game too, "I changed my game to a skiing game because
I thought it would be more exciting and fun than the Mr. Fraction
game" (see Fig. 4.7).

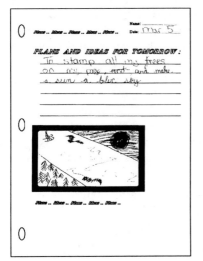 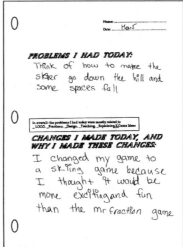

**Figure 4.7.** Miriam's designer notebook entries from March 5.

Both Miriam's and Amy's explanations for changing their game sounded very similar, even if they resulted in different game ideas. To my mind, these changes reflected a complex interaction among different factors that might have had an impact on Amy and Miriam. For one, the previous discussion showed that Miriam and Amy were both engaged in elaborating their game ideas. They might have felt that the idea of a monster (although this idea did not appear later in either Amy's or Miriam's game was more compelling and had more exciting aspects than did Mr. Fraction. In previous research I discussed the importance and the type of collaboration between students in design projects (Kafai & Harel, 1991a). Miriam and Amy's optional collaboration provides a further example of how two students can interact and influence each other in their decisions, even when they might head in different directions in their games.

A second factor might have been the game ideas of other students to their right and left. They might have compared these game ideas with their own and realized that most of the other students' ideas were more centered around games. Harel (1988) also documented in the Instructional Software Design Project the adoption of the Sesame Street screen between Debbie and Naomi as an example of the impact of other classmates' designs. Debbie "adopted" or imitated Naomi's original Sesame Street screen showing four fractions representations, three of which represented the fraction one half and the fourth a different fraction. A further factor might have been the classroom discussions and brainstorming sessions around games and ideas that the teacher conducted with the students at the beginning of the project. All these factors may have contributed to Miriam's and Amy's decision to change game ideas. In addition, both Amy and Miriam were at the very beginning of the design process. In the postinterview, Amy explained from her experience when the timing for change is right or not.

> *Yasmin*: How do you decide when you are already too far in your game and can't change anymore?
>
> *Amy*: Well, you can always change it, but sometimes you don't want to change it cause you think if you change it, you don't have time to do another one [game]. But at the point where it's at the end where they're about to win or if there's levels and you're on the last level 3 or something and there are three levels. Something like that.
>
> *Yasmin*: Do you think about these things when you start out with your game?
>
> *Amy* [nodding her head]: Yeah, I try to think of a game idea that won't get me bored.
>
> *Yasmin*: How do you know that in advance?
>
> *Amy*: Well, I didn't but I tried to. And so, if it seemed fun I continued.

In this interview segment, Amy explained the criteria that guided her decision to change: "won't get me bored," "fun," and "don't have time to do another one." Design decisions were influenced by many factors; the social context, be it a friend or other classmates, was one factor among many others. What Harel (1988, pp. 207–217) called *long-distance* and *short-distance* imitation does not necessarily lead to imitating other people's ideas. Amy and Miriam changed their initial game ideas but both decided to do something very different from each other. One might argue that this impact went to the detriment of fractions and to the advantage of the game idea. We shall see that it did not stop

Amy from exploring fractions further, but now in a different context.

## March–April: The Map Game

Amy's new game idea centered again around fractions. Her first representation of the map appeared in her notebook design: a rectangle cut into 21 pieces, one of them colored in. It also describes her idea of situating her fraction questions around the map: "This is what fraction of the map?" But she chose not to implement this idea in the end (see Fig. 4.8).

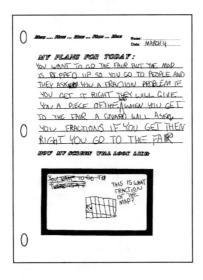

**FIG. 4.8.** Amy's designer notebook entry from March 4.

This is an interesting new idea for her game. First of all, with her map representation, Amy left the world of stereotypical textbook and worksheet representations of halves and fourths when dividing her map into 21 parts, even though she was still attached to fractions representations as area. Second and more important, she assigned a meaning to the fraction representation: a map that had been ripped into pieces. Furthermore, her description of the new game made clear that the map, or fractions, had a functional position in the game because the player had to reassemble them to get to the fair. These three aspects made Amy's choice a very special one.

Amy's Logo code included the elaboration of her introduction and was more explicit about the setting and conditions of her game, as shown in Fig. 4.9.

```
to start
ht cc
pr [You want to go to the fair but the map was ripped up
by someone who didn't like you. Everybody has a fraction
of the map. You are to go to the people one at a time and
they will ask you a fraction problem. If you get it right
you will get a fraction of the map. When you get the
whole map you will be at the fair gate. The guard at the
gate will ask you three hard fraction problems. If you
get them right you will go inside the fair and get a
surprise! After you are done reading this press start2
and press enter.]
end

to start2
pr [After you are done reading this press play and then
enter. Then the people will appear.]
```

**FIG. 4.9.** Amy's Logo code on March 4.

On the same day, I saw that Amy was writing a new introduction, so I asked her to give me some more information about her new game idea.

*Amy*: I am going to, you know, when you go to a fair and your map is ripped up and lots of people, like different people have gotten different parts of the map. And you go around [to see different] people and they ask you fractions problems. And if you get them right, then they give you a piece of the map and if you get it wrong, then you go to the next person and they give you a piece of the map if you get it right. And if you get there, when you get there, the guard is standing at the door and he'll ask you really hard fractions questions. And if you get them right, you go into the fair and you win.

*Yasmin*: So the map is the place where it is connected to the fractions?

*Amy*: When you get all the map you finally get to the fair and then the guard will be standing there and ask you fraction questions.

*Yasmin*: Let me ask you something: what do you think, right now, will be your biggest problem with this project?

*Amy*: I have no idea right now [waving her hand]. Beats me.

Once Amy had defined her game idea, she began working on the first instructional sequence. Most of her planning and implementations in the following weeks were focused on game features. For example, to give the player the ability to manipulate figures, the program had to read and interpret choices given by the player. But at the same time, Amy was also involved in explorations and considerations of different fractions representations. For now, I focus on Amy's work on creating a blueprint for her instructional presentations of fraction questions for the third graders and how she dealt with upcoming programming problems. I call this section "The Blueprint for the Instructional Quiz." Later, I go back to Amy's ideas and designs around fractions. That section of Amy's work is titled "Consideration of Fraction Problems."

## March: Creating the People—The Blueprint for the Instructional Quiz

Once Amy had finished writing the introduction for her new game, she started working on a set of procedures that would define her instructional quiz. Amy first experimented with some new features, such as COLORUNDER that she used in one of her procedures. She also learned about the DRIVE procedure: how to use the keyboard keys to manipulate shapes on the screen. Some students wanted to know about a such procedure. On March 8, I told a few students about this procedure and put the program on one of the computers at the pods, accessible to everyone ( see Logo code in Fig. 4.10).

The programming behind the DRIVE procedure was a simplified form of what one finds in commercially available games using joysticks (or the Nintendo cross). In DRIVE, only four directions are recognized: up, down, left, and right. Similarly, in Nintendo, pressing the A or B button initiates certain actions, such as throwing stones or jumping high. In the same way, pressing the S-key stops DRIVE from continuing. Because most students are familiar with the use of joysticks or keys as the input device in game playing, I felt that the complex operations of this procedure would be fairly easy for them to understand.

|  |  |
|---|---|
| `to drive :key` | The DRIVE procedure takes as an input parameter the variable :KEY, which reads in a keystroke. |
| `if :key ="u [seth 0 fd 5]` | If the U-key is pressed, have the turtle face up and move five steps forward. |
| `if :key ="r [seth 90 fd 5]` | If the R-key is pressed, have the turtle face to the right and move five steps forward. |
| `if :key ="d [seth 180 fd 5]` | If the D-key is pressed, have the turtle face down and move five steps forward. |
| `if :key ="l [seth 270 fd 5]` | If the L-key is pressed, have the turtle face the left and move five steps forward. |
| `if :key ="s [stop]` | If the S-key is pressed, stop the procedure and go out of the DRIVE procedure. |
| `drive readchar` | This is the recursive call, where the DRIVE procedure calls itself and reads in |
| `end` | the next key pressed. |
| | |
| `to start` | The procedure START is nec essary to start DRIVE. |
| `drive readchar` | Calls DRIVE and reads in first key stroke. |
| `end` | |

**FIG. 4.10.** Logo code of the DRIVE procedure.

The DRIVE procedure introduces students to an interesting programming concept—recursion. A recursive procedure is one that calls itself as a subprocedure. There has been much research about some of the problems that beginning programmers experience with understanding recursion (see Harvey, 1985; Kurland &

Pea, 1985; Papert, 1980). In the case of the DRIVE procedure, the only action that can end this procedure is to press the S-key. Otherwise, DRIVE waits for the next keystroke.

On March 8, Amy copied the first parts of the DRIVE procedure.

```
to drive
if :key ="u [seth O fd 5]
if :key ="r [seth 90 fd 5]
end
```

Amy thought about using this procedure in a particular way. She had designed her "people" on the SHAPES page, which she then stamped in the middle of the screen. She placed the player at the bottom left-hand corner of the screen. The player's task was to move the turtle over the figure using the different keys. Once the player hit one of the "people" with the turtle, a fraction problem appeared. Amy took advantage of the fact that each turtle could "read" or report on the background or shape color under the pen by using the Logo command COLORUNDER. The default color of the background was black (or white for the shapes) but could be changed into a different color. By March 12, Amy's procedure read as shown in Fig. 4.11. She also changed the name to MOVE.

| | |
|---|---|
| `to MOVE :key` | |
| `pu` | PEN UP so that the pen does not leave a trace. While moving forward, Amy forgot the END. |
| `IF COLORUNDER = 15 [problem1]` | If the color under the turtle pen reports the color number 15 (red), then go to the procedure PROBLEM1, which presents the first fraction problem. |
| `if :key ="u [seth 0 fd 5]`<br>`if :key ="r [seth 90 fd 5]`<br>`if :key ="d [seth 180 fd 5]`<br>`if :key ="l [seth 270 fd 5]`<br>`if :key ="s [stop]`<br>`move readchar`<br>`end` | |
| `to problem1`<br>`tell 3 setc 4 st` | Amy has not yet designed and programmed her first fraction problem. |
| `end` | |

**FIG. 4.11.** Amy's Logo code.

The instruction IF COLORUNDER = 15 [PROBLEM1] was a conditional statement, another programming concept to which students were introduced in the Game Design Project. IF was used a reporter here, and required at least two inputs. The first input included an expression that was either true or false. The second input specified the action to be taken if the first expression happened to be true. If the first expression was false, Logo simply went on to the next instruction in the procedure. IF the turtle pen read a color under it with the number 15, then it executed the commands placed in the brackets, which was to call procedure PROBLEM1. So PROBLEM1 was executed only IF COLORUNDER = 15 was true. Otherwise, the turtle moved according to the given key strokes. In this particular context, Amy used MOVE to call her procedure PROBLEM1, which presented the first fraction problem to the player.

*Making the People.* After installing the MOVE procedure, Amy first worked on SHAPES to design the faces of the people. On March 11, she wrote "I could not make a good face on shapes." The next day, however, she confirmed her success (see Fig. 4.12).

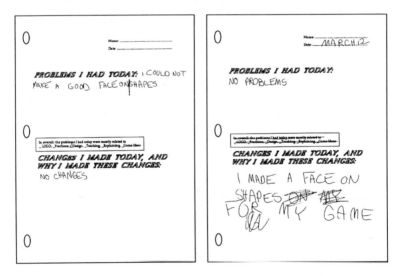

FIG. 4.12. Amy's designer notebook entries from March 11 and 12.

The round face, however, evolved into separate face and body forms on the SHAPES page. Her PLAY procedure stamped these figures (composed out of shapes 1 and 2) in the middle of the screen.

Amy had now designed the first of her people and placed it at the middle of the screen. Fig. 4.13 shows the Logo code for this, and Fig. 4.14 shows the screen with the player in the starting position at the lower left corner.

```
to play
rg tell 0 pu setpos [-10 20] pd   Places upper part of per-
                                  son's body and stamps it.
setsh 1                           stamp
pu setpos [-10 0] pd setsh 2      Places lower part of per
                                  son's body and stamps it.
stamp pu setpos [-120 -50]
setc 10
setsh 3 pu                        Places player in lower
                                  left corner.
end
```

**FIG. 4.13.** Amy's Logo code on March 12.

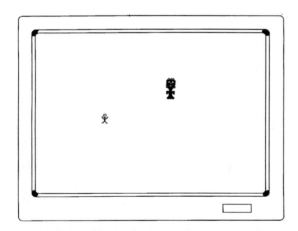

**FIG. 4.14.** Screen printout of Amy's scene where the player meets the first of the people.

*Preparing the First Fraction Problem.* Now that the MOVE procedure and the people were ready, Amy returned to the computer on March 14, working on her first fraction problem. She decided to use shapes for both the pictorial and the symbolic representations for the question. In her notebook designs, Amy explored different representations of one half, such as the tilted triangle and the circle (see Figs. 4.15 and 4.16).

```
to problem1
rg cc ct
ST
tell 1 pu setpos [-95 75] pd
setsh 4 setc 15 stamp pu          Places circle shape one half.
setpos [-70 75] pd setsh 5        Places question mark shape.
stamp pu setpos pu
setpos [-25 75] pd                Places question.
label [Please type a,b or c for ]
pu setpos [-30 60] pd
label [your answer.]
type se [a = 1/\2 b = 2/\2        Choices are printed in com
                                  mand center.
c = 3/\2]  char 13
answer                            Calls procedure ANSWER.
end
```

**FIG. 4.15.** Amy's Logo code on March 14.

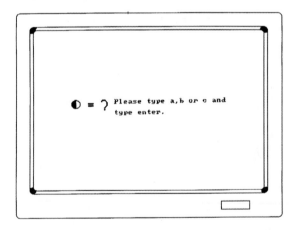

**FIG. 4.16.** Screen printout of Amy's first fraction question.

*Debugging Problems.* There was an unexpected bug in the PROBLEM1 procedure. Every time the player moved the turtle over the figure, the first fraction problem (PROBLEM1) appeared but the turtle also left a trace of exactly five steps (see Fig. 4.17 and 4.18).

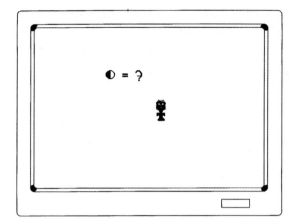

**FIG. 4.17.** Screen printout of Amy's problem scene.

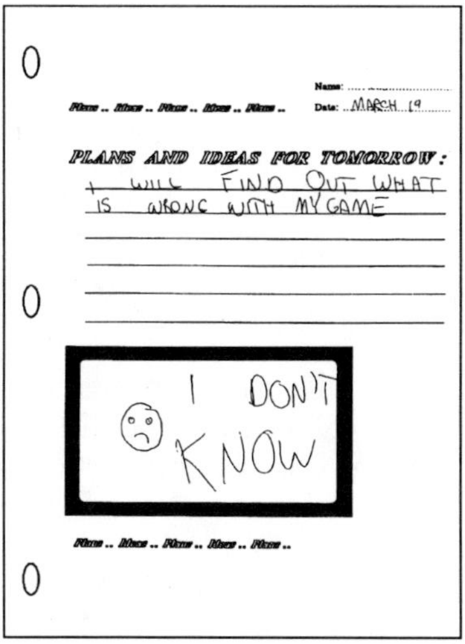

**FIG. 4.18.** Amy's designer notebook entry from March 19.

The way to correct this problem was to put PENUP (short: PU) in front of the SETHs in MOVE. Now each time the player moved the turtle over the person, the fraction problem appeared as programmed but the turtle left no traces (see Fig. 4.19). However, note that this was an unnecessary repair. The problem disappeared once Amy had programmed the ANSWER procedure. But it showed again how personal aesthetics, "to have it look right," play an important role in students' design.

```
To MOVE :key
IF COLORUNDER = 15 [problem1]
```
If the color under the turtle is the color number 15 (red), then go to the procedure PROBLEM1, which presents the first fraction problem.

```
if :key ="u [pu
seth 0 fd 5]
if :key ="r [pu
seth 90 fd 5]
if :key ="d [pu
seth 180 fd 5]
if :key ="1 [pu
seth 270 fd 5]
if :key ="s [stop]
move readchar
end
```

```
to problem1
tell 3 setc 4 st
```
Amy has not yet designed and programmed her first fraction problem.

```
end
```

**FIG. 4.19.** Amy's Logo code.

In the meantime, Amy also programmed her answer choices for the procedure ANSWER. She included three different answers, only one of which was the correct choice "a" (see Fig. 4.20).

```
to answer
name readlistcc "z
```
Reads in value into variable z.

```
if :z = [a] [ pr [Correct!
You get one-fourth of the
map and you have to get
three more fourths to get
```
a = correct answer.

```
the whole map. ] rg pu setpos
```
Shows one fourth of map shape.

```
[-75 -10] setsh 11 setc 6
pd stamp wait 150 play2]
```
Calls procedure PLAY2 to continue game.

```
if :z = [b] [type [That's
wrong.You do not get a
fraction of the map.]wait 100
```
b = wrong answer; message printed out that game is over.

```
rg pu setpos [-40 55] pd ht
label [Game Over] wait 100 rg]
if :z = [c] [type [That's not
correct.You did not get a
fraction of the map.]wait 100
rg pu setpos [-40 5] ht label
[Games Over] wait 100 rg ]
end
```
c = wrong answer; message
printed out that game is
over.

FIG. 4.20. Amy's Logo code.

By March 26, Amy had completed her set of procedures for
the first instructional fraction sequence. It was composed of the
following parts:

| | |
|---|---|
| play | Sets up the person to meet. |
| sta | Allows the player to meet the person. |
| move | Allows the player to meet the person. |
| problem1 | Poses fraction problem. |
| answer | Evaluates the player's choices and gives feedback. |

Amy organized her instructional sequences around this set of
sophisticated procedures: the arrow key procedures and conditional statements. She made everything work, and solved the
problem with the MOVE procedure and the line drawing. The advantage of using this structure as a blueprint for the coming fractions questions was that Amy knew that all of this worked. The
only values she needed to change were the shapes for the people;
she also needed to add shapes for the map and the fraction question. The structural components of this procedure set could be
maintained. At the same time, Amy developed an interesting alternative to procedural abstraction.

## March–June: Using the Blueprint for Other Fraction Problems

During the subsequent weeks Amy developed a programming
strategy: She copied the whole sequence and then modified the
necessary parts. She changed the names of the procedures, some
just by adding a "2" as in PROBLEM2 or PLAY2 to distinguish
them from the first set. On March 24, she copied the PLAY pro-

cedure into PLAY2 and modified it correspondingly (see Fig. 4.21).

```
to play2
rg ct
setc 1
pu setpos [0 20] pd setsh 15        New shape (SHAPE 15) for the
                                    second person's upper part.

stamp pd
pu setpos [0 0] pd setsh 16         New shape (SHAPE 16) for the
                                    second person's lower part.

stamp pu setpos [-105 -55]
setsh 3 setc 10                     Sets player in lower right
                                    corner.

type se [Type moving to start
to move.] char 13
end
```

**FIG. 4.21.** Amy's Logo code.

On March 26, she copied the rest of the procedures. I pointed out the places where the procedures had not been changed yet (see Fig. 4.22).

```
to problem2
tell 1 pu setpos [-125 75] pd       New fractions shape.
setsh 17 stamp
tell 2 pu setpos [-85 75] pd
setsh 5 stamp                       Places same question mark
                                    shape.

tell 3 pu setpos [-55 75] pd
setsh 6 stamp
cc type se [Type a = 1\/\4 b =      New answer choices are given.
2\/\4 c = 3\/\4] char 13
pu setpos [-30 75] label
[type a,b, or c for your answer]
end                                 Still no procedure call for
                                    ANSWER2.

to moving
move2 readchar
end

to move2 :key
if colorunder = 1 [problem2]
if :key ="u [pu seth 0 fd 5]
if :key ="r [pu seth 90 fd 5]
if :key ="d [pu seth 180 fd 5]
if :key ="l [pu seth 270 fd 5]
if :key ="s [stop]
```

```
move2 readchar
end

to answer2
name readlistcc "x
if :x = [a] [pr [Correct! You get
two-fourths of the map and you
have to get two more fourths to
get the whole map. ] rg pu setpos
[-75 -10] setsh 11 setc 6 pd                The second shape for one
                                            half of map has not been
                                            added yet.
stamp]
if :x = [b] [type [That's wrong.
You do not get a fraction of the
map.]]
if :x = [c] [type [That's not
correct.You did not get a fraction
of the map.]] wait 250
play2                                       Old procedure still called
                                            for PLAY2.
end
```

**FIG. 4.22.** Amy's Logo code.

Amy's programming is worthwhile of discussion for two reasons. The first reason concerns Amy's reuse of her procedures for the instructional sequence; the second reason focuses on the interdependence between game design and her programming.

All of Amy's procedures for the following fraction quizzes had the same names; different problems were referenced through different numbers.

| PLAY | PLAY2 | PLAY3 | PLAY4 | . . . . |
|------|-------|-------|-------|---------|
| MOVING | MOVING2 | MOVING3 | . . . . | |
| MOVE | MOVE2 | MOVE3 | . . . . | |
| PROBLEM | PROBLEM2 | PROBLEM3 | . . . . | |
| ANSWER | ANSWER2 | ANSWER3 | . . . . | |

Amy used the identical structure for her different instructional sequences. First, she presented the target: The user had to use hand–eye coordination to move the turtle over a colored target figure (PLAY, MOVING, MOVE). Upon hitting the colored target figure, a fraction problem appeared and answer choices were given (PROBLEM). The correct or incorrect answers elicited corresponding feedback: getting parts of the map or not. Then the next instructional sequence started (ANSWER).

Logo is a modular language, because it allows complicated problems to be broken down into simpler modules or components. These modules can be solved independently of each other and re-combined for a solution to the original problem. Amy chose to create her modules around a set of procedures and to modify them accordingly. Amy recognized procedures as "entities, as things one could name, manipulate or change" (Papert, 1980, p. 153). From a software design point of view, Amy had adopted a structure that she knew was efficient and bug free. The reuse of procedures allowed Amy to be efficient in her programming pro-duction (see Fig. 4.23). Amy finished her first fraction problem on March 24, her second on April 3, and her third on May 6. Through this approach, she produced and covered a large part of her game structure in a short amount of time. Amy was not the only one who was "reusing" already written procedure parts; other classmates such as Shaun, Sid, and Albert did the same for their fraction problems. Amy also began to improve a few fea-tures of her project. The first concerned the user control, which changed from the confusing instructions about typing two proce-dure names to typing just one command. She gave the player some control. All the subsequent procedures called each other at the end. She also changed her instructional strategy. The player advanced to the next fraction quiz in the first two fraction prob-lems irrespective of giving a correct or incorrect answer. In the last two problems, only correct answers brought the player to the next fraction problem. The incorrectly answered question was re-peated again for the player (see Fig. 4.24).

A second point of discussion applies to the interdependence between Amy's programming of instructional sequences and the game design, in particular the map design. As Amy finished her first instructional sequence, she was still undecided about how many quizzes she would create and implement for her students. Her first map design (March 4) had 21 parts. By the end of March, when she designed the first map shape, she first divided the map into halves and then into fourths. As Amy was deciding on the parts of her map, she realized that the initially projected 21 problems would be too time consuming to implement. As Amy settled on the map equally divided into four pieces, she might have decided to repeat the same instructional sequence. In her choice of repeating the instructional sequence, Amy also relied on her experience that many games use redundant play patterns.

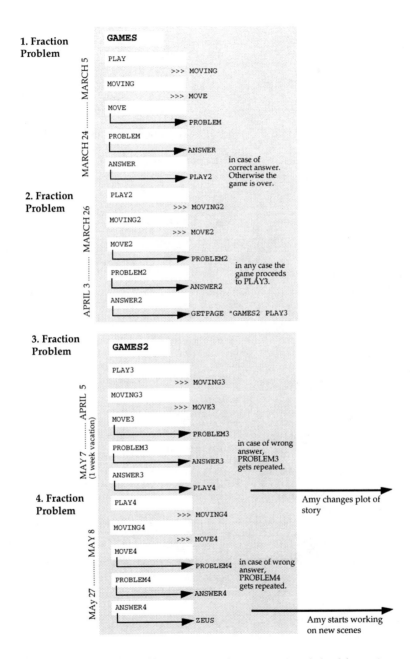

**FIG. 4.23.** Overview of Amy's implementation of the blueprint for the instructional quiz.

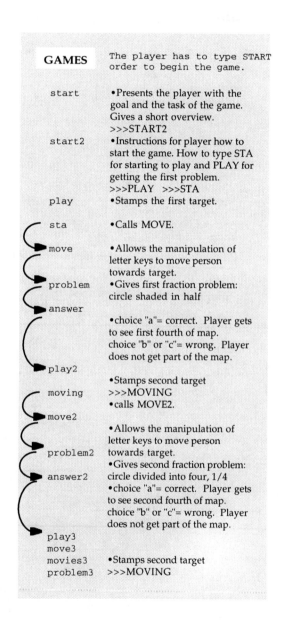

| GAMES | The player has to type START order to begin the game. |
|---|---|
| start | •Presents the player with the goal and the task of the game. Gives a short overview. >>>START2 |
| start2 | •Instructions for player how to start the game. How to type STA for starting to play and PLAY for getting the first problem. >>>PLAY  >>>STA |
| play | •Stamps the first target. |
| sta | •Calls MOVE. |
| move | •Allows the manipulation of letter keys to move person towards target. |
| problem | •Gives first fraction problem: circle shaded in half |
| answer | •choice "a"= correct. Player gets to see first fourth of map. choice "b" or "c"= wrong. Player does not get part of the map. |
| play2 | •Stamps second target >>>MOVING |
| moving | •calls MOVE2. |
| move2 | •Allows the manipulation of letter keys to move person towards target. |
| problem2 | •Gives second fraction problem: circle divided into four, 1/4 |
| answer2 | •choice "a"= correct. Player gets to see second fourth of map. choice "b" or "c"= wrong. Player does not get part of the map. |
| play3 | |
| move3 | |
| movies3 | •Stamps second target |
| problem3 | >>>MOVING |

**FIG. 4.24.** Overview of Amy's first page GAMES as of April 22.

## March–June: Collecting Pieces of the Map— Considerations of Fraction Problems

So far we have followed Amy's initial game ideas and how she set up the structure for the instructional quiz. Amy's involvement with fractions began at the same time and was mostly reflected in the explorations of different fractions representations in her notebook design. Let us go back to the first days and look at Amy's designs of fractions (see Fig. 4.25). Here, Amy designed two different representations of one half using a triangle. Amy did not implement any of these designs in her Logo program.

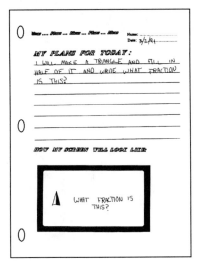

FIG. 4.25. Amy's designer notebook entries from February 28 and March 1.

Children's familiarity with the fraction one half and the particular place it holds among fraction concepts for children have been well documented in the research literature (Kieren & Nelson, 1978; Lesh & Landau, 1983). One half is the easiest and most familiar fraction for young children, and they are exposed to it early. Harel (1988) noted in her thesis that most of the instructional designers started in their software design by representing halves. She analyzed in depth Debbie's particular misconceptions about one half and how she overcame them through explaining and representing in various forms this concept to other students.

Amy's beginning, then, replicated the observations from other design projects. What may be more particular to Amy is that she designed different representations in her notebook of one half, still using geometrical-shaped objects. Most other game designers also choose one half as their "starting fraction," but only very few of them have explored variations in their notebook designs or program implementations. Amy's subsequent designs still involved a representation of one half, but used a circle this time (see Fig. 4.26). She became more concerned with the instructional context. If we look back at Amy's programming development, this was about the time when she finished implementing the MOVE procedure and started working on the other parts of her blueprint.

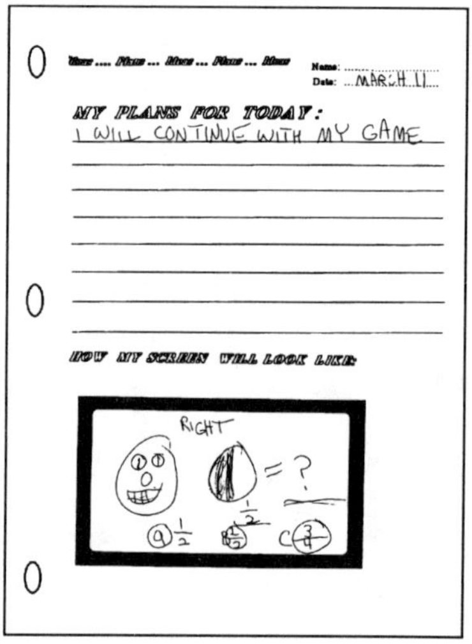

FIG. 4.26. Amy's designer notebook entry from March 11.

*First Fraction Problem.* Amy's Logo code for her first fraction problem was the procedure PROBLEM1 (see Fig. 4.27). Like many other game designers, Amy did not create representations of fractions using the turtle. Instead, she designed them on the SHAPES page. Similar to the PLAY procedure, where she used SHAPES and stamped them on the screen, Amy used SHAPES to represent her fraction question. One shape displayed a circle cut into half with one side shaded black; another formed a question mark. She presented the player with three choices; the first one, a, was always the correct one (she later changed this strategy about "a" always being the correct answer).

```
to problem1
rg cc ct
ST
tell 1 pu setpos [-95 75] pd
setsh 4 setc 15 stamp pu          Places circle shape one half.
setpos [-70 75] pd setsh 5        Places question mark shape.
stamp pu setpos pu
setpos [-25 75] pd                Places question.
label [Please type a,b or c for ]
pu setpos [-30 60] pd
label [your answer.]
type se [a = 1/\2 b = 2/\2        Choices are printed in com
                                  mand center.
c = 3/\2]   char 13
answer                            Calls procedure ANSWER.
end
```

FIG. 4.27. Amy's Logo code on March 11.

In the postinterview, Amy reflected on her game and its features. She emphasized that she liked making fractions.

> *Yasmin*: When you think about your project, how it is right now, what are the three best things about it?
>
> *Amy*: Even though the people don't look that good, I like making them. And I like the fractions. I like making the fractions. It's fun and it's easy.

I believe this expresses an important aspect of Amy's relationship with her game and fractions in general and with Logo programming in particular. Even though Amy was concerned like all her classmates about the aesthetics of her designs, making the shapes was the part she enjoyed most: "I like making them [the people]. I like making the fractions." Here, the difference between the process and products of design comes out most clearly. Furthermore, it shows one of the reasons why students are attracted to programming—they like the process of making things.

Amy's first instructional dialogue included feedback to the player's choice in the procedure ANSWER. (Her first instructional screen is shown in Fig. 4.28; the Logo code is shown in Fig. 4.29.)

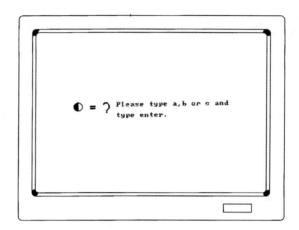

**FIG. 4.28.** Amy's first instructional screen.

```
to answer
name readlistcc "z
```
Reads a value into variable z.

```
if :z = [a] [ pr [Correct!
You get one-half of the
map and you have to get
one more half to get
the whole map. ] rg pu setpos
```
a = correct answer.

Shows one fourth of map shape.

```
[-75 -10] setsh 11 setc 6
pd stamp wait 150 play2]
```
Calls procedure PLAY2 to continue game.

```
if :z = [b] [type [That's
```
b = wrong answer; message saying game is over.

```
wrong.You do not get a
fraction of the map.]wait 100
rg pu setpos [-40 55] pd ht
label [Game Over] wait 100 rg]
if :z = [c] [type [That's not
```
c = wrong answer; message saying game is over.

```
correct.You did not get a
fraction of the map.]wait 100
rg pu setpos [-40 5] ht label
[Games Over] wait 100 rg ]
end
```

**FIG. 4.29.** Amy's Logo code.

For the correct answer, the player received one half of the map and could continue the game. Two days later, on March 26, Amy rephrased her feedback for the correct answer choice to

```
if :z = [a] [type [Correct, You get one-third of
the map and you have to get two more halves to get
the whole map.]
```

This was an interesting mistake on Amy's part. Here, she obviously interpreted the remaining parts of one third as halves. In her next session, on March 28, she corrected this mistake and the answer choice read

```
if :z = [a] [type [Correct, You get one-fourth of
the map and you have to get three more fourths to
get the whole map.]
```

This reply also coincided with Amy's map shape design, which was now concluded. Amy might have decided by now not to implement the initially projected 21 fraction problems (as discussed earlier in this chapter).

Another important observation can be made here. Amy broke away from standard representations of fractions in designing the shape for the map. I have already discussed Amy's choice of the map design and emphasized her move away from the standard representations of halves and fourths. On March 4, her first plan showed a map divided into 21 parts, one of which was colored in, whereas on March 25, her representation of a piece of a map appears as one fourth (Fig. 4.30). It is unclear what happened in Amy's thinking between March 4 and March 25. However, her change to fourths in her map design indicated a return to stereotypical representations of fractions. The design of the map shape may have influenced Amy in redesigning the answer choice. But most important, the map design represented for Amy a choice that led away from the anonymous representations in textbooks. She made fractions personal in attaching meaning to them and this may have been the most important step in her conceptual development. Harel (1988, 1991) had noted in Debbie's developing understanding of fractions the importance of the house scene, where all the shapes were presented as halves.

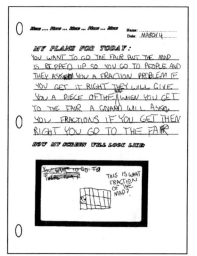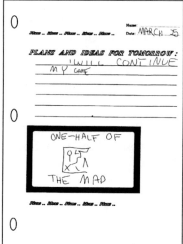

**FIG. 4.30.** Amy's designer notebook entries from March 4 and 25.

*Second Fraction Problem.* Amy continued using the blueprint for her instructional quiz to design three further questions and replies. For her second problem, which she started on March 26 and finished on April 3, she chose to design a representation of one fourths using a circle (see Fig. 4.31). What is most interesting about these designs is that Amy played around with one fourth on the same representation, using a circle cut into four parts. On March 26, three out of four parts were shaded in; on March 28, one out of four parts was shaded in.

Although most children understand the concept of a whole, it is more difficult for them to understand how one whole is comprised of different fractions parts (Lesh & Landau, 1983). Very often, students do not see the other part of the representation, the nonshaded area, as a fraction as well. I see Amy's two representations as a sign of flexibility in moving between two different views of the same representation for one fourth.

*Third Fraction Problem.* On April 3, Amy started thinking about her third fraction problem. Here she chose a fraction, one third, that most children consider very difficult, especially if they have to divide a circle into three equal parts. In my pre-interview, I asked Amy to divide a circle into three parts. Several of her attempts cut the circles into four parts.

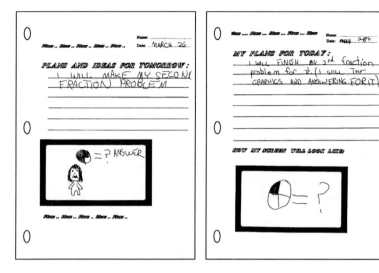

FIG. 4.31. Amy's designer notebook entries from March 26 and 28.

In the end, Amy decided to cut the circle into six parts and she told me that each person would get two pieces. In her notebook design of April 3, Amy crossed out a circle that looked like the typical one third representation of circles that most children draw: a circle cut into two halves and one of the halves divided again into two parts. Right next to it, she drew another circle divided into three parts and one of them shaded in (see Fig. 4.32). In the subsequent weeks she created more representations of one half (April 11): a circle divided into nine parts, three of which were shaded in (April 29); and a circle divided into three parts (May 3). On April 26, she drew the representation that became her third fraction question. She designed six squares, three of which were shaded black. Right next to it she wrote the symbolic representation "3/6 = 1/2."

*Fourth Fraction Problem.* After Amy finished her third fraction problem on May 7, she immediately drew a new one of a rectangle divided into eight parts, two of which were shaded in black. In the subsequent days, she went on to more complicated representations of circles: she creates a circle for 3/7 (see Fig. 4.33). She never implemented this design, and I am not sure why. It might be that she realized that it was difficult using the SHAPES.

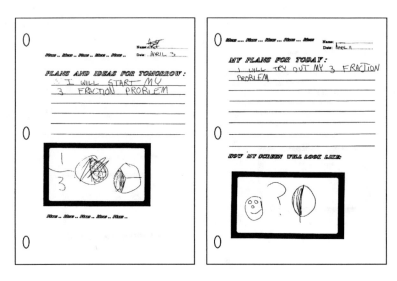

**FIG. 4.32.** Amy's designer notebook entries from April 3 and 11.

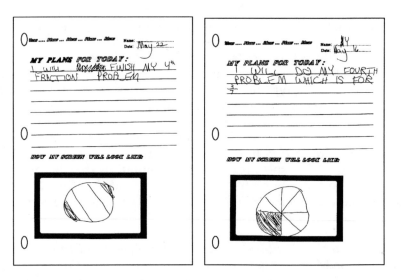

**FIG. 4.33.** Amy's designer notebook entries from May 7 and 16.

On May 21, Amy returned to the representations of thirds, and designed a double representation of two thirds. On the left side, two thirds of the circle's area was shaded in, whereas three smaller circles were drawn on the right side, one of which was shaded black. Again, as in the second fraction problem, Amy played with the complementary function of fractions that 1/3 and 2/3 equal one whole. But this representation also showed a further growth in Amy's development: She displayed one fraction using an area, the most typical representation for fractions, and the other fraction using discrete objects, circles. This is one of the first occurrences of a group representation of a fraction. On May 22, Amy designed a circle divided into five unequal stripes and the end stripes were shaded in (Fig. 4.34).

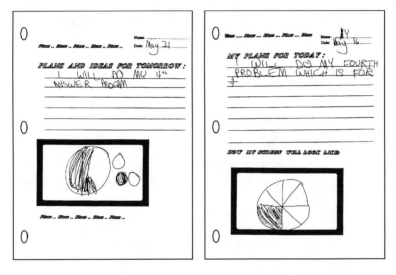

FIG. 4.34. Amy's designer notebook entries from May 21 and 122.

What fraction did Amy try to represent here: 2/5 or 2/3? I am not sure how to explain Amy's intention behind this design. I see it as evidence that she was exploring different ways of representing fractions but not all of them were correct. We supported students in writing down all their ideas and plans in their notebooks, but made clear that not everything had to be implemented.

*Summary.* A good way to summarize Amy's involvement with fractions in the context of her game is an overview of her designs over the four months of the project. I arranged all her notebook entries regarding fractions over this time period in an overview on two pages (see Figs. 4.35a and 4.35b). Amy often repeated many designs several times in her notebook entries, but due to space restrictions, I included only the first entries of a new design.

In this overview, it stands out clear that Amy dealt with fractions consistently throughout the project. She explored various fraction representations for her instructional screens, yet remained attached mostly to the representations of fractions as area. In her later designs, she also created group representations. One of her other classmates, Jero, was very similar to Amy in these explorations (see Figs. 4.36a and 4.36b). Amy also designed many more representations than she implemented. She explored multiple ways of representing a fraction: for example, using either the circle or the triangle for 1/2; alternating between 3/4 and 1/4 using different shadings, and using 1/2 and 3/6 for reducing fractions and creating representations for this. For 2/3, she often designed representations for 1/3 or 2/3, but never implemented those. Some of her representations also explored more "unusual" fractions, such as 3/9 (April 29), 3/7 (May 16 and May 17), and 2/5 (May 22), which were not the typical textbook fractions. Nevertheless, most of Amy's development of fractions remained rather limited when compared to the students in Harel's Instructional Software Design Project (1988).

At the end of the first phase of the Game Design Project, I asked Amy what she would do differently if she could start her game all over again. Interestingly, Amy was more concerned with the instructional content of her game than with her game idea.

> *Yasmin*: So, this is like a make-believe question: If you could start all over again, what would you do differently?
>
> *Amy*: The explaining program. 'Cause when I'm finished with the game, I'm going to go back and do explaining programs for each problem. And I would do more background for the people.
>
> *Yasmin*: The explain program, that's an interesting aspect. What are you thinking about?
>
> *Amy*: Well, if they get it wrong, I was going to do, "Please try again," but I decided to do an explain program by telling

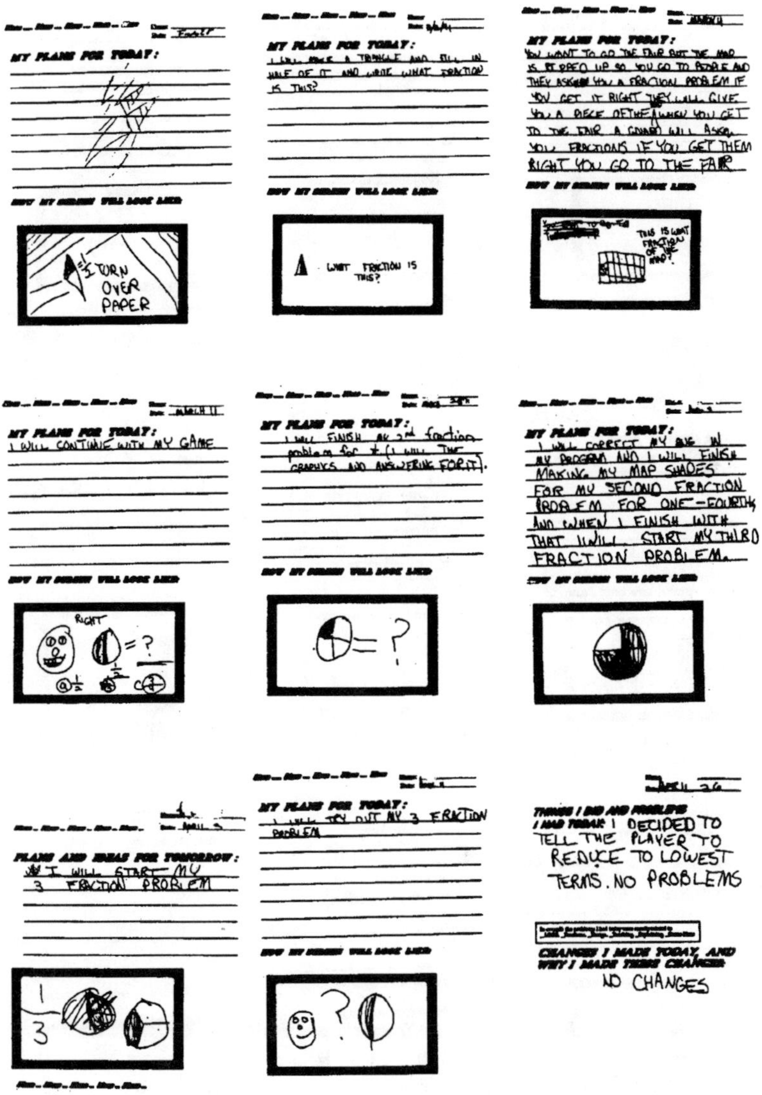

**FIG. 4.35a.** Overview of Amy's notebook designs of fraction representations from February 28 until April 26.

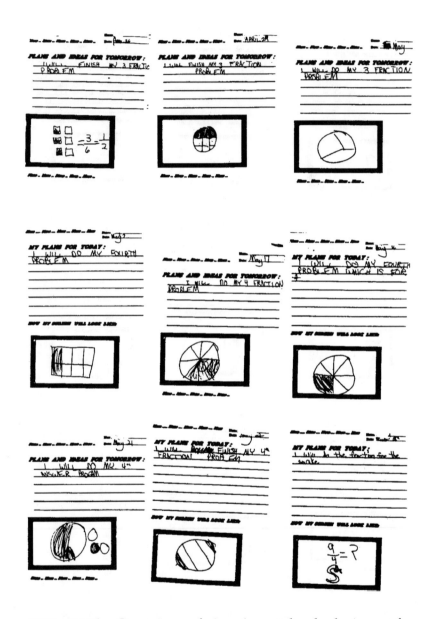

**FIG. 4.35b.** Overview of Amy's notebook designs of fraction representations from April 26 until June 18.

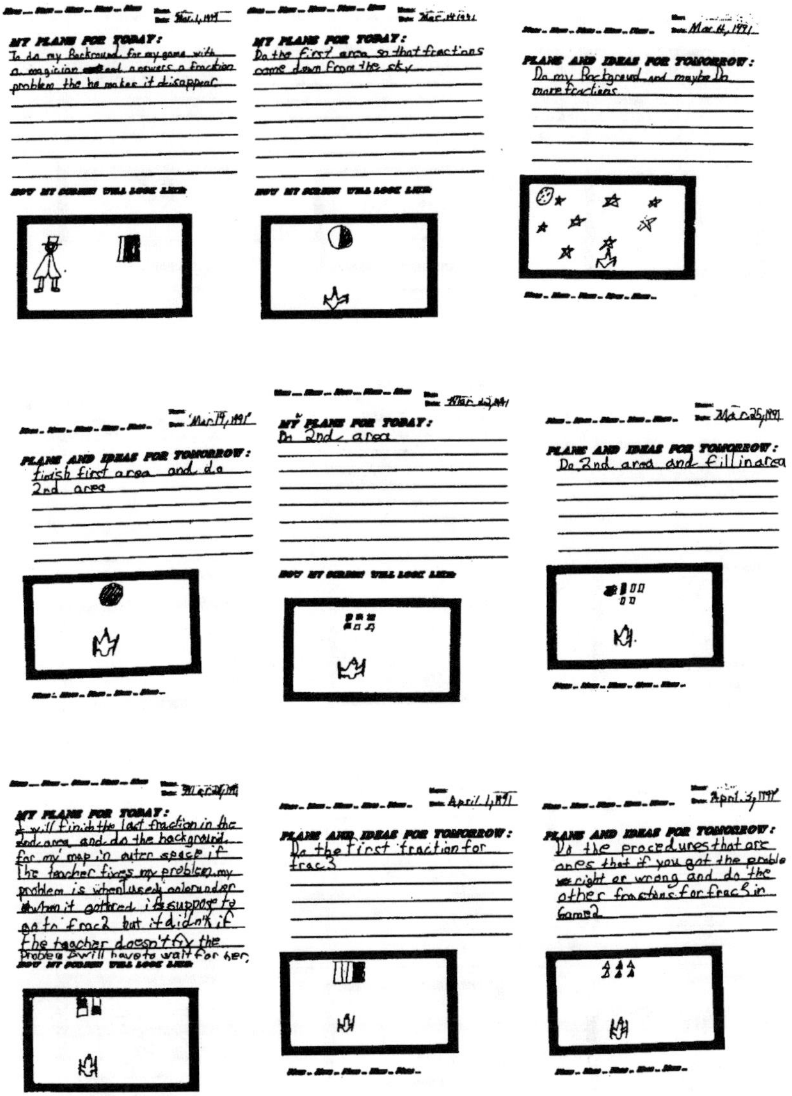

**FIG. 4.36a.** Overview of Jero's notebook designs of fraction representations from March 1 until April 3.

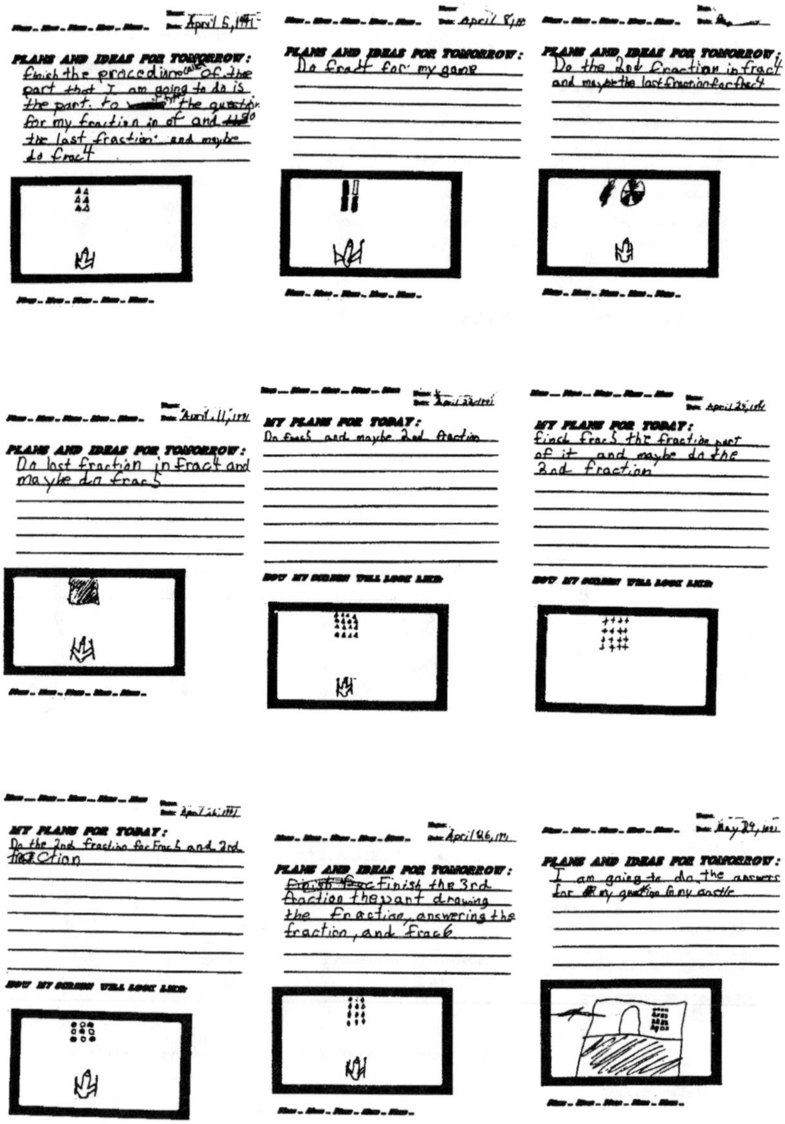

**FIG. 4.36b.** Overview of Jero's notebook designs of fraction representations from April 5 until May 29.

them why they're wrong. And that they should try again cause they're not going to learn if they don't take it.

*Yasmin*: What do you want to include, specifically, in the explain program?

*Amy*: I want to say...I don't know. I was just going to explain, like what is this [draws a circle]? And they get it wrong. And then I'd say, "No, this equals one half because one half is shaded in."

*Yasmin*: Would you explain something else?

*Amy*: And I'd say that you'd have to try again.

*Yasmin*: Can you think of different kinds of help you can provide?

*Amy*: No.

By the time of this postinterview, Amy had completed most parts of her game. Nevertheless, she was aware of its limitations: missing explanations and visual enhancements. Amy's concern about her missing explanations may serve as a further indicator of her involvement with fractions in her game.

## April–November: Greek Myths
## Changing the Plot of the Story: From the Fair to the Home of Zeus

On April 29, Amy decided to change the plot of her game. In her notebook, she wrote about "I changed the plot" (Fig. 4.38). This was a first indicator for Amy's move towards the narrative. The fair became Zeus' home and many of her game features adopted elements from Greek mythology. (For a more detailed discussion of the narrative elements in students' games, I refer the reader to chapter 3.) The Logo code in Fig. 4.37 shows her new introduction:

```
to start
ht cc
pr [You want to go to the home of Zeus but the map was
ripped up by the Greek God Hades. All of the Greek Gods
and Godesses have a fraction of the map. You are to go to
the Gods and Godesses one at a time and they will ask you
```

a fraction problem. If you get it right you will get a
fraction of the map. When you get the whole map you will
be at the gate of Zeus's home. The bull at the gate will
ask you three hard fraction problems. If you get them
right you will go inside Zeus's home and get to become
the God or Godess of fractions and meet Zeus! ]
wait.for.user start2
end

**FIG. 4.37.** Amy's Logo code on April 29.

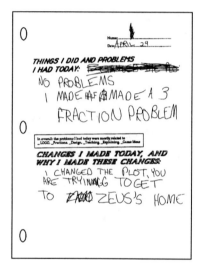

**FIG. 4.38.** Amy's designer notebook entry from April 29.

One of the reasons for Amy's change was a game presentation
that the teacher and I gave on April 26. In the previous weeks, we
had been asked repeatedly by the students about our own games
and whether we would show them. Let me give a synopsis of our
games. The teacher's game was situated in a sea environment. In
a sequence of scenes, the player went from fishing to diving and
meeting a sea star to opening a sea shell. It contained a mix of
fraction problems and information about the inhabitants of the
sea environment. For example, in the scene where the diver
opened the shell, the player was told that pearls were formed
around sand kernels that got inside the shell. Several animations
were included in this game: for example, of a man swimming,

seaweed with changing colors, and so on. At the time of the presentation, the game had no title, introduction, or directions, and
only three fraction questions had been incorporated.

My own game was called The Fraction Sphinx. The introduction presented the story of a sphinx guarding the entrance of a city
and asking all visitors fraction questions. After the introduction,
the player sailed across the ocean on a ship, accompanied by music, and was given the first fraction problem: a yellow square to be
divided into four equal parts. One of the yellow parts was sub-
divided into five smaller green parts. The player was given an array of choices. After choosing an answer, he or she was asked
whether another answer was possible as well. At the time of the
presentation, I had accomplished only one fraction problem, but
the title screen with moving letters and music, the introduction,
and the directions were all finished. The presentation of our unfinished games had considerable impact on some students and
raised an important issue about the function and use of examples
in design projects.

Once Amy switched her game context, she started involving
other students in her quest of finding out about Greek mythology.
This concerned various aspects. She frequently consulted her
classmate Albert about different myths (Amy: "He knows") and
asked others, including me, about spelling names correctly:

*Amy*: How do you spell "Zeus"?

*Yasmin*: What do you mean?

*Amy*: Zeuuus!

*Yasmin*: You mean like "zoo" where the animals are?

*Amy*: No, like in Greek.

*Yasmin*: Oh, the god, it is  Z-e-u-s.

*Amy*: So I was close.

*Miriam* [sitting right next to her]: I told you!

On the next day, Amy started working on the music that
would become part of her introduction (see Fig. 4.39). She also
included STARTUP in her program, which meant that the game
would start automatically once the player selected the GAMES
page. Other than that, Amy continued designing and implementing her fraction problems.

```
to startup
song
end

to song
tone 523 5 tone 587 5 tone 523 5 tone 659 5 tone 523 5
tone 698 5 tone 523 5 tone 784 5 tone 523 5 tone 880 5
tone 523 5 tone 988 5 tone 523 5 tone 1047 5 tone 523 10
end
```

**FIG. 4.39.** Amy's Logo code.

In the postinterview, four months into the project, I asked Amy again about her decision to change her game.

> *Yasmin*: Do you remember three months ago when we first started out with the project, what were your first ideas and plans?
>
> *Amy*: Well, [my] first idea was you're trying to go to the fair, but I changed it because I thought it was pretty boring. But I didn't make a lot of change. I just changed the directions because basically you [the player] did the same thing. So, it wasn't really like changing my game. I did change the plot but I didn't change what programs I really . . .
>
> *Yasmin*: What are some other ideas that you had?
>
> *Amy*: I was going to do something about the sea or I was going to do something about space.
>
> *Yasmin*: Why didn't you use those ideas?
>
> *Amy*: Because I thought of the other idea and I thought it'd be more fun. 'Cause I didn't have any real good ideas with the space and the sea thing.

She explained that her new story plot did not imply a major change in the game. The sequence of player actions and the fraction questions were the same. In another part of the postinterview, Amy spoke about the importance of the time point for making a decision to change the game: "[B]ut sometimes you don't want to change it, because then if you change it you don't have enough time to do another one." Amy's experience as a designer was that if a person has invested a certain amount of time in one idea, it is more difficult to change. I interpret Amy's changes in the light of her insight. She felt comfortable implementing the change in the plot of her story because she would not lose any of the programming work she had done so far. Instead, the new story offered a more compelling and fun background for her game.

Two further aspects of Amy's game change are intriguing. First, design activities offered opportunities for integrating other subject matters: Amy brought in a third subject, Greek mythology, on her own. The second aspect concerns the presentation of the teacher's and researcher's games to the students. I use this presentation to discuss the implications of using examples in design activities, or model cases as Perkins (1986) would say.

*Integration of Subject Matters.* The initial conception of the Game Design Project integrated the learning of programming with the learning of fractions in the context of games. With her change of the game context, Amy inadvertently integrated a new subject matter—Greek mythology. Writing about and knowing Greek myths is traditionally part of the language arts curriculum. Amy's choice showed how one can integrate different school subjects, such as mathematics, history, programming, arts, or writing, into one design enterprise. But there is another important point to be made with Amy's decision: the opportunities that design activities offer for bringing different subjects together. Harel and Papert (1990) argued that learning several things together can be easier than learning each of these things separately. They emphasized that learning different subjects in the same context can be supportive of each other. In Amy's case, the introduction of Greek mythology was supportive to her game design and offered a more compelling background for her instructional sequences. One might argue that her mix and meld of subject matters was not very profound, not nearly so much as people usually strive for when they are constructing crossdisciplinary curricula. This might hold true in the case of Greek mythology and fractions, yet it is important to remember that Amy chose to introduce this subject matter herself. She initiated all the thinking and searches for further information to place into the context of her game. The integration of several subject domains at the same time raises questions regarding the sequencing of learning components and the teaching of design skills as a separate subject. One argument against the integration is that students first have to learn the skills before they can apply them in a design project. This would mean, for example, that students first learn design skills, then the knowledge (fractions) and the skills (mathematical operations). Only after these prior steps have been completed could students combine all three in a design project. Amy provided a compelling case against that argument.

*Use of Examples in Design Activities.* In the beginning of the Game Design Project, we were confronted with the issue of how to provide support to the students for this complex and challenging task. I discuss here two different strategies and their implications that we both used in the project: providing examples and conducting discussions.

The teacher's and researcher's presentations were one method of bringing examples into design projects. We wanted to show students that designing games to teach fractions is something they can do, and also that adults are involved in this activity. Furthermore, we wanted to extend the classroom community, because we felt that students would be more receptive to our advice and suggestions if we presented these as designers instead of as teachers. We were aware of the potential impact of these presentations. However, after the student designers were two months into the project, we decided that whatever impact our design solutions might have would be counterbalanced by the fact that most students were well advanced into their own projects.

Another strategy was to provide examples of what had been done before. For example, we could have shown students a number of different educational games on or off the computer. In classroom discussions, we could have evaluated these games according to a number of criteria, such as their fun, teaching strategies, graphics, sounds, user interface, and so on. By doing so, we could have provided students with a sense of what some other designers believe educational games to be. Instead of presenting examples of educational computer games, we could have discussed games the students knew or had played with, what they thought was fun about them, and what could be learned from them. We chose to use the discussion strategy at the beginning of the Game Design Project. We had several classroom discussions where students presented their ideas of how to build a game to teach fractions. The advantage of this option was that we established a discourse in the classroom of what educational games are, a discourse that was informed by the students' knowledge and ideas.

The problem with the first strategy of giving examples relates to setting standards. Teachers and researchers are more than just a part of the classroom culture; they are also points of reference for the students of what is acceptable and right. For example, when a teacher says, "This is a good game," many students feel compelled to see that game as a right and acceptable one. In design projects, we want to move away from this issue of right or wrong. Designers talk about a design being done well or poorly, rather than being right or wrong. A designer might argue that the means or the medium chosen was not an adequate choice, or that a particular color or composition or sequence was not the right choice. Right or wrong also implies that there is only one right answer to a given problem. In design, there always is a range of solutions to a given problem. Furthermore, there are often no definite answers to a design problem. Design projects often have no real ending, as well as having no one right answer. There are always features that can be added, modified, or deleted to improve the design.

As to the impact of the teacher's and researcher's game presentations— some students decided to switch particular features of their games. For example, Jero, who for some time had considered changing his game, now started a new story in which he implemented both the swimming scene (from the teacher's game) and the ship crossing the ocean (from the researcher's game). He also switched his story context and narrative. Amy changed her story to Greek mythology. In her case, this did not require a structural or conceptual rearrangement of her game. It involved rewriting her introduction: The "people" became "gods," which was a matter or renaming; the end goal of the "fair" became the arrival at "Zeus' home." Amy did not change her programming of the structure of her game. In other words, most of her changes were on the surface level. These changes mostly benefited her story context. Her game was now placed in a larger context of Greek mythology. She could borrow and transfer the elements of her game and make the player part of it.

## May: Arriving at Mount Olympus—Zeus' Home

By the end of May 24, Amy had finished her first set of four fraction questions and reached the point where the player had all four pieces of the map. In early May, Amy had changed the plot of her story to Greek mythology, but she kept the map structure of her

initial plot because it allowed her to carry over all of the programming she had done during the previous two months.

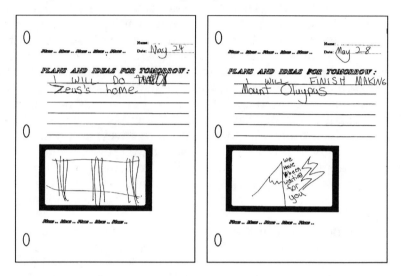

**FIG. 4.40.** Amy's designer notebook entries from May 24 and 28.

The parts of her game shown in Fig. 4.40 extended the story
from the Greek mythology.  Instead of arriving at the fair, the
player now reached "Zeus' home."

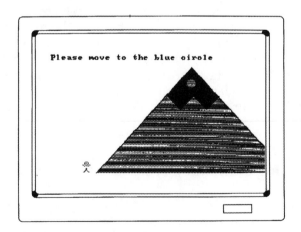

**FIG. 4.41.** Screen printout of Mount Olympus in Amy's game
Greek Myths.

For the last part of her game, Amy created a scene, Mount Olympus. She still used the same means of movement—the player had to move the Turtle to a target—but the placement of the target had changed (at the top of the screen instead of the middle) (see Fig. 4.41). Amy then proceeded to design the home of Zeus.

## June: Changing to Narrative—Meeting Zeus at Home

In the last days before the summer, Amy followed up on her design of Zeus' home. Her extension to a different game format stood out most clearly in the following scene: when the player arrived at Mount Olympus, he or she came into Zeus' home and saw pieces of gold (Fig. 4.42). Instead of the player moving around using the arrow keys, Amy had now programmed all the animations and interactions: She told a story.

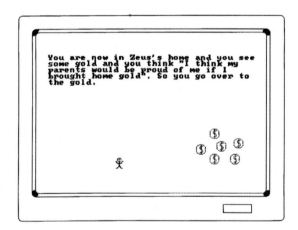

FIG. 4.42. Screen printout of the last scene in Amy's game Greek Myths. Note the use of dollar symbols for the six pieces of gold.

Amy's Logo code for the screen printout is shown in Fig. 4.43:

```
to Z2
rg ct
pu setpos [120 -50] pd              Stamps all the pieces
                                    of gold.
setsh 23 setc 6 stamp
pu setpos [85 -75] pd stamp
```

```
pu setpos [85 -35] pd stamp
pu setpos [95 -55] pd stamp
pu setpos [115 -75] pd stamp
pu setpos [65 -60] pd stamp
pu setpos [-125 -80] setsh 3
setc 2 pr [You are now in Zeus's
home and YOU see some gold and
you think "I think my parents would
be proud of me if I brought home
gold". So you go over to the gold.]
seth 90 repeat 19 [fd 10 wait 3]          Animates player to
                                          walk.

wait 100
ct pr ["Look at these big pieces of
gold!" you say.]
z3                                        Calls next procedure
                                          Z3.

end
```

**FIG. 4.43.** Amy's Logo code.

This is the first instance where Amy changed the instructional context. Amy now provided actors and dialogue that posed the fraction question (instead of just having a fraction problem appear with the corresponding answer choices). There are two interesting aspects connected with Amy's move. The first one relates to her introducing the narrative in her game. She realized now the intentions she had announced weeks earlier with "I changed the plot of the story." The second aspect relates to her fraction question. Amy placed six coins in the lower right corner of the screen. Her question addressed the equivalency of fractions for 2/6. Amy could have used the coins to provide a pictorial representation of 2/6, but she choose not to do so. This expressed a remarkable difference to the representations designed by the students in Harel's Instructional Software Design Project (1988). Nicole, one of the instructional designers, created a screen in which she used currencies such as dollar bills and quarters to show their relation to fractions (for a more detailed analysis, I refer the reader to chapter 6). The next screen that appeared is shown in Fig. 4.44; the accompanying Logo code is shown in Fig. 4.45.

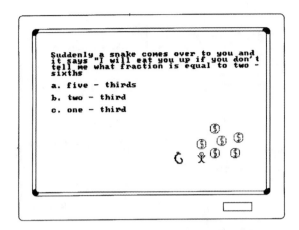

**FIG. 4.44.** Screen printout of the last scene in Amy's game Greek Myths.

```
to z3
setc 2
pd stamp pu setsh 24 seth 90          Moves snake towards
                                      player.
setpos [-130 -80] wait 50
repeat 20 [fd 8 wait 2] stamp
ct pr [Suddenly a snake comes
over to you and it says "I will
eat you up if you don't tell me
what fraction is equal to two-sixths]
pr []       pr [a. five-thirds]
pr []       pr [b. four-sixths]
pr []       pr [c. one-third]
answer5
end
```

**FIG. 4.45.** Amy's Logo code.

In her notebook, Amy had designed a new fraction representation: an improper fraction 9/4. But a quick look at the screen implementation tells us that Amy did not use this fraction in her question. Instead, she decided to focus on the equality of fractions (see Fig. 4.46).

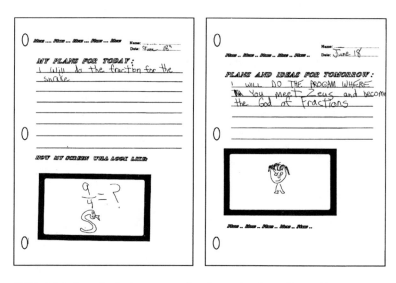

**FIG. 4.46.** Amy's designer notebook entries from June 18.

Amy then started working on the design of the final scene, which she  implemented after the summer.  She described the ultimate goal of the game "becoming the god of fractions."  At the end of June, Amy had implemented the major part of her game on three LogoWriter pages (see Fig. 4.47 for an overview).  That the design of the game was not finished could be seen from the procedures names that Amy had already written but left empty.

## September–October:  Connecting Myth to Math— Becoming the God of Fractions

After the summer, Amy worked on finishing her game.  Her first task was the last scene, the home of Zeus.  This scene was planned, but not implemented, before the summer (see Amy's notebook entry from June 18).  I interviewed her on September 24 about her plans for the second phase of the Game Design Project:

> *Yasmin*: So what are your plans?
>
> *Amy*: Well, you see, this is the end of the game where he [the player] made it to Zeus well, he gets to meet Zeus. So you get to choose if you want to go home or if you want to stay with Zeus.

*Yasmin*: Oh, with Zeus. So you [the player] are now in the home of Zeus? [I am referring to the house I see on her screen.]

*Amy*: No, this is your home. You see I am doing one ending of the game and I am doing the other ending [Amy is programming two endings for her game].

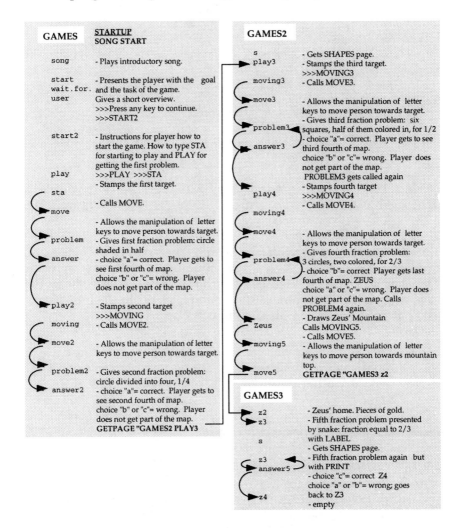

FIG. 4.47. Overview of Amy's game Greek Myths on June 19.

**FIG. 4.48.** Screen printout of the last scene in Amy's game Greek Myths.

In terms of programming, Amy was working on two procedures, Z4 and ANSWER6. In Z4, the player met Zeus (see Fig. 4.48) and was given two choices, either to go home or to live with Zeus forever.

The procedure ANSWER6 read in the player's choice and provided feedback. Each scene concluded with the message GAME OVER and credited Amy with the design of the game. The final overview of her game is shown in Fig. 4.49. In the interview, I asked her what else she planned to work on.

> *Yasmin:* So this is what you plan to do for the big fair, exhibition. Are there any other things you plan to work on? Any other improvements or changes you want to make?
>
> *Amy:* I am going to go through it after I finish and see if there is anything I need to finish up. That's basically it.

Most of Amy's work in the second phase of the project dealt with the final touches for her game. For example, she included the procedure WAIT.FOR.USER instead of WAIT in some of her procedures for the correct answer choices before the player continued with the next problem. Furthermore, for some of the incorrect answers, she added the message GAME OVER by Amy. In addition, she included the names of Athena, Aries, Apollo, and Aphrodite for her Greek gods in the first four fraction problems.

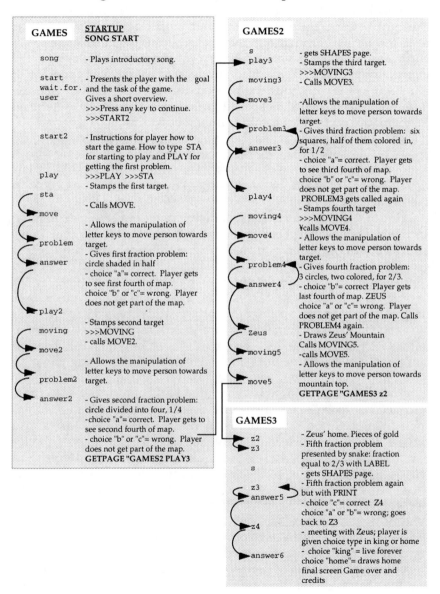

**FIG. 4.49.** Overview of Amy's game on November 14.

## Summary and Discussion of Amy's Case

I found Amy to be an interesting and rich student for a case because of her continuous engagement with fractions—which was
reflected in her game design, her programming, and her notebook
entries—and in her development of a programming strategy for the
instructional quiz. These different aspects were taken together in
Amy's mind throughout the project and proved to be a rich example of the benefits of an integrated design project involving
mathematics and programming, among other things.

The following four intellectual landmarks, taken together,
characterize significant developments in Amy's thinking about
game design and about fractions. The interesting aspects in her
development of fractions were located at different time points in
the Game Design Project.

Her first move was to make a distinction between instructional
software (as she had seen it a year before at another class) and
educational computer games. Amy started of with the idea of
creating a piece of software using a stereotypical fraction
representation (a triangle cut into halves) accompanied by an
instructional quiz. A few days later, after thinking about the task
of creating a game and seeing other students' ideas, she had
realized that instructional software is different from educational
games. With her fraction design, she had satisfied the fraction
component of the game but had not created an interesting game.

In her second move, Amy integrated a fraction concept into the
game design. She designed a map that had been ripped into parts
and needed to be reassembled by the player. Amy's idea of the
map in pieces had equivalents in many children's stories and
movies that involve treasure hunts and maps that indicate the lo-
cation of the treasure. In this particular context, Amy integrated a
fraction concept—the part–whole relationship—with the game
idea. Amy succeeded in attaching meaning to fractions in a manner very similar to the instructional designers in Harel's study,
who designed screens representing fractions by using measuring
aids in kitchens, different representations of money, wagons,
baseballs, and houses. However, if we look at Amy's conceptual
development in terms of her representational level of fractions, we
see that throughout the project Amy remained attached to the
part–whole concept of fractions. Her map design was probably
the best example of representing fractions as area. In the later

designs, Amy also started using "group representations" for two thirds and for improper fractions. Yet her boldest attempt remained her integration of a fraction representation with the map design, even though Amy continued to use fraction representations such as halves and fourths.

Amy's third move was related to programming. She provided the player with different interactions. She had the player move to a figure in order to answer a fraction question before the player could receive and start reassembling pieces of the map. In this approach, the player had to actively manipulate the figure in order to receive the fraction question and to construct the map. With this idea Amy took a more "constructionist" approach, whereas most of her teaching and quizzing adopted a more "instructionist" stance.

Her last move, toward the end of the project, was combining the narrative of the game with fractions. We saw how Amy introduced the idea of Greek mythology into her game. The last scenes of her game broke away from the more traditional game format and placed the player, through the narrative, in various encounters with gods. Amy also gave the user, in the last scene of the game, the choice to either "go home" or "become the God of fractions." These four different shifts characterized the different levels of Amy's conceptual development and learning of fractions.

In her game development, Amy created an interesting integration between Greek mythology and her map idea. Her change of the story plot in early May had implications only in the later part of the project, when Amy turned to a different game format. Instead of allowing the player to advance in the game through active manipulation, she placed the player in the position of a listener participating in a fantastic story. Amy became more creative and attentive to details in her designs and narrative when combining game design and fractions.

Amy's programming style showed a move from drawing-oriented programming towards more dynamic interactions and use of feedback. Amy's Habitat program, which she designed before the Game Design Project, is a typical example of the programs she and most of her classmates implemented. In drawing-oriented programming, students use the turtle mostly as a drawing tool to create graphical scenes. In contrast, interactive programming places major emphasis on controlling the flow of information between a player and a program, providing feedback if necessary, and inviting users to be involved in manipulations. This last type of programming requires students to think more deeply about possible interactions and the structure of their programs.

Amy's blueprint of the instructional quiz that she designed for her fraction questions is one good example. Here, Amy developed a programming strategy (keeping in mind the time constraints of the project), that would allow her to deal with the instructional component of the game in an efficient manner. The reuse and adaptation of an already written programming code is a useful strategy often employed by expert programmers.

The pedagogical implications of Amy's development in the Game Design Project are manifold. For one, Amy is a bright student in many subjects and we need to ask ourselves if her particular game ideas were something that could be achieved only by good students. One might suppose that Amy successfully appropriated the game design task only because she was a fluent programmer and a good student. However, this was one factor among many others. Other students apparently as bright and fluent as Amy created impressive projects but did not appropriate the idea of fractions and games in the same integrated fashion. Amy's participation in Project Headlight for many years made her an experienced programmer and allowed her to be creative. But this may be one of the most important points we want to communicate about the Project Headlight experience.

Another important point is that there was still room for improvement in Amy's case, in particular her thinking and involvement with fractions. We saw in Amy's case many important moments in which she connected to fractions, through her thinking about game design, her thinking about the narrative, and the creative use of the map.

# SID AS A GAME DESIGNER

DESCRIPTION OF THE GAME

Gemini and Swartz Fraction Journey is a very exciting game. At the beginning it tells you why you're on this fraction quest and what your mission is. It also tells you what the town **Peaceville is like and what Destrution is like.** After reading the directions you begin on your dangerous, exciting, educational and <u>daring game</u>.

DIRECTIONS

I know the directions seem crazy but you have to follow them. So for now we will just call them WILD AND <u>CRAZY</u> **DIRECTIONS**. At the beginning of the game you put your disk in and go to LogoWriter. Put in the game disk. Then just go to games3 and follow the directions. When you get to a green place with two trees and a door you type walk and then enter.

1. On the first problem it really is easy but read the directions carefully.
2. On the second problem you should look over the words and there you will find the fraction problem.

Sid's documentation for his game Gemini and Swartz Fraction Journey. The formatting in bold face, underlining, and capital letters was included in the original printout.

## Introduction

Sid had written the "wild and <u>crazy</u> **directions**" at the end of a six-month-long project. His writings did not reflect the process in which Sid was involved while designing and programming his game. As a matter of fact, for the major part of the project, Sid was engaged in designing two other games that he abandoned before he focused on Gemini and Swartz Fraction Journey. In the final two months of the project, Sid accomplished as much in the design of his game and its instructional purpose as most other students accomplished throughout the whole project. Part of

Sid's behavior in the Game Design Project might have reflected his general attitude toward schoolwork. He was likely not to finish or to forget homework. In school, he also seemed to have a hard time staying focused while working on assignments. One of the goals of this case study is to take a closer look at Sid's particular itinerary designing the different games.

Sid was a 10-year-old African-American boy who came to the Hennigan School at the beginning of fourth grade. He had an outgoing attitude and smiled a lot, yet he had a hard time getting accepted by his classmates. As one of them said about Sid, "He always minds other people's business"—something that is not always appreciated. In fact, many of his classmates seemed to take his outgoing interest as a matter of intrusion. In the middle of the school year, when students proposed choices for their line-up mates, Sid's name did not appear on any of these lists. Quite frequently, I saw him sitting by himself at the computer pods. Sid was not easy to interview, as some of the later interview segments show. He often told me, "I don't know," and it was unclear whether that reflected his indecision, his not knowing, or his unwillingness to talk.

Sid's case provided important insights into a wide range of issues covering the time frame of the project, fractions involvement, game ideas, and Logo programming.

*Time Frame.* I selected Sid for a case study because he did something that many of his classmates considered doing during the Game Design Project: He changed his game. Other classmates had similar difficulties in settling down on one particular game idea or considered starting over again several times. But Sid switched his game idea twice, and came only in the end to something that he liked and felt comfortable with. The additional seven weeks in the second phase of the project provided him with the necessary time to program and implement his game. He did so in a very straightforward and efficient manner that belied his difficulties during the first months of the project. My analysis shows that Sid's efforts in the beginning were, in fact, important stepping stones toward the completion of his third game.

*Fractions.* Sid's involvement with fractions was rather sparse. He created and implemented a total of five instructional situations. The number of fraction problems that Sid designed did not differ from that of most his classmates. However, Sid only worked on them in the last month of the Game Design Project. For the major part of the project, Sid was not involved with fractions.

He grappled mostly with finding a game context to situate his instructional interactions. An important design issue became clear: The design of the instructional content to teach fractions was interdependent with the design of the game context. Even though fractions were not central in many of the students' games, obviously the design of the instruction could not be completely divorced from the game design process.

*Game Ideas.* Another appeal of Sid's case was the variety of his different game ideas: from a basketball court, to a maze, to a fantasy travel. Each of Sid's games had a different theme. His first idea, a game using the basketball theme, orients itself on a real-life situation. Only two other games in the class did the same. Both were designed by girls and dealt with teaching situations. It could be that Sid felt that his game was too different from a real basketball game and that the many features were too difficult to implement. His second game, the maze, emulated another student's idea. Maybe Sid did not feel comfortable pursuing this idea that so closely resembled his classmate's game. His third game chose the context of a fantasy story in which fractions are the obstacles to be overcome in the quest for a princess. This game idea and story are very uniquely Sid's.

*Logo Programming.* Sid's programming process during the project revealed his fascination with animation, something he shared with other game designers. In the first two games, Sid experimented with programming the manipulation of arrow keys and the movement of figures before he formed a context to implement them. In his third game, however, Sid overcame many of his problems with programming constructs and proved himself to be an efficient programmer. Another issue of Sid's programming related to his use of procedures and superprocedures. Sid used a combination of procedure calls and superprocedures to create links between the different parts of his games. However, his first two games were fragmented, because many procedures had no connection with each other. The fragmentation displayed in the structure of his programs could also be considered a reflection of his dissociation with his game idea.

All 16 game designers designed and implemented a complete game. Some of them even designed two complete games, such as Trevor. Sid was the test case for this kind of project because of the long time and the many iterations it took him to find ideas with which he could identify and to which he could relate. Finding a design idea and implementing it means taking a risk. It is an official announcement to the rest of the class: "This is what I think is an interesting game idea. This is how my game will look." This statement requires explanation, which might be particularly difficult in the early stages when only glimpses and sketches of the future game can be seen.

*Structure of Sid's Case.* I structured his case into three major segments. Each segment presents the design of a different game that Sid started and implemented to a certain extent. Only the third and last game, Gemini and Swartz Fraction Journey, was brought to completion. Sid's project development was very linear, one game after another. Fig. 4.50 provides an overview.

---

The first phase (March–June)

| March–April | Game 1: *Fractions Slam Dunk* |
|---|---|
| March | Designing the basketball court |
| March | Dunking the ball |
| April | The fan club |
| April–May | Game 2: [*Maze Game*] |
| May–November | Game 3: *Gemini and Swartz Fraction Journey* |
| May | Variations on the introduction |
| May | Classroom presentation |
| May | The little hut: preparing the first animation |
| June | Meeting with Garvin: constructing the dialogue |

The second phase (September–November):

| October | Soldiers from Loft—2 fraction questions |
|---|---|
| October | Sparzi's castle—2 more fraction questions |
| October | Revising the conversation with Garvin |
| November | Ending of the game |

---

**FIG. 4.50.** Overview of Sid's project development.

In the following presentation of Sid's case, I describe day-by-day development of the different games to provide a sense of Sid's progress and struggles. The chunking of the segments in each game closely followed Sid's own focus with the graphical aspects of his game (this applies mostly to his first game) and the different scenes in his fantasy story of Gemini and Swartz Fraction Journey. The following case presents an overview of the different games that Sid developed in this project from March until November.

## March–April: Fractions Slam Dunk (Game 1)

Sid had a good start. Immediately, the first day of the project, he gave his PLANS FOR TODAY for the game: "I am going to make a game with math, addition, subtraction, and multiplication. I am going to make Michael Jordan dunk a basketball in the hoop. If the answer is right the ball will go in. If the answer is wrong, the ball will bounce off." When he came back from the computer work, he said in his PLANS FOR TOMORROW: "I will continue what I am doing today. I will make more people and have more math problems. This time I am going to have a timer. This time I am going to have certain levels." (See Fig. 4.51 for Sid's designer notebook entries.)

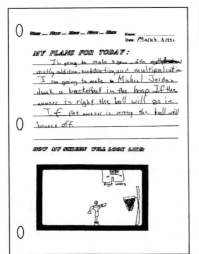 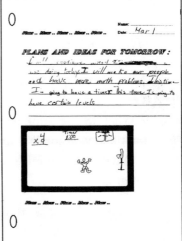

FIG. 4.51. Sid's designer notebook entries from March 1.

Sid wrote a math division problem on the top of his designs even though he did not like math classes. When the students discussed their different game ideas in class and how those could be combined with fractions, Sid confessed, "I hate fractions." Maybe this is one reason why he did not mention fractions but instead cited division. Sid wrote two lines of code on that day that would be the start for his basketball court:

```
to play
pd setbg 9                              Sets the background in blue.
```

In the interview about game ideas that I had with most students in the first days (March 4), Sid sketched out his design.

*Yasmin*: So what is your plan, Sid?

*Sid*: Me? Personally, what I am trying to do here is to make a basketball court and I'll have players going back and forth, back and forth. And then I make the player, the guy, with the ball go back and forth, back and forth. And I will have him insert a letter like A, to press A and that gives you a fraction. And I have him answer this and you will dunk the ball if you get it right. So, if you get the right answer, then the guy is going to come up and dunk the ball.

*Yasmin*: Dunk it. Great. So what happens if I get the wrong answer?

*Sid*: The ball is going to bounce off and I might have another guy come and catch it.

*Yasmin*: Okay, so then the other side is going to make the point. Good. Can I ask you something?

*Sid*: What?

*Yasmin*: What do you think is the biggest problem right now?

*Sid*: I don't know. Actually I don't have a problem right now.

*Yasmin*: What do you think could become a problem?

*Sid*: Nothing.

Sid's choice of the basketball theme for his game setting was not surprising, knowing his interest in sports in general and in basketball in particular. I had many casual conversations with Sid in which he updated me on current basketball events, or just went over the list of famous basketball players and names of teams with me. In a later interview (October 7) with another research assistant, Sid stated his admiration again:

*Cora*: What kind of heroes do you admire?

*Sid*: Well, sport heroes.

*Cora*: Sport heroes. What kind of specialties do you like about them?

*Sid*: They take their time, they practice. If they make a mistake, they don't show it. The mistake can turn into something else.

He told me that he often went with his father to basketball games. This was not the first time that Sid used the basketball idea for one of his programs. In his pre-interview, he talked about a procedure called JORDAN in which he has "a man going up and dunking into the basket." Sid was picking up an idea that he had before and transforming it into a game. Turkle (1984) wrote about the holding power of playing games. In her various interviews, it became clear that playing games has a particular personal resonance for each player. We might see an analogy in making games. Sid's choice of the theme of basketball resonated with his personal interests. We will see, however, that this does not always result in a holding power for making games.

## March: Designing the Basketball Court

In his ideas and plans Sid was now farther ahead. On March 4, he worked on SHAPES and prepared two procedures: MOVE, which stamped a player and a hoop on the right side of the screen, and GUYS. In his notebook, he wrote in PLANS FOR TODAY, "Today I am going to make Michael Jordan move to get ready to dunk the ball" (see Fig. 4.52).

```
to move
setbg 9
tell [1] st
setsh 2 setc 2 pu
setpos [135 -10]          Places one part of the hoop.
pd stamp
setsh 3 setc 2 pu
setpos [145 -30]          Places other hoop part.
```

```
pd stamp
end

to guys                                 Will be implemented later.
tell 2
```

**FIG. 4.52.** Sid's Logo code.

On the next day, Sid wrote in PLANS FOR TODAY, "I am going to make my players move and make music and a booth of fans and people" (Fig. 4.53) and added by the end of the session, "I am going to make the second basket and more players." He also created his first superprocedures, which included an interesting syntax error: He called the subprocedures as if in a listing, separated by commas as one would do in a real sentence.

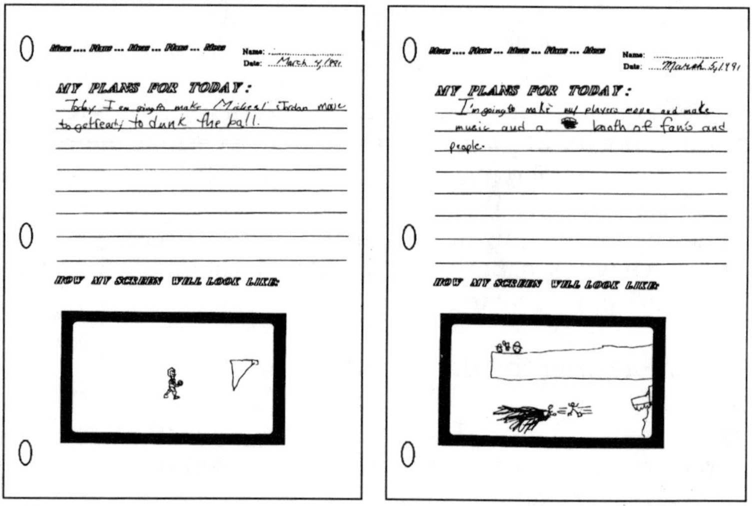

**FIG. 4.53.** Sid's designer notebook entries from March 4 and 5.

Sid next worked on animating his players. As he stated in his plans in the first interview, he made them go back and forth, from the left to the right (see Fig. 4.54).

```
to b                                    Sid's first superprocedure.
rg cc ct ht
move, guys, player                      The commas produce an error
                                        message.
end
```

```
to move                          Stamps different part of the
                                 hoop.
setbg 9
tell [1] st
setsh 2 setc 2 pu setpos [135 -10]
pd stamp
setsh 3 setc 2 pu setpos [145 -30]
setsh 4 setc 2 pu setpos [150 -50]
pd stamp
end


to guys
tell 2                           Not completed yet.

to player
tell [3] st
tone 50 20                       Makes some sounds.
tone 20 20
tone 40 20
tone 80 20
tone 160 20
tone 30 2
setsh 13 setc 4
setpos [-30 -40]                 Places one player.
seth 270 pu
repeat 10 [fd 10 wait 7]         Makes him move to the left.
setsh 26 setc 15
pu setpos [55 -40]               Places another player.
st seth 90 pu
repeat 20 [fd 5 wait 4]          Makes him move to the right.
seth 270 pu
repeat 20 [fd 5 wait 4]          Makes second player move to
                                 left.
end
```

**FIG. 4.54.** Sid's Logo code.

From the pre-interview (February 26) with Sid, I knew that he (like many other students) was interested in animation—how things move. I found out about this when I asked him more specifically to evaluate one of his programs, the sea habitat.

*Yasmin*: What are the three things that you like best about your program?

*Sid*: The diver . . . surfer, and the fish.

*Yasmin*: Why the diver, surfer, and fish?

*Sid*: 'Cause they move.

*Yasmin*: They move. What is good about the moving?

*Sid*: That they move, like, how they move. Like they move slow and you can see how their legs move. How they move; how they, like, go up and down.

Like other students, Sid professed his interest in animation. What he did not say but what I think was one of the major motivating forces in programming animation is that he, Sid, did the programming to make this happen. He controlled the movements (see also Albert's case, discussed later in this chapter, in particular the demon scene). There were two other interesting aspects in his programming. Sid experimented with TONE and he tried to compose melodies. Furthermore, in writing his superprocedure B, Sid made an interesting bug: He listed all the procedures to be called but divided them by commas, as one does in a real sentence. It showed that Sid understood the concept of superprocedures but had yet not mastered the syntax.

## March: Dunking the Ball

On March 12, Sid continued with his basketball game, now concentrating on the slam dunking scene. He wrote two procedures, called WRITE and GUY. Sid implemented two players in his game: They started at different positions and ran back and forth on the basketball court (Fig. 4.56). No interaction or control was possible from the player's side, except for pressing the "d"key, which introduced the first fraction. Fig. 4.56 shows the Logo code that Sid added on March 12.

```
to write
print [IF YOU WANT TO SEE THE STAR
MICHAEL JORDAN DUNK THE BALL DIG! DIS!
PRESS THE UGLY D KEY BOOYEEEY!]
END
to guy
pu setpos [5 -40] pd setsh 26 seth 90
pu repeat 1 [fd 5 wait 5]              Unnecessary use of repeat.
seth 270 pu repeat 1 [fd 5 wait 5]
pd stamp
end
```

FIG. 4.55 Sid's Logo code.

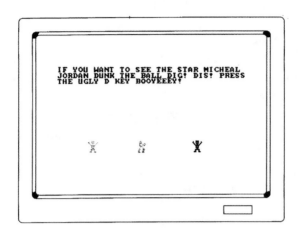

**FIG. 4.56.** Screen printout from the procedure on March 12.

During the subsequent week, Sid did not come to school because of illness. His notebook entry in PLANS FOR TODAY from March 19 stated that "I am going to finish up my program." This idea of finishing up persisted for a long time. On March 19, I had a conversation with Sid while he was sitting at the computer. Sid was not as communicative as most of the other students were. In retrospect, I think of a couple of reasons that might account for his rather stern attitude: Maybe he did not feel comfortable talking about a game that he wanted to finish and was not satisfied with.

*Yasmin*: So, Sid what are you working on right now?

*Sid* [difficult to understand]

*Yasmin*: So, you are nearly done, you tell me?

*Sid*: Yeah.

*Yasmin*: What is the last part you are working on now?

*Sid*: The fractions and the guys to make them.

*Yasmin*: To make what?

*Sid*: To make them dunk the ball.

*Yasmin*: How does this work?

*Sid*: It's easy.

*Yasmin*: I don't know.  What will it do? . . . So you will ask a
  question?

*Sid*: I ask a question.

*Yasmin*: What happens then?

*Sid*: You have a procedure that when you have to answer the
  question.

*Yasmin*: What happens with the answer?

*Sid*: Well, if you get it right, you dunk the ball; if you get it
  wrong, he doesn't dunk the ball.

*Yasmin*: Do you already have some ideas about what kind of
  question you are going to ask?

*Sid*: Yeah.

*Yasmin*: For example?

*Sid*: I don't know.

*Yasmin*: You haven't thought about it?  That's OK, you have
  time.

*Sid*: OK.

*Yasmin*: What do you think people should know about fractions?

*Sid*: I don't know.  I don't really want to do it about fractions.
  I'd rather do math.

On March 20, he wrote, "I am going to finish up my game by
making the half time."  Sid was the first of the game designers to
announce this idea of finishing.  Other students thought of changing game ideas or game features, but nobody else considered ending his or her game at this point in time, three weeks into the project.  Nevertheless, Sid continued to work on his game for another
month.  On March 20, he added the procedures WRITE, D, and
MUSIC to his program.  Most of the students had been only briefly
introduced to the Logo command TONE.  With TONE, two input parameters were required.  Sid's music programming presented a
rather interesting variation: He systematically varied the frequencies as well as the duration (see Fig. 4.57).

```
to write
print [IF YOUR MICHAELS
BEST FAN DIG! DIS! PRESS          Prints out on top of screen.
THE D BUTTON AND THEN
```

```
COMES A FRACTION AND
THEN A SLAM.] ht                    Hides the turtle.
end

to d                                Will be called if player
pu setpos [-110 5]                  hits the d-key.
SETSH 5 pd stamp
print [Press lhalf or 3fourths]
end

to music
CC RG HT CT CG                      Clears the screen of text and
                                    graphics.
label [              HALF    TIME !
SO  LETS  HAVE SOME MUUUUUSIC ! !]
tone 115 10          tone 200 20
tone 300 30          tone 400 40
tone 500 50          tone 600 60
tone 700 70          tone 800 80
tone 900 90          tone 1000 100
tone 300 20          tone 200 20
tone 5000 20         tone 1000 20
end
```

**FIG. 4.57.** Sid's Logo code on March 20.

Let us look at what Sid had accomplished thus far. First, he had programmed the basketball court and the animation of the players. Sid's procedure names such as PLAY and MOVE clearly indicated his intentions. Second, Sid had been exploring music features. He complained on March 12 that one could not hear any of the tones that he had programmed. One problem was that he had forgotten the second input parameter in TONE; also, his frequencies were very low, so even if TONE had been programmed correctly, one could not hear them. Later in the project, Sid worked on more experimentations with music. His rather systematic variations of frequencies showed how he tried to get a sense and grasp of the sound. Third, Sid had introduced his first fraction question three weeks into the project. On the SHAPES page, he designed a circle cut into halves with one side shaded in. In that sense, Sid started his representation in a very traditional way, like most of the other students (see also the similar analysis in Amy's case). Fourth, Sid had installed a superprocedure, called B, which called some of his other procedures. He also had corrected the comma mistake because it produced an error message. From the very beginning, Sid programmed all his different scenes in procedures. Sid did not sit down and say, "I am going to design the basketball court and I have one procedure that draws the hoop, another that describes the player." Rather, he made them up as he went along. There was no indication that Sid wrote his Logo code first and segmented it later. This was in very strong contrast to other classmates, for example, Albert, who put everything up into one big procedure at the beginning. Papert (1980) introduced procedures as powerful ideas, describing them as "mind-sized bites." For Sid, the procedures were different ideas that he implemented. One could call them, by analogy, "idea-sized bites." Each of his new ideas or plans was assigned a procedure name.

On March 25, for the first time, the title of the game appeared Fraction Slam Dunk. By now, Sid has implemented a complete instructional scene with two hoops, two players with different motions and the fraction one half (Fig. 4.58). He also has further plans. When his teacher and I met later in that day, we discussed students' individual projects, among them Sid's. In the teacher's conversation with Sid, we found out more about his plans. He talked about including different levels in his game: Each time the player got a fraction right, he or she would see a ball dunked. Then the player would come to the next level and at the end get a big medal. At this time, Sid was not very concerned about his end user. As the teacher played Sid's game, she told him that she did not know what to do because Sid did not provide any information or instruction.

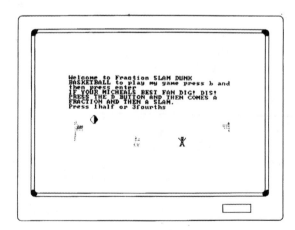

**FIG. 4.58.** Screen printout of Sid's program GAMES March 25.

Another interesting observation about Sid's game design was his concern with his game idea. At the end of computer time, Sid repeatedly marked the category GAME IDEAS, on the notebook sheet CHANGES I MADE and PROBLEMS I HAD TODAY. I had included an additional box where students could simply check the corresponding options:

> *In overall: the problems I had today were mostly related to* LOGO__, FRACTIONS__, DESIGN__, TEACHING__, EXPLAINING__, GAME IDEAS_X_.

Here, Sid had frequently checked the category GAME IDEAS in the preceding days and checked it again in the coming weeks (March 25 and 26 and April 2, 3, and 8). This may be a further indication that Sid was not happy with his current implementation of Fraction Slam Dunk.

## March–April: The Fan Club

On March 25, Sid's PLANS FOR TOMORROW were "I am going to make the man dunk the ball," but on March 26, he introduced a new idea: "I am going to make the levels for my games." At the end of that day, he wrote, "I am going to make my fans jumping say things out loud."

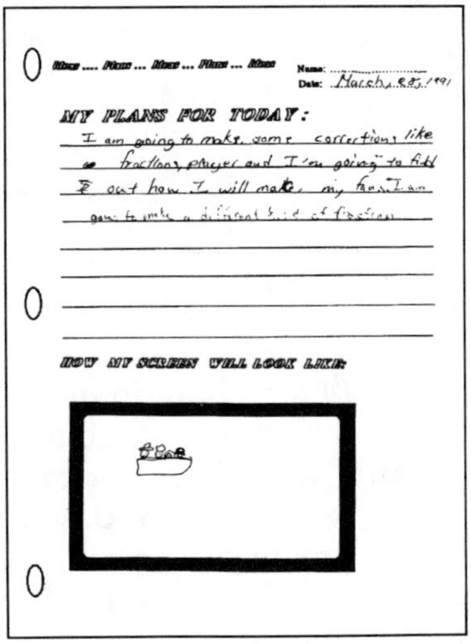

FIG. 4.59. Sid's designer notebook entry from March 28.

On March 27, he wrote, "I am going to make more problems with my mixed problems like . . . , some fan seat and fans," and later, "I am going to correct some things and make some more players." On March 28, he wrote, "I am going to make some corrections like fractions, players and I am going to find out how I will make my fans. I am going to make a different kind of fractions" (Fig. 4.59). Sid's ideas continued. On April 1 and the following days, he introduced in his plans, "I am going to make my girl fan jump up in the air, then I will make harder fractions."

On April 3, he wrote, "I am going to make the fans dance in the crowd, make characters run over the basketball course. Then I am going try to finish up my game," and his PLANS FOR TOMORROW were "I am going to make some more dancers and music and the end of the game" (Fig. 4.60).

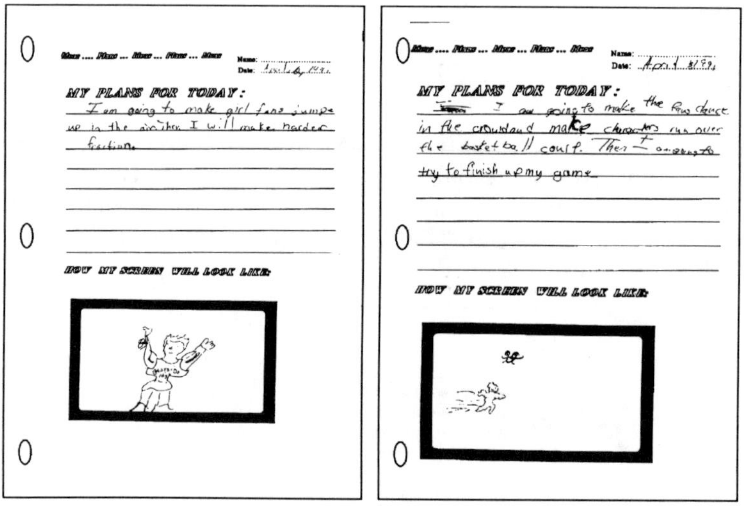

**FIG. 4.60.** Sid's designer notebook entries from April 2 and 3.

On April 5, he wrote, "I am going to make some dancers and music and the end of the game then I am going to make some character run around the court," and "I am going to make my character move tomorrow." Sid was still working on his animations. Several times in the preceding weeks he had asked me how to control the speed of the animation. He wanted his shape (he could not tell me exactly what it represented) to move slower. He pointed to the screen and imitated the moving gesture. I suggested to him that he change some of the parameters in his REPEAT statement. I told him that he could also make it move at different speeds, first slow and then fast. On April 8, he stated, "I am going to make my character move around the court," and later, "I am going to solve my questions and am play my game on my own." His problems were, "I did have some problems today like I couldn't find out why my man couldn't dunk the ball." On April 9, he wrote, "I am going to solve my questions and play my own game," and later, "I changed some of my characters today" (see Fig. 4.61).

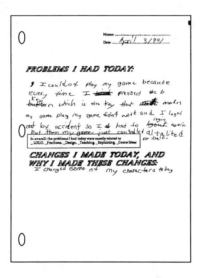

**FIG. 4.61.** Sid's designer notebook entry from April 9.

On April 22, I mentioned to Amy and Barney that I had found out how to use the arrow keys with the DRIVE procedure (previously we had used the letter keys). I installed a program with the DRIVE procedures for students to try out and copy on one of the free computers. Amy came over with her notebook. She first tried out the procedure and exclaimed: "Oh it works!" and then she copied the code. I indicated to her that she only needed to change a few things in her procedure. Several other students, Barney, Trevor, Jero, Sid, and Darvin came and looked. Sid kept running back and forth between the two computers (his seat was on the other side of the pod). Sid also copied the wrong numbers for the up-arrow. So did Jero, mumbling the numbers.

Amy (in a demanding, teasing voice): "You should take your note-book and write it down!" At the end of that computer session, Sid wrote in his notebook that he had a lot of problems: "I had a lot of problems today one problem was that when I was using drive I couldn't . . . (illegible) and in his PLANS FOR TOMORROW that "I am going to make some fans make a lot of balls and use a new presedure." On April 24, he wrote that he had problems with the MOVE procedure: "Last time everything was working, now it doesn't anymore."

At this point, I stopped documenting Sid's game design in de-tail. I included Sid's numerous notebook entries describing his plans and ideas for his Fraction Slam Dunk game (see also overview in Fig. 4.62) in order to show that Sid had many ideas— fans, dancing girls, music, timers, booths, dunking balls, moving players—for his game. He listed many ideas during the first five days of the project, and implemented many of them in Logo pro-cedures. But 3 weeks into the project, the first signs of discontent with his game and wanting to finish became evident. Why then did Sid continue another 4 weeks working on his Fractions Slam Dunk before abandoning it? In the following paragraphs, I present some of the reasons that might underlie his switch.

The first reason applies to Sid's style of programming. As I described before, Sid wrote procedures like "idea-sized bites" that represent his individual ideas. He still worked on his dancers and made more music and animation. But he did not implement them. Sid's game became very fragmented. All his later proce-dures are not connected to the core of his first procedures. Only the early procedures were called in his superprocedures. I inter-preted this fragmentation of Sid's programs to mean that he did not feel comfortable including them. They were not working. They did not offer appealing animation. The increasing fragmentation in his program was a sign that Sid did not see connections among the pieces and did not want to make connections.

Sid's personal style of working through problems might have been another reason. In an interview with a research assistant, Sid stated how he handled problems:

| Entry | Ideas and Plans | Implementations | Events |
|-------|-----------------|-----------------|--------|
| MARCH 1 | - game with math; dunk a ball; right answer, wrong answer; more people; timer; different levels | play | |
| MARCH 4 | - make player move; dunk a ball | move | |
| MARCH 5 | - make music; player move; booth of fans; people; second basket | guys player | |
| MARCH 12 | - dunk ball | | |
| MARCH 19 | - I am going to finish my program. - make half time | write d music | First time Sid mentions that he wants to finish his game. |
| MARCH 20 | - dunk ball | | |
| MARCH 25 | - make levels for game; make fans jump + say things loud | 1half 3fourths basket | GAME IDEA PROBLEM |
| MARCH 26 | - mixed problems; some fans; make more players | dunk | GAME IDEA PROBLEM (from his notebook )show g |
| MARCH 27 | - corrections of fractions; players; make fans; more players | | |
| MARCH 28 | - girl fan jump into air; harder fractions | dance m | |
| APRIL 1 | - girl fan jump into air; harder fractions; fans dance in crowd | | GAME IDEA PROBLEM |
| APRIL 2 | - fans dance crowd; characters run across court; more dancers; music | | GAME IDEA PROBLEM |
| APRIL 3 | - dancers; music; characters move | da | Sid mentions again that he wants to finish game. |
| APRIL 5 | - characters move on court; solve my questions; play my own game | | |
| APRIL 8 | - solve my questions; play my own game | | GAME IDEA PROBLEM |
| APRIL 9 | - fix all problems; music and band; make dancers dance | 2f b a | |
| APRIL 10 | - ask kids questions how they like my game; make dancers move | wa dis | 1. Evaluation Visit of Third Graders |
| APRIL 11 | - make characters move | bang | |
| APRIL 12 | - dancers move; make fans; more balls | fraction two | |
| APRIL 22 | - dancers move; make fans; more balls; more enemies | enemy | |
| APRIL 23 | - two more enemies; change my enemies | | |
| APRIL 24 | - make two enemies move | | |
| APRIL 26 | - make two enemies move; | | |

FIG. 4.62. Overview of Sid's plans and implementations for the first game. In the Ideas and Plans column, I provide a summary of his notebook entries, in the Implementations column I describe the corresponding procedures that were implemented at that time, and in Events I describe other notes or activities that happened during this time.

> *Cora*: You got a good idea.  What is the first thing you do?
>
> *Sid*: First, I start from the hard things then I just go through the small ones so I can work my way down.  Like, if I want to have a major thing, I would do that right away, so I can get it out of my face.  You know, just keep on doing it.  So I feel that the game should end.
>
> *Cora*: Also, if you have a good idea, you work on it immediately?
>
> *Sid*: Also, I have different ideas.  So I have to think for a while, then make my decision which I am going to do.
>
> *Cora*: Where do you get most of your ideas?
>
> *Sid*: I get my ideas like . . . first, when I started the game, well I am just typing that stuff.  I get ideas.  So I just keep on doing.

Sid has an interesting approach in dealing with problems and new ideas.  He stated that "I start from the hard things then I go through the small ones."  A few moments later, he said that he gets ideas from just typing.  These two statements about his styles of dealing with problems and ideas seemed contradictory (Turkle & Papert, 1990).  His first statement was much more representative of that of a planner having reviewed the list of problems to work on and identified the most difficult one.  His second statement seemed to speak more from a bricoleur's point of view: getting ideas as he was working and integrating them into the design.  I saw his statement as evidence that both styles can coexist in the same person.  Sid had many ideas that he presented in his notebook, not of all which were implemented.  In fact, he started with the hard problem—making the players move and dunk the ball.  These two ideas were prominent in his entries and programming and kept reappearing in his plans.  His dissatisfaction with his current implementation and the hard problems might have pushed him to give up.  A further reason was Sid's methods of dealing with problems.  In the same interview, he stated that he erased ideas when they didn't work.

> *Cora*: If you have a problem in  your programming, like your program won't run, after you spend so much time?
>
> *Sid*: Yes, it happens.

*Cora*: What is the first thing you do? What is the first thing you think about doing?

*Sid*: I think I'll try and if this doesn't work and I still cannot get help, I'll erase the idea.

Papert (1980, p. 113) described as one of the advantages in programming the possibility of making mistakes that are simply part of the programming process. I agree with him on the point that undoing mistakes should be easy and part of the process. Yet, in Sid's case, this attitude raised critical issues, because he had such a hard time concentrating and finishing work. It might have been very important for him to continue working further until he reached a breakthrough instead of giving up too easily. When Sid started his second game, he "officially" erased his first game completely.

This led me to a fourth reason for ending his game, which was Sid's dissatisfaction with his game idea itself and his persistence in wanting to finish the game early on. One aspect of this dissatisfaction might have been the student evaluation on April 11. Sid was not happy with how the evaluation went. Before the evaluation, he wrote that "I am going to ask the kids that are in another class questions. I am going to ask them how they like my game and 4 other questions." Later, he complained that his student-evaluators did not pay any attention to his game at all: "They [the two girls] just talked about boys."

On April 29, Sid continued working on his enemies. In his program, he had problems running the TONE commands, even though he used the correct syntax. (Very frequently for unknown reasons, the computer put hidden characters into the students' programs and produced error messages. The only solution was to copy the procedure to a different place.) Sid told me that he had a problem. When I asked him what his problem was, he told me that TONE caused a problem but he had fixed it. He also announced clearly in his PLANS FOR TOMORROW that "I am going to make a games two." Figure 4.63 shows Sid's first game as it was on April 29.

FRACTION SLAM DUNK BASKETBALL

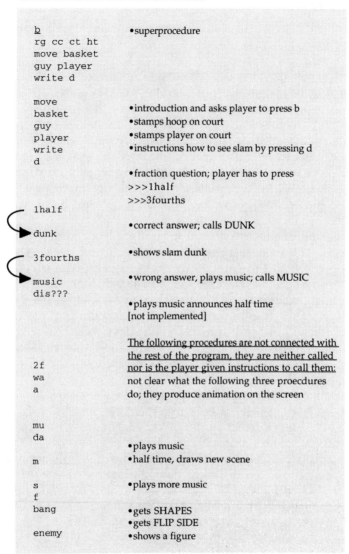

| | |
|---|---|
| <u>b</u><br>rg cc ct ht<br>move basket<br>guy player<br>write d | •superprocedure |
| move<br>basket<br>guy<br>player<br>write<br>d | •introduction and asks player to press b<br>•stamps hoop on court<br>•stamps player on court<br>•instructions how to see slam by pressing d<br><br>•fraction question; player has to press<br>>>>1half<br>>>>3fourths |
| 1half<br>dunk | •correct answer; calls DUNK<br><br>•shows slam dunk |
| 3fourths<br>music<br>dis??? | •wrong answer, plays music; calls MUSIC<br><br>•plays music announces half time<br>[not implemented] |
| 2f<br>wa<br>a | <u>The following procedures are not connected with</u><br><u>the rest of the program, they are neither called</u><br><u>nor is the player given instructions to call them:</u><br>not clear what the following three proecdures<br>do; they produce animation on the screen |
| mu<br>da | •plays music<br>•half time, draws new scene |
| m | |
| s<br>f<br>bang | •plays more music<br><br>•gets SHAPES<br>•gets FLIP SIDE |
| enemy | •shows a figure |

FIG. 4.63. Sid's first game, Fractions Slam Dunk on April 29. Note that his program did not have a clear structure. The left column displays Sid's procedures in the order that they appeared in his original program code. The right column provides a summary of the procedure content.

Sid was not the only one who wanted to change his game. After class, the teacher came to me and updated me about the students' work.

*Joanne*: Did you hear? Miriam and Jero both want to change their game. Jero told me his wasn't exciting.

*Yasmin*: Yes, I told him he could do it if he really wants to.

*Joanne*: I want first to talk with them about it before they start all over. It could be that they only need a little bit of encouragement; someone tells them, "This is great!"

Based on my previous interpretations, it is doubtful whether encouragement would have helped Sid continue his game. His disenchantment had gone beyond that stage. Sid worked very hard on two aspects: the animation and many features of a real-life basketball game. Many of his procedures moved shapes of players or fans. He described many features of the basketball game: the game action (players moving back and forth, ball dunking, fans dancing and talking), the participants (players, fans, people), and the rituals (half-time, music, dance). It was my assumption that Sid was not satisfied between his implementations in Logo and the experiences he knew from going to real basketball games. He tried to carry over many of the important aspects, but his attempt to make his game so real may have made it harder for him and rendered the discrepancies more visible. The animations may have been another source of his dissatisfaction. Another game designer, Albert (whose case I present in detail later in this chapter), also created animations. For his crucial scene of the demon jumping out of a chest, Albert spent three months on planning and preparations before actually implementing it. Sid made several attempts, but those may not have satisfied him.

## April: Maze Game [Game 2]

Sid's second game began on April 29 with a notebook entry, "I am going to make a games two." Sid did not make any drawings, provide further descriptions or give this new game a name. Remember that Sid had announced one month previously that he wanted to finish his first game and start working on a new one. A few days later, in a conversation with his teacher, Sid described his new game idea.

> *Sid*: Now I want to have, let's see . . .
>
> *Joanne*: Where do you want to have the man move?
>
> *Sid*: Oh, I know what I do, to move them forward.
>
> *Joanne*: Is there a purpose? Are they trying to get to something?
>
> *Sid*: Yeah. There is gonna be like, ahm, like shapes coming, like enemies coming towards him and he has to move away and so then I am gonna have like . . .
>
> Joanne: He has to move around the enemies?
>
> Sid: Yes, and so I am gonna have like one of those street things in the middle, you know, those sewer tops right here [pointing to the screen] and I am gonna have like tar stops, tar that stops the wheels of the cars. He has to move around them.
>
> *Joanne*: Have you made your enemies?
>
> *Sid*: No, but I am going to do that.
>
> *Joanne*: That's what you need to do. So you are up to the point now where your enemies are moving. So you can move your enemies around and he can try to avoid them.
>
> *Sid*: Thank you.
>
> *Joanne*: You are welcome.

This conversation is an example of the kind of scaffolding or prompting a teacher can provide for students. The teacher's question "Is there a purpose?" provided an interesting example for one of Perkins' (1986) four design questions about structure, purpose, model case, and argument. Here, the teacher used it for two purposes. First, she wanted to get information on what Sid wanted to do with the figure in his game, and to understand the purpose of his programming (she had helped him with a programming problem before). Second, she wanted to understand the general context of the game. In the process of raising this question, she also made Sid be more explicit about his own underlying game plans and goals, none of which had been documented in the notebook. In this conversation, the teacher helped Sid clarify his own game ideas and what he needed to work on. Through this conversation we also found out that Sid was trying to implement a maze. His friend Darvin has worked since the beginning of the project on a similar idea: He designed a maze through which a skater had to run avoiding ghosts (see Fig. 4.64).

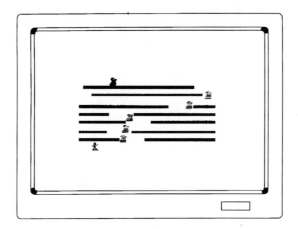

**Figure 4.64**. Screen printout from Darvin's game Run.

Sid emulated some of Darvin's ideas in his new game, but instead of having ghosts, Sid chose tar and sewers (see Fig. 4.66 for a screen that shows this implementation). Sid officially deleted his old game. His first procedure PLAY drew a vertical line on the right side of the screen and set the background to red. The music that Sid programmed seemed more like an alignment of different notes than a melody (see Fig. 4.65).

```
to play
setsh 0 pu setpos [110 -55] pd fd 200
setsh 8 pu setpos setbg 4
end

to music
tone 224 25   tone 623 50   tone 900 25
tone 324 25   tone 3129 50
end

to mu
tone 9000 24    tone 800 23   tone 70 22
tone 10 21   tone 06 2   tone 01 9
end
```

**FIG. 4.65**. Sid's Logo code on May 20.

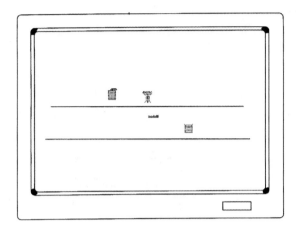

**FIG. 4.66.** Screen printout from Sid's second game as of May 6.

On the following day, May 1, Sid copied the DRIVE procedure again (he had a nonfunctional version in his first game). I discuss this episode in more detail, because it showed how students often dealt with an array of bugs in their programs. After they had successfully removed one bug, others were still embedded in other procedures. In Sid's case, his first problem was in a new procedure, DRIVE, which he now wanted to use in his program. His second problem was smaller: some of his code in other procedures drew lines where it was not supposed to. During the computer time, Sid announced, "I want to do the arrow thing."

> *Yasmin*: I cannot remember the numbers [I am referring to the ascii code,] did you write them down [in your notebook]?
>
> *Sid*: I cannot find it anymore.
>
> *Yasmin*: I think Amy has it written down. Why don't you go to her and ask her if she can give you her book so that we can copy the numbers.
>
> *Sid*: But I don't want to have numbers, I want the arrow keys.

Sid's statement clarified one issue for me: He still did not understand that each arrow key, and for that matter any keyboard key, was represented by an ascii code. Sid went to Amy and copied the numbers. There were still a few problems with his DRIVE procedure:

```
to drive :key
if :key = 72 [seth 0 fd 5]
if :key = 80 [seth 180 fd 5]
if :key = 77 [seth 90 fd 5]
if :key = 75 [seth 270 fd 5]
if :key = 115 [stop]
drive ascii read char
```
READCHAR has to be written as one word.
END is missing.

```
to start
drive ascii read char
```
READCHAR has to be written as one word.

```
end
```

After Sid and I fixed together his END and READCHAR bugs, his procedure ran correctly. Sid pointed out to me another problem in another procedure: It drew an extra, unwanted line when he ran his new procedures SET1 and SET2. The following printout shows Sid's new program code:

```
to set1
st setbg 9 setsh 0 seth 90 pu
setpos [-150 -30] pd fd 300
```
Draws a horizontal line.

```
setsh 0 seth 90 pu setpos [-150 -85]
pd fd 400
```
Draws a second horizontal line.

```
setsh 1 setc 6 pu setpos [-55 -10]
pd stamp
```
Stamps different shapes along lines.

```
setsh 2 setc 2 pu setpos [0 -15]
pd stamp
set2
end
```
Calls procedure SET2.

```
to set2
setc 1 setpos [-150 -20]
```
PENUP is missing here.

```
setsh 8 startup
end
```

His teacher then joined Sid at the computer, and the following conversation ensued:

*Sid*: See it's working. Every time I do it, every time it does SET2, it just draws a line.

*Joanne*: Why?

*Sid*: I don't know.

*Joanne*: Yes, you do.  If you don't want it to draw a line, what do you have to do?

*Sid*: PENUP.

*Joanne*: Yes, of course you know why! [Sid looks at his procedure.] If you don't tell the turtle to do PENUP and you set the position, each time it draws a line when it gets to this position.

*Sid*: Oh here [he is now at the procedure SET2].

*Joanne*: If you put it here it's fine [pointing to the beginning of the line].

*Sid*: Let's see now. [He returns to the graphics screen and runs the program from the beginning.]

*Joanne*:  Did it draw a line?

*Sid* [joking]: Yes.

*Joanne*: Did it draw a line?

*Sid*: Where?

*Joanne*: From here to there?

*Sid*: No.

*Joanne*: No. OK.

Sid did not finish this, his second game, either.  He designed some more shapes, elements for the new environment, but never created a title, introduction, or directions.  In the three weeks that Sid worked on his second game idea, he was not involved in any fractions.  His main concerns were directed toward programming problems.  Even though I called this phase his second game, I think it really represented a transition phase in his game development, for the following reasons.

Sid's programming of game features was very sketchy in the beginning of his second phase.  He replicated the design start of his first game: He started out with preparing the environment in which the instructional context would be located.  He programmed some features of the environment, such as the obstacles on the street, the arrow-key procedure, and music.  These procedures were connected with each other through procedure calls (see Fig. 4.67).  The central feature of Sid's second game was his the inclusion of the DRIVE procedure.  Sid used this procedure in his first game, but it did not function there. During his first game, Sid was more concerned with programming the animations on the screen. Instead of having the player move the shapes around, he programmed movement. I see this as an exploration of another facet of animation. Sid picked up a combination of game ideas for his second game. The strongest influence was the maze from Darvin's game. The teacher's questions prompted him to concretize some of his ideas, but the goal of the game (why does the man have to avoid all the obstacles?) and how the instructional content of fractions would be included were still unclear. Sid did not develop this game idea fully.

**[No name]**

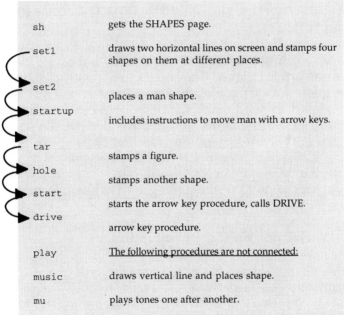

| | |
|---|---|
| sh | gets the SHAPES page. |
| set1 | draws two horizontal lines on screen and stamps four shapes on them at different places. |
| set2 | |
| startup | places a man shape. |
| | includes instructions to move man with arrow keys. |
| tar | |
| hole | stamps a figure. |
| | stamps another shape. |
| start | |
| drive | starts the arrow key procedure, calls DRIVE. |
| | arrow key procedure. |
| play | The following procedures are not connected: |
| music | draws vertical line and places shape. |
| mu | plays tones one after another. |

**FIG. 4.67.** Overview of Sid's second game [Maze game] as of May 17.

At this stage, three months into the project, a critical issue for design projects emerged. There would always be students who had problems identifying with the task at hand. None of Sid's programs were finished. All his thinking and messing around with different ideas and Logo procedures did not bring him very far. Also, Sid was not involved with fractions at all. Compared to the other game designers, Sid accomplished very little in this time and he definitely did not seem to be on task. What had Sid learned in this time? Why did it take him so long? I believe that we saw Sid in a kind of incubation phase, as his later development showed (see also Harel, 1988; Kafai & Harel, 1991a). It is correct that all his messing and thinking around looked aimless. Yet, for students with Sid's personality and working habits, it seemed more normal. It took him more time to overcome his old working habits, to find an idea that he liked and would work on.

## May–November: Gemini and Swartz Fractions Journey [Game 3]

From May 7 until May 24, Sid was already indicating his intention of starting a third game. The entries in his notebook often stated: "I am going to start games three" without giving any hints what the new game would be. The following notes and designs in his notebook lacked the detail that he provided for the scenes in his first game. My interpretation was that Sid had abandoned the notebook as a planning tool to sketch out elements of scenes that he would implement later in his programs. As we saw in the subsequent weeks, Sid was beginning a new game format, that of a fantasy story.

## May: Variations on the Introduction

On May 17, Sid started his third game by writing an introduction. This indicated an important difference in Sid's design approach. In his previous two games, he began programming immediately the game context (basketball court or maze) and the actors (players or skaters). In his first game, the title screen did not appear until four weeks into the project. The Logo code in Fig. 4.68 includes Sid's new introduction.

```
to start
print [WELCOME TO STRIKERS FRACTION
JOURNEY TO BEGIN TYPE BEGIN]   CT
END
```

```
TO BEGIN
PR [MANY, MANY YEARS AGO THERE LIVED A
GREAT SCIENTIST IN A TOWN CALLED
PEACEVILLE.  IN PEACEVILLE PEOPLE WERE
PEACEFUL.  BUT THERE WAS AN EVIL PART OF
THE TOWN.  IT IS CALLED DESTRUTION.  IN
DESTRUTION TH.]

TO START
setbg 1
```

**FIG. 4.68.** Sid's Logo code on May 17.

During the next session, on May 20, Sid rewrote his introduction for the first time: "Striker, the great scientist" became "King Austin." His new title was "Welcome to King Austin's Fractions Journey." The Logo code is shown in Fig. 4.69.

```
to start
cc rg ct
ht setc 9 fill
pu setpos [-120 20]
label [WELCOME TO KING AUSTIN'S
     FRACTION]
pu setpos [-120 0]
label [JOURNEY. TO START TYPE
BEGIN.]
tone 40 20        tone 37 10
tone 30 10        tone 20 50
tone 40 30
END


TO BEGIN
CT cc rg ht setc 14 fill
repeat 5 [pr[]]
PR [MANY, MANY YEARS AGO THERE LIVED A
GREAT KING IN A TOWN CALLED PEACEVILLE.
IN PEACEVILLE PEOPLE WERE PEACEFUL.  BUT
THERE WAS AN EVIL PART OF THE TOWN.  IT
WAS CALLED DESTRUTION.  IN DESTRUTION
THERE LIVED AN EVIL WITCH.  HER NAME WAS
MERVIN DA FAY.  MERVIN HAD GREAT, GREAT
MAGICAL POWERS.  IN PEACEVILL THERE
WAS A SECRET ROOM IN THE ENGRUM PALACE.
IT WAS CALLED THE ENCHANTED ROOM.to
start type st2]
END
```

```
to s
shapes
end
```

**FIG. 4.69.** Sid's Logo code on May 20.

In his notebook entries, Sid described familiar sounding plans: "I am going to make some characters," and later, "I am going to make my characters move." He started working on the next scene, the background for his first animation sequence, and called it "the little hut." In contrast to his previous games, Sid dedicated more attention this time to setting up the context for his game. He included music in his new introduction and provided more information on his game context: the places and the main characters. The story outline clearly defined two groups of actors, the good and the evil. In this introduction, Sid's story plot began to grow.

## May: Classroom Presentation

On May 28, Sid rewrote the introduction once again, embellished his beginning screen, and continued working on his first scene. The title and story context had become "Welcome to Gemini and Swartz Fraction Journey." For a moment, I stop documenting Sid's progress in his game and focus on his classroom presentation. Beginning in May, we started inviting students to give short presentations of the state of their current games to their classmates. I report on this classroom presentation in more detail for two reasons. First, Sid had just began his third game. In the conversation with his classmates and the teacher, he explained features of the game in more detail than he wrote in his notebook. Second, this conversation among game designers provided another example of how peers can ask "the design questions" of purpose, structure, and argument. (I provided another example of such a conversion with his teacher in early May during the second game.) Sid was sitting in front of one of the classroom computers. The content of the screen was projected on an additional TV monitor. This allowed his classmates sitting behind him to follow the game. When Sid started his program, a first problem appeared as the title wrapped around the page:

```
to start
cc rg ct
ht setc 9 fill
pu setpos [-120 20]
print [WELCOME TO GEMINI
AND SWARTZ'S
```

This title is too long; it wraps around the page and overwrites the beginning of the first words.

```
FRACTION JOURNEY]
pu setpos [-30 -25]
setsh 1 setc 6
```

Stamps the figure shapes of the main characters on the title screen.

```
pd stamp
pu setpos [20 -40] setsh 2 setc 4
pd stamp
pu setpos [40 -40] setsh 6 setc 10
pd stamp
pu setpos [-120 0]
label [JOURNEY. TO START TYPE BEGIN.]
tone 100 5          tone 100 5
tone 500 10         tone 600 50
tone 100 20
END
```

After a brief comment from another student, Sid continued the game. The teacher asked Trevor to read the introduction and directions aloud because they were difficult to see on the monitor for the students sitting farther away:

```
TO BEGIN
CT cc rg ht setc 14 fill
repeat 5 [pr[]]
PR [MANY, MANY YEARS AGO THERE LIVED A
GREAT KING IN A TOWN CALLED PEACEVILLE.
IN PEACEVILLE PEOPLE WERE PEACEFUL.  BUT
THERE WAS AN EVIL PART OF THE TOWN.   IT
WAS CALLED DESTRUTION.   IN DESTRUTION
THERE LIVED AN EVIL WITCH.   HER NAME WAS
MERVIN DA FAY.   MERVIN HAD GREAT, GREAT
MAGICAL POWERS.   IN PEACEVILL THERE
WAS A SECRET ROOM IN THE ENGRUM PALACE.
IT WAS CALLED THE ENCHANTED ROOM.]
PR [TO CONTINUE TYPE intro]
END
```

*Sid*: This is it for the moment.

*Joanne*: What's gonna happen next?  Can you tell us?

*Sid*: I have a hero who comes to this little hut in the wood. And there will be this old, old man. I'll show you on the SHAPES page . . . [The rest is not audible. As Sid continues the outline of his story, his voice gets very low.] and then they go on a journey.

*Yasmin*: I couldn't hear you.

*Sid*: I have the hero. He comes to this little hut in the forest. So, OK, there is this old, old man who gives them information on where the King's daughter went. To get them help . . . [unclear] . . . and he gets them tools to fight the robbers. The journey starts. And then there will be little figures coming at them and he has to tell them with a fraction.

It was hard to hear what Sid described of his game. But the little that was audible gave an idea of what Sid later implemented in his game. (For example, the meeting with the old man who would be named Garvin.) Next, his classmates asked several questions about Sid's game:

*Albert*: When does the person ask a fraction question?

*Sid*: It never asks them, I mean the screen asks them. I have the monster coming at you. To kill the monster you have to answer this fraction.

*Amy*: Why are you trying to kill her? You are trying to kill the witch?

*Sid*: No, because the dragon, he is filled with magic power but the witch is not.

*Amy*: So, the witch can turn into different forms?

*Sid*: Yes.

*Joanne*: You might want to say that the witch can take the form of other evil creatures.

*Albert*: What is this [pointing at screen] supposed to be?

*Sid explains*: I couldn't really make the hut so this is where he will travel.

*Shanice*: What you are trying to say is . . . when the monster throws a fraction at you, you don't solve it before it hits you, you die?!

*Sid*: No, you get less power.

*Albert*: It says that there is the witch and the hero is going to kill the witch. But the witch hasn't really done anything bad. So it's just like "Hi" I kill you [he imitates a gun with his hand, pulling the trigger with his finger].

*Class*: No, the witch has kidnapped the princess.

Most of his classmates' questions were directed at clarifying the story of his game. Students discussed the meaning of his screen design (little hut), instructional context (feedback to right or wrong questions), character traits of actors, justifications for the story (kidnapping of princess), and design issues (wrapping around of title). Albert's question about the fraction revealed the students' concept of how to integrate fractions—by asking questions. Sid's reply to Shanice's question about incorrect answers showed how he integrated a Nintendo concept—getting less power—into his game. To use Perkins' (1986) terminology, students were asking the design questions of structure, purpose, model case, and argument, but in relation to the development of his story. Sid's classmates asked him: What is the meaning of your story? What will happen? What are the intentions of your characters? How will you pose your fraction question? What will happen if you don't answer correctly? The questions also indicated that students still had some problems figuring out the "story" behind Sid's game, and so Sid himself probably did as well.

Another way to look at these interactions is that Sid's classmates were trying to make sense of his game, to find the logic behind the actions and characters. But this was not logic in the formal, abstract sense; it was the logic of the story that Bruner (1990) also described as the narrative mode of thought. Albert's last question about the reasons for killing the witch indicated this most clearly. In Albert's understanding of the story, Sid has violated the narrative mode because the hero had no reasons for killing the witch. But other class members corrected him and pointed out that the witch had kidnapped the princess and hence punishment was justified.

In all, this presentation and his classmates' remarks and questions most likely had a profound impact on Sid's thinking and design of the game. They helped him clarify the inconsistencies in his story and set up a meaningful and coherent beginning for his game. With their questions, his classmates gave him pointers about where his narrative needed improvement, and what features to add. I think it is reasonable to say that Sid decided on many of these features as the questions were posed. He had not thought about them before. They gave his game a structure and a purpose to direct his future programming. These questions also proved another point to Sid: His classmates had interest in and recognition of what he was working on.

## May: The Little Hut—Preparing the First Animation

After finishing the introduction, Sid started programming the first scene where his two main actors, Gemini and Swartz, are on their way to the little hut. Fig. 4.70 shows a screen printout, which makes the Logo code easier to understand. This is Sid's Logo code for the little hut scene:

```
to st2
rg cc ct
```
Clears the screen from text and graphics.

```
setbg 1
```
Sets background to blue.

```
print [TO GET TO THE
LITTLE HUT TYPE GO.]
pu setpos [-150 -85]
pd fd 200
```
Draws the horizontal and vertical lines.

```
rt 90 fd 400 rt 90
fd 200 rt 90
fd 400 pu setpos [-75 -65]
setsh 12 setc 12 pd stamp
```
Stamps the door shape.

```
end

to go
tell 1
```
Talks to Turtle 1.

```
pu setpos [155 -65]
pd setsh 2
```
Sets the shape of Gemini.

```
seth 270
```
Directs the heading to left.

```
tell 2
```
Talks to Turtle 2.

```
st pu setpos [135 -65]
pd setsh 6 pu
```
Sets the shape of Swartz.

```
seth 270
repeat 20
```
Directs the heading to left.
Makes both shapes move at the same time towards the door.

```
[tell 1 st pu fd 9 wait 3
tell 2 fd 9 wait 3]
rg cc ct ht
house
end
```
Clears screen.
Calls next procedure HOUSE.

```
to house
st pu setpos [-150 85] pd
setsh 3 setc 4 seth 180 pu
repeat 17 [fd 10 wait 2]
end
```

In this scene, Sid programmed the seemingly simultaneous movement of two shapes. In order to do this, Sid had to use two turtles (Logo provided four turtles, numbered 0, 1, 2, and 3) and position them. He did this in the first seven lines of the procedure GO. The next statement included a REPEAT statement that told first Turtle 1 and then Turtle 2 to move five steps forward, and repeated this sequence 20 times.

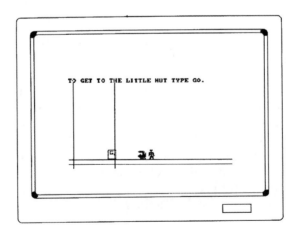

**FIG. 4.70.** Screen printout from the ST2 and GO procedures on May 29.

On the screen, both figures arrived at the door positioned at the left of the screen. The WAIT 3 statements were necessary to slow down the movement of the figures. (In Albert's case, I discuss in detail what programming was necessary to coordinate the actions of different turtles and shapes for animation on the screen.)

In Sid's case, it is important to remember the results of his first game, where he also tried to employ animation for his players but did not use such a sophisticated technique. I argued in my evaluation of Sid's game change that one reason for abandoning his game may have been dissatisfaction with the programmed animations. In the Fraction Slam Dunk, Sid moved only one turtle at a time. I suggested that he wanted to create the atmosphere of action on a real basketball court by having several players move, but was not able to achieve this effect. In the meantime, several game designers had employed the effect of moving more than one turtle at a time. During the classroom presentations or while playing his classmates' games, Sid probably saw these effects and became able to verbalize his intentions. On May 30, Sid asked me how he could move things at the same time. In his initial programming, Sid used SETPOS in his REPEAT statement, with the result that his figures always returned to their starting position with the beginning of each REPEAT.

## May–June: Meeting with Garvin—Constructing the Dialogue

After concluding the little hut scene, Sid continued his story. This was his last big scene before the summer. His main actors, Gemini and Swartz, now met an important source of information, Garvin. Sid included some animation in this scene (in the procedure MOVE, where Garvin came from the top down to the bottom), but his main thrust was the dialogue between Garvin and Gemini. This was Sid's effort to thicken plot of his story. The following excerpt from Sid's Logo code includes the full dialogue spread over seven procedures:

```
to move
pu setpos [125 -85]
pd setsh 2                        Positions Garvin at the upper
                                  left corner of screen.
seth 270
pu repeat 17 [fd 10 wait 2]       Moves him to the bottom.
pd stamp
```

```
talk1                          Calls next procedure TALK1.
end

to talk1
pr wait 30 ["Hello Gemini" "hello
Garvin".Garvin I am going to
need some information on Sparzi
the dragon."Sit and my crystal
ball will tell"] wait 50
sit                            Calls next procedure SIT.
end

to Sit
pu setpos [-80 -85]
setsh 8 pd                     Stamps a ball.
stamp
ball                           Calls next procedure BALL.
end

to ball
pu setpos [-100 85]
setsh 11                       Moves ball shape over screen.
setc 9 pu seth 180
repeat 15 [fd 10 wait 10]
pd stamp                       Stamps the shape.
talk2                          Calls next procedure TALK2.
end

to talk2
CT ht cc
pr [Sparzi the dragon,lives in
the western part of Destrution.
He has great magical powers.If
you wish to fight him you will
need these weapons.]
wep                            Calls next procedure WEP.
end

to Wep                         Stamps an array of weapons on
                               screen.
pu setpos [-125 -5] pd
setsh 10 setc 1 pd stamp
pu setpos [-105 -10] pd setsh 14
setc 4 pd stamp
pu setpos [-105 -5] pd setsh 9
setc 8 pd stamp
pu setpos [-70 -5] pd setsh 15
setc 15 pd stamp
move                           Calls next procedure MOVE.
end
```

```
to move
ct ht
print [thank you!
I apreiciate it.                    Note spelling mistake.
So long Garvin!]
end
```

### Gemini and Swartz's Fraction Journey

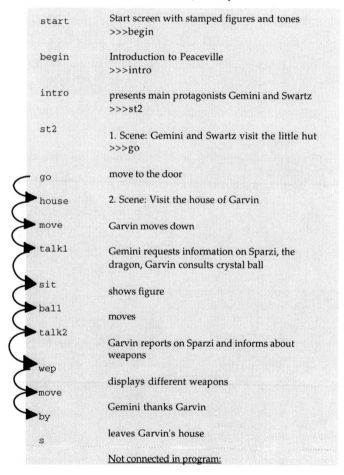

| | |
|---|---|
| start | Start screen with stamped figures and tones<br>>>>begin |
| begin | Introduction to Peaceville<br>>>>intro |
| intro | presents main protagonists Gemini and Swartz<br>>>>st2 |
| st2 | 1. Scene: Gemini and Swartz visit the little hut<br>>>>go |
| go | move to the door |
| house | 2. Scene: Visit the house of Garvin |
| move | Garvin moves down |
| talk1 | Gemini requests information on Sparzi, the dragon, Garvin consults crystal ball |
| sit | shows figure |
| ball | moves |
| talk2 | Garvin reports on Sparzi and informs about weapons |
| wep | displays different weapons |
| move | Gemini thanks Garvin |
| by | leaves Garvin's house |
| s | |

Not connected in program:

**FIG. 4.71.** Sid's third game, Gemini and Swartz's Fraction Journey, by the end of June.

With this procedure sequence, Sid had set up the context for his game and both of his characters were now ready to go on the fraction journey. We can also see that Sid has changed his programming style. In his first game, Sid used a superprocedure to connect the different procedures into one unit. He switched over to calling each procedure from the preceding one, except for the cases in which the player was asked to type in a procedure name. On June 19, the last day of the first phase, Sid wrote in his notebook: "I am going to continue my game." An overview of Sid's program before he headed off for the summer is shown in Fig. 4.71.

## September–November: The Second Phase

Before the summer, Sid did not work on any fraction problems. He set up the context for his new game, and wrote the introduction and directions. Second, he had designed and implemented two different scenes (the little hut and the dialogue with Garvin) that constituted the context for the fraction journey. In contrast to his two other games, Sid had connected all the procedures with each other, either by calling them from the preceding procedure or by asking the user to type in the procedure name. This represented an interesting switch in his programming strategy. Sid had learned how to segment his programming into separate procedures and how to arrange them in a superprocedure before the Game Design Project started. However, this was not his personal programming style, even though Sid had placed each of his different ideas in individual procedures before (see his first game). By implementing the style of "daisy chain" programming (because every procedure was connected with the next), he wrote the program more like a story, where one paragraph follows the next.

In the subsequent two months, Sid completed his game, which is "about two people who go into an adventure for this princess. They have to fight the evil dragon, not a dragon, like a magician, an evil magician who can change himself into anything." Instead of describing his design process day by day, I decided to present an overview that summarizes the most important events during this time (see Fig. 4.72) and printouts from the most important screens to provide the reader with a sense of Sid's graphical work. Several aspects marked the design of Sid's third game in the sec-

ond phase. The first aspect related to Sid's splitting up his introduction procedure and distributing it over two pages. The second
aspect concerned Sid's design of fraction questions, which he accomplished between October 15 and November 5. The third aspect concerned he rewriting of the story. Whereas the first two
aspects mostly dealt with decisions in design and programming,
the last aspect applied to the plot of his story.

| Date | Scenes | Procedures | Events |
|---|---|---|---|
| MAY 17<br>MAY 20<br>MAY 24 | -Variations on the introduction | `start begin` | |
| MAY 28<br><br>MAY 29 | -The little hut scene | `st2 go` | Classroom Presentation |
| MAY 31 | - Talking with Garvin | `house move talk1` | |
| JUNE 18<br>JUNE 19 | - Going to the house | `by tree walk` | |
| SEPTEMBER 30<br><br>OCTOBER 15 | - Soldies from Loft: First fraction question | `enemy f k e` | |
| OCTOBER 21 | - Sparzi's castle | `castle sparzi`<br>`fight` | Sid splits up his introduction on two pages: |
| OCTOBER 22 | - Second fraction question | `t soldier a ft` | |
| OCTOBER 25 | - Introduction split up onto two pages | `GAMES begin`<br>`GAMES1 v`<br>`GAMES intro` | |
| NOVEMBER 4 | - Third fraction question | `problem sparzi2`<br>`e f` | |
| NOVEMBER 5 | - Fourth fraction question | `problem3`<br>`problem4` | |
| NOVEMBER 7 | - Ending of game | `a b c` | |
| | Final Touches | | |
| NOVEMBER 15 | - Game Fair | | |

FIG. 4.72. Overview of Sid's implementation for his third game. In
the Scenes column, I describe the theme of the game scenes; in
Procedures, I provide the procedures for the corresponding game
scenes; and in Events, I describe other activities that happened during this time.

## October: Soldiers from Loft—Two Fraction Questions

In October, Sid started programming his first fractions questions. The structure that he chose for his first question was also applied to the following three questions. The enemy, either a soldier from Loft or Sparzi the dragon, asked the player a fraction question. If the question was not answered correctly, the game was over. Otherwise, the next question appeared. The programming of these questions followed the same pattern: One procedure printed the question on the screen and provided the player with choices. The player typed one of the given letters, which called the corresponding procedure.

```
to enemy
setbg 3 ct pu setpos [30 -70]
setsh 7 setc 4 setc 3              Displays the soldier with changing
                                   colors.

setc 4 setc 5 setc 2 setc 5
seth 0 pu repeat 5                 Moves him forward.
[fd 100 wait 2]
print [I am a soldier
from Loft.                         Prints on top of screen.
Answer this problem.]
cc type se                         Prints choices in command
                                   center.

[WHAT EQUALS ONE WHOLE? Type e
if it's 1/2 type a if it's
2/3 or type f if it's 4/4
and press enter.] char 13
end

to f                               Correct answer.
RG CC CT
PRINT [YOUR .........
.........RIGHT!!!]
END

to k                               Wrong answer.
PRINT [SORRY .....
.........YOUR WRONG]
TONE 5 100
t                                  Calls next procedure T.
end

TO e                               Wrong answer.
PRINT [SORRY BUT NICE TRY.}
END
```

In the three following questions, Sid addressed similar problems. The second and third questions presented a shape in the form of a circle cut into four parts and asked the player to identify either 3/4 or 1/4. The fourth problem asked what given fraction equals 3/4 (6/8).

## October–November: Sparzi's Castle—2 More Fraction Questions

In his last scene, Sid programmed the frame of a castle and created an elaborate design of Sparzi, the dragon (Fig. 4.73). Sid designed five different shapes that had to be juxtaposed to create the entire dragon, which he then placed over the castle as a dominating figure.

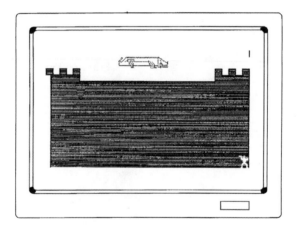

**FIG. 4.73.** Screen printout from Sid's procedure CASTLE.

This is Sid's Logo code for the scene of Sparzi's castle:

```
TO CASTLE
RG CT cc
pu setpos [-147 95] pd fd 150 lt 90 fd 7 rt 90 fd 10 rt 90 fd
10 rt 90 fd 10 lt 90 fd 10 lt 90 fd 10 rt 90 fd 10 rt 90 fd
10 lt 90 fd 10 lt 90 fd 10 rt 90 fd 10 rt 90 fd 20 lt 90 fd
200 lt 90 fd 20 rt 90 fd 10 rt 90 fd 10 lt 90 fd 10 lt 90 fd
10 rt 90 fd 10 rt 90 fd 10 lt 90 fd 10 lt 90 fd 10 rt 90 fd
10 rt 90 fd 170 pu setpos [-137 -15] pd setc 8 fill
```

```
pu setpos [-102 25] pd setsh 14 setc 4 pd stamp
sparzi
end
to sparzi
cc ct
pu setpos [-40 75] pd setsh 15 setc 8
pd stamp
pu setpos [-25 75] pd setsh 16 setc 8 pd stamp
pu setpos [-10 75] pd setsh 17 setc 8 pd stamp
pu setpos [5 75] pd setsh 18 setc 8
pd stamp
pu setpos [20 75] pd setsh 19 setc 8
pd stamp
fight
end
```

## October: Revising the Conversation with Garvin

In May, Sid had programmed a long dialogue between Gemini and Garvin in preparation for the meeting with Sparzi, the dragon. In this second phase of the project, Sid made two changes in his story. The first was a revision of the dialogue between Gemini and Garvin, which was to be considerably shortened (see Fig. 4.74).

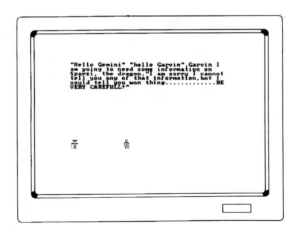

FIG. 4.74. Screen printout from Sid's changed procedure.

His second change was that he split his introduction procedure BEGIN into two procedures, BEGIN and V. He placed 12 lines of the procedure BEGIN on a separate page and included GETPAGE calls from one page to the next. The reasons for this change were not clear to me. The only explanation I have is speculative. Toward the end of the Game Design Project, many designers started talking about how many pages their game had. What students had seen in the beginning as an impediment to their programming turned into a feature. The more pages there were, the better the programmer was. The number of LogoWriter pages became synonymous with the size of the project. Could it be that Sid wanted to create more than the two pages that he had so far? Or was Sid's use of GETPAGE of a more playful nature, and he liked the effect that it created in his game when the player watched the program alternate between the two pages? I do not have a definite answer for this.

## November: Ending of Game

During the last days of the project, Sid touched up his game. He corrected some of his typos (but not all). He created an ending for his game (see Fig. 4.75). He included more WAITs in his procedures to slow down some scenes.

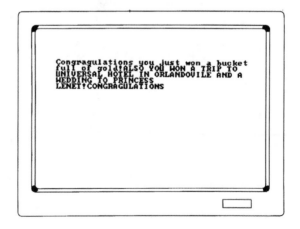

**FIG. 4.75.** Screen printout from Sid's procedure ENDING.

To my mind, Sid's greatest accomplishment in this project is that he succeeded presenting a full-fledged game on the day of the Game Fair. Looking back over his development during the previous six months, it was not always evident that he would succeed in reaching this goal (see Fig. 4.76).

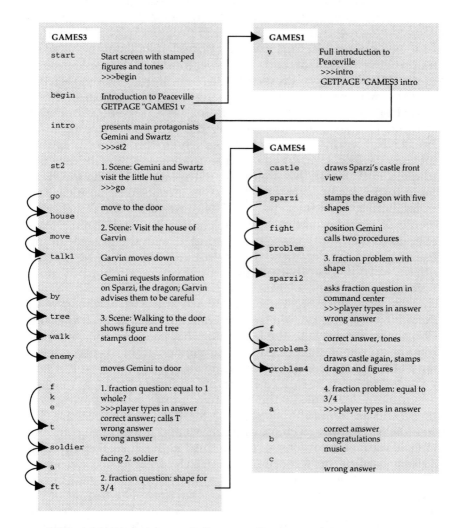

FIG. 4.76. Overview on Sid's game Gemini and Swartz Fraction Journey on November 13.

## Summary and Discussion of Sid's Case

I found Sid a particularly interesting case for the Game Design Project because his game progress emphasized the importance of the time frame for the development of his learning and thinking.

The aspect of the Game Design Project that had the major impact on Sid's development was of a rather general nature. Sid changed his attitudes as a designer and problem solver. I reported in the beginning about his persistent problems in staying focused and bringing work to an end. In the beginning of the game design, Sid displayed many of these attitudes. He started two games but did not finish either of them. Much of his programming efforts seemed unfocused. Toward the end of May, it was questionable what Sid had accomplished during the previous three months. The teacher and I often asked ourselves this very question. However, with his third game, Sid learned how to finish his work independently, and this involved many aspects: developing a theme for his game, creating characters, designing graphics, and implementing all of these things. His third game also indicated a change of strategy about how to handle this challenging task. Whereas in the first two games, Sid started with the programming of animations and manipulations, in the third game, he started with an introduction that involved little programming but more thinking about what his game would be like.

Sid's programming took off toward the end of the project when, after the summer, he worked hard to finalize his game under time constraints. In the beginning, his programming seemed rather intermittent and eclectic. He implemented in his procedures many of his ideas for his game but never connected most of them in a coherent way to form a full game. I labeled his approaches and implementations in the first two games as "experimentations," and as "stepping stones" for the third game, because Sid used to explore how to create animations and how to program the manipulation of arrow keys. In the third game, his programming strategy became more sophisticated. He created sequences of procedures connected to each other. Like Amy, he learned to use a "blueprint strategy" for his instructional quiz: The format of his questions did not change in his Logo code except for the necessary adaptations of detail. In the end, Sid succeeded in creating a computer game with all the necessary ingredients.

Sid's game development went through different stages. It moved from a reality-based to a fantasy-driven game format. His first idea was the implementation of a basketball game. As one explanation for his abandoning of this game idea, I offered that Sid was concerned about the missing realism in his animations of moving basketball players and other features compared to either real basketball games or commercially available video games. In his second game, he created an already more imaginative environment with the design of a maze with obstacles. In his third game, the fantasy aspect came into full play in his narrative. Sid created an imaginary world with two cities, enchanted rooms, evil witches, and two partners—Gemini and Swartz—who are on their way to save a kidnapped princess. Sid's game had all the ingredients of a good story and a happy ending (if the player answered all the questions about fractions correctly).

Sid's thinking about fractions during the project was rather sparse. First of all, for the major part of the project, Sid did not deal with any fractions either in his written designs or in his actual programming. He was mainly concerned with getting his game started. Fractions may have been in the back of his mind all along, but all his fraction questions were designed in the last month (of the six-month-long project). There was little evidence in his notebook writings, interviews, or program implementations that he was thinking about fractions.

A further point is that none of Sid's game ideas explicitly or implicitly integrated fractions or aspects of them. At first glance, the two factors of game and fractions seemed to be unconnected in Sid's game. However, the analysis of his design development showed how both components evolved to be tied to each other. In Sid's game, the design of instructional content was interdependent with the design of the game context. He did not start designing and implementing any fraction questions before his game context was settled. In the representations of fractions that Sid finally designed in his four instructional interactions for his game, he remained close to the basic part–whole relationship of fractions and only represented halves and fourths.

The pedagogical implications of Sid's case are wide ranging. The question we have to ask is whether Sid's experiences as a game designer can be meaningful for us as educators and researchers, even if most of his work was in bits and pieces and he didn't finish many of his ideas and his first two games. One important issue is Sid's tendency to easily change ideas, erase programs, and start new things. This also happens to be one of the advantages in programming. Many ideas can be tried out, and a student should feel comfortable to do that. The debugging of ideas is an essential part of the programming process (Papert, 1980). It is rare that a program works correctly the first time. It might have been particularly important for Sid to stay on task, over a long period of time, and to keep on trying. In his game development we saw a clear example how long it took him to overcome his working attitude and to stick to one idea.

A child like Sid is often lost and unsuccessful in a typical school environment and will always score lower than Amy and Albert on school tests. But here he was able to find his way and express himself, just as Amy and Albert did. He was able to produce a finished product that was his own, that he could share and be proud of, side by side with Amy and Albert. The extensive time frame given to him and his classmates proved to be essential for his development.

# ALBERT—A CASE OF A GAME DESIGNER

Albert's cover design for his game Mission: Town.

## Introduction

Albert was a 10-year-old boy who came into Mrs. R.'s classroom and the elementary school at the beginning of fourth grade. I joined the classroom at the beginning of the school year (which was the fourth grade) to get to know the students and the teacher. Albert was rather quiet and demure, yet playful from time to time with his classmates. He was generally well liked by the boys and girls in his class. Very often I saw Albert in the classroom with his head resting on his left arm which was lying on the table, while working on assignments. His posture could lead an outside observer to believe that he was bored or sleepy; rather, it indicated his engagement with the work at hand. Albert was meticulous in all his work: His designs and writings were characterized by his chiseled and precise way of drawing lines, figures and filling in the spaces (see Albert's cover design). His style of working through things was also meticulous, one task after another until the whole was completed. Albert took his time. When Albert described himself, he mentioned that he never gave up easily, and liked to draw, read and entertain people with magic.

Two aspects struck me in Albert's approach to the Game Design Project. The first aspect was his persistence in planning and implementing a particular game scene–the demon scene. The second aspect was his programming development in the project that resulted in a particular organizational structure of LogoWriter pages. Whereas the first aspect also applied to many of his classmates, the second aspect was something entirely unique to Albert.

*Design Style.* Albert's approach to planning and implementing were crystalized in one particular scene that was central to his game: A demon jumping out of a chest and asking a fraction question. This scene appeared first in his notebook plans on March 20, and reappeared frequently until its final implementation. In his note taking during the subsequent three months, he described step by step what he planned to do, what he had accomplished and what he still had to do. His sense for fine-tuning in programming game and graphics features was one of his trademarks. Albert simultaneously maintained several threads throughout the project, such as designing the shapes, determining characters of the play, working on fractions questions, and changing the plot of the game. The design and programming of the animation features of this scene, the making of shapes, and the choreographing of different interactions reflected Albert's particular style of design and programming. They were also testimony to his ability to project and maintain long-term goals in planning and problem solving.

*Logo Programming.* The second aspect refered to Albert's personal organization of his program. This aspect of Albert's approach only emerged fully in the second phase of the project (after the summer) when Albert worked on finalizing the implementation of his game. In those last weeks, Albert added more scenes to his games, but he also started to use LogoWriter

Pages in a different way to organize and structure his game. His game had grown to dozens of different scenes distributed over different pages. His initial "one big procedure on one page" programming style changed to "several procedures organized in one superprocedure on one page." Each page became the repository for an event consisting of several scenes on its own.

Albert's approach raises many questions about distinctions such as planners/bricoleurs and to what extent one can observe them in the long process of designing a product such as a game. The purpose of this case study is to show how Albert, in fact, had many details of his game "planned out" but continued to do "bricolage."

*The Structure of Albert's Case.* Albert's program implementation was divided into two phases. In the first phase, students were concerned with finding game ideas and implementing them, whereas the second phase started with general agreement among the students, teacher, and researcher that the remaining two months would be dedicated to finalizing the game.

---

The first phase (March–June)

| March | Designing the ccenery: The haunted house |
| March | Choosing the cast of actors: creatures, demons, bullies, wizards, punks, gangs, guys with knives and magic users |
| March–June | Thinking about the inside the house: the demon scene |
| April | First fraction |
| May | Albert's game at the end of the first phase |

The second phase (September-November)

| September–October | Reorganization of the game |
| October | Creating links between pages |
| October | Programming style |
| October | Dramatic moments |

---

FIG. 4.77. Overview of Albert's project development.

The themes/sections shown in Fig. 4.77 characterize Albert's programming progress over the six months of the game project. Their segmentation is mainly oriented at the themes of scenes that Albert implemented in his game.As the main organizing principle for my sections, I looked at how the screens were conceived, designed, implemented, and modified from the first day, when he started out, to the last day of the game fair, when he presented the final version of his game. Albert was never working on just one theme alone at a given point of time. His notebook entries, paired with the implementations in his programs and the interviews, indicated that Albert followed several themes in parallel. Even though Albert started out with one idea of what his game would be, he also defined and refined the details of his game as he implemented the first features. My decision, then, was to focus on the big themes as they appeared in Albert's progress, which did not necessarily appear every day. Some, in fact, spanned a period of three months.

The following sections focus on three parts of Albert's game: the design of the haunted house, the scene of the demon jumping out of the chest, and asking a question and Albert's organization of LogoWriter pages. The other parts of his work are presented only in summary form.

## March: Designing the Scenery–The Haunted House

On March 5, Albert described his first idea for the game, the horror house, that he was going to implement over the weeks to come (see Fig. 4.78). In fact, the first day of the project (March 1), Albert started by playing with specific Logo commands but did not count these as part of the project. Many of his classmates also started their projects in a similar way (see chapter 3 for a more detailed description and discussion). He wrote in his Designer's Notebook: "I'm doing tone colorunder." These were commands that the teacher had introduced a few days before the start of the project, while the students were still programming their habitat program (see the introduction of Amy as a game designer). He did not save these explorations with Logo commands because, as he explained to me, he had not started his game yet. At the end of this day, he wrote in his PLANS FOR TOMORROW: "I will start my game. I'm not sure of what I want to do but I'll know by March 4" (not realizing that he would have chorus on that particular day and therefore have to wait until March 5 to start). When his teacher saw this notebook entry, she asked Albert why he had chosen this particular day, March 4. He answered that he just picked a date. Months later, in the postinterview, Albert provided a better explanation: He told me that very often on his way home or over the weekend, he thought about his projects and what he was going to do the next day in school.

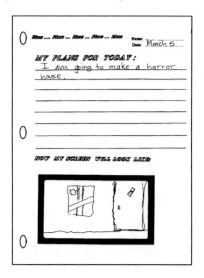

FIG. 4.78. Albert's designer notebook entry from March 5.

On March 5, Albert's START procedure looked as shown in Fig. 4.79 and provided a good example of his programming style (see also Fig. 4.80).

```
to start
rg setsh 13 pu setpos [-155 -40] seth        Draws the ground line of
90 pd fd 320 pu setpos [25 -40] seth         the house.
180 pd fd 20 setpos [110 -40] seth
180 pd fd 20 pu setpos [125 -60] seth        Draws the upper doorstep.
270 pd setpos [10 -60] seth 180 fd 20
pu setpos [125 -60] seth 180 pd fd 20
setpos [-5 -80] seth 0 pd setpos [140       The center line of the
                                             lower doorstep.
```

```
-80] seth 270 fd 10
```

**FIG. 4.79.** Albert's Logo code from March 5.

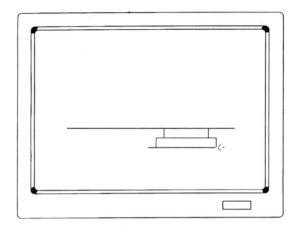

**FIG. 4.80.** Screen printout from the START procedure on March 5.

What is interesting about Albert's programming style was his way of programming the door steps on the screen. Albert used the turtle pen as a drawing tool, and his instructions said: take the pen, place it down at this position, draw a line of this length, then take the pen up, orient it this direction, and so on. Albert showed that he understood how to use SETPOS (which placed the turtle at any given position on the screen using the Cartesian coordinates) and SETH (which oriented the direction of the turtle independently of its previous orientation, i.e., SETH 180 turned the turtle always with its head down). He was introduced to both commands only a few weeks before. He also did not forget to lift the pen up and down every time. He used to his advantage the fact that if one moves the turtle with SETPOS to a new position with the pen down, then the pen of the turtle leaves a trace: Instead of telling the turtle to draw a line of so many steps, he just determines the new position and then moves the turtle from the old position. The trace left of this move becomes part of the drawing.

Another programming solution to Albert's screen design could have taken advantage of the regularly shaped areas of the door steps. He could have decomposed the picture into several rectangles. My explanation for his programming is that Albert considered the design of the front side of the house not so much a programming problem but a drawing one.

Toward the end of this day (March 5), I interviewed Albert about his initial plans, as I had done with all his other classmates. He described his ideas of the game:

> *Yasmin*: So, you weren't here yesterday. You were at chorus. Can you tell me a little bit about your plans for the project?
>
> *Albert*: Ok, I'm gonna make a haunted house . . . ahm . . . in the beginning, I'm making the front right now [he is pointing towards the screen] and it's gonna say, "Your friends dare you to explore the haunted house. You have to . . . " [his voice trails off and then continues]. And so it's gonna give you a choice to say, "If you want to be here or if you want to go back and check it out." And if so, your object is to explore the whole house and without getting killed or murdered or kidnapped [he smiles].
>
> *Yasmin*: That's a very dangerous place, your house.
>
> *Albert*: Yeah.

Albert had outlined the basic format and content of his game: the setting of the game (the haunted house with secret rooms), the task (exploration), potential actors (murderer, guys with knives), actions (collecting stuff, door opening and people coming at you, knife cutting) and the graphical arrangement. In his mind, he had constructed a vision of what his game would look like that was to determine considerably his design process in the following weeks.

But Albert's ideas of his game also showed another feature, that of a realistic planner. The first drawing of the haunted house and the actions foreseen seemed to be aspects that Albert felt comfortable designing and implementing.

> *Yasmin*: Does it have to do with fractions?
>
> *Albert*: Yeah, you have to explore. There is a number of rooms and I am not sure what fractions, how many rooms, I am going to make. So, it's going to explore, **you have to ex-**

**plore this fraction of the house** without getting killed.
And . . .

*Yasmin*: So how can you avoid getting killed?

*Albert*: Well, you can collect stuff, like you got a map as to
where stuff is and what rooms are and if there are any secret rooms. Because there are going to be a few secret
rooms that you can go in. You have to find those to explore the whole house. So, then I haven't figured out what
I am going to do.

*Yasmin*: So, what is it all about? These dangerous things hap-
pening in your house? Are fractions dangerous?

*Albert*: Well, I am going to make something like I am not sure I
am just going to have murder in it . . .

*Yasmin*: So are fractions dangerous things? Or . . .

*Albert*: One thing, fractions come in as, or, I can have some
game: A murderer is in the house and it could say, "One
third of the game is coming at you."

I have highlighted one phrase in Albert's answer because it
showed a first but very fragile idea of how to integrate fractions
into his game design: to think about *exploring parts of the house* as
*exploring fractions*. Otherwise, in Albert's initial ideas and plans,
there was little space accorded to the educational content of the
game, the fractions. Albert was still more concerned about the
features of his game and the situations in which the fraction
questions would be asked or take place. Later on, when I asked
him if the fractions part would be challenging for him, he was
very tentative—in contrast to the programming problem that he
saw he must solve for his game:

*Yasmin*: If you think about your project now, what do you
think might be the biggest challenge for you?

*Albert*: Ahm . . . right now . . . I think the biggest challenge that
I am gonna make here, is making the robbers coming at
you or something. When you open a door, something, the
guys come at you, and making all that happen.

*Yasmin*: So, it has to do with Logo programming?

*Albert* [nods yes]: I can also have, once you type in you want
to open the door, it shows you and the guy will step out

with the knife and the guy will go like this [he indicates a cutting movement with his arms and laughs].

*Yasmin*: Are there any challenges related to fractions for you?

*Albert*: I don't think I will have any problems but I might come across some of them that might be kind of difficult.

Albert's concerns were already ahead of his actual programming. He was concerned with implementing the different interactions between the player and figures of the game. These were aspects that he dealt with weeks later.

The next day, March 6, Albert changed the content of the START procedure and included the introduction for his game as he had explained it to me in the interview in the day before. The drawing of the front was now placed in a procedure that he called HOUSE. His procedure START now introduced the player to the context, the task of the game, and read:

```
to start
rg pu setpos [-150 60] label [Your
friends have dared you to explore]
setpos [-150 45] label [a haunted
house! If you want to chicken] setpos
[-150 40] label [out type chicken, but
if you want to ] setpos [-150 30]
label [enter the house type house.]
end
```
LABEL prints the text in yellow letters on the screen.

```
to house
rg setsh 13 pu setpos [-155 -40] seth
90 pd fd 320 pu setpos [25 -40] seth
180 pd fd 20 setpos [110 -40] seth
180 pd fd 20 pu setpos [125 -60] seth
270 pd setpos [10 -60] seth 180 fd 20
pu setpos [125 -60] seth 180 pd fd 20
setpos [-5 -80] seth 0 pd setpos [140
-80] seth 180 fd 10 setpos [-5 -90]
seth 0 fd 10
```
Albert added these lines to the HOUSE procedure, which draws the outline.

In the subsequent weeks, Albert programmed the other features of the house: the window, the door, and the numbers. The HOUSE procedure grew in the same fashion, programmed line by line with SETPOS and SETH until it displayed the front view of the haunted house. Fig. 4.82 provides an overview of the individual parts of the house, which he implemented step by step.

Another plan that Albert wrote on March 6 was, "to finish start and make the inside." By "inside," he meant that he had started already thinking about the scenes following the house front, but it would take him three weeks before he finished HOUSE and started working on the program parts that dealt with the inside of the house. On March 19, he wrote in his PLANS FOR TODAY that "To finish house I just need to do the window and I'll be all set." The code for final procedure HOUSE (accomplished on March 27) was as shown in Fig. 4.81.

```
to house
rg repeat 10 [tone 294 15 tone 262 7
wait 10] setsh 13 pu setpos [-155 -40]
seth 90 pd fd 320 pu setpos [25 -40]          Draws the ground line of
                                              the house.
seth 180 pd fd 20 setpos [110 -40]
seth 180 pd fd 20 pu setpos [125 -60]         Draws the upper doorstep.
seth 270 pd setpos [10 -60] seth 180 fd
20 pu setpos [125 -60] seth 180 pd fd
20 pu seth 270 pd setpos [10 -80] pu          The center line of the
setpos [-5 -80] seth 0 pd setpos [140         lower doorstep.
-80] seth 180 fd 10 setpos [-5 -90]
seth 0 fd 10 pu setpos [30 -40] seth 0
pd setpos [30 60] seth 90 setpos [105         The door frame.
60] seth 180 setpos 105 -40] pu setpos
[55 50] seth 90 pd setpos [80 50] seth
180 fd 10 seth 270 setpos [55 40] seth
0 fd 10 setsh 3 pu setpos [65 45] pd          Stamps SHAPE 3 with
stamp pu setsh 3 setpos [75 45] pd            number 13 twice.
stamp pu setpos [-96 -8] setsh 0 seth 0
pd fd 60 seth 90 fd 60 seth 180 fd 60         The window frame.
seth 270 fd 60 pu setpos [-71 52] seth
180 pd fd 60 pu setpos [-61 52] seth
180 pd fd 60 pu setpos [-96 27] pd
repeat 13 [fd 3 seth 140 fd 3 seth 90]        First crack in the
                                              windows.
pu setpos [-95 14] pd repeat 9 [fd 3          Second crack in window.
seth 140 fd 3 seth 90] pu setpos [-1
18] setc 6 pd fill ht pu setpos [-150         Fills in background in
                                              color yellow.
70] label [You walk up to the house.
you can, a. ] setpos [-150 60] label
[go in or b. chicken out.]
name readlist cc "user.input
if :user.input = a [inside]
```

```
if :user.input = b [house]
end
```

FIG. 4.81. Albert's Logo code by March 29.

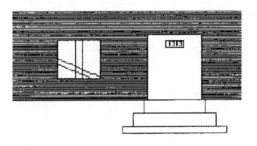

MARCH 5    Begin programming of doorsteps.

MARCH 6    Finish programming of doorsteps.

MARCH 8    Begin programming of door.

MARCH 12   Finish programming of door.

MARCH 13   Stamping of doorknob.

MARCH 14   Begin programming of windowframe.

MARCH 19   Programming of window cracks.

MARCH 20   Finishing of window cracks.

MARCH 22   Adding color to background

MARCH 26   Programming of choices: INSIDE or HOUSE.

FIG. 4.82. Overview of Albert's programming of the HOUSE procedure. It shows how Albert systematically worked on implementing all the features, one after the other, of the front view of the house.

## March: Choosing the Cast of Actors–Creatures, Demons, Bullies, Wizards, Punks, Gangs, Guys with Knives, and Magic Users

While Albert was programming the front view of the haunted house, he began "messing around" to determine the specific char-acters of his actors asking fraction questions. It is important to remember that although Albert was considering different actors in his notebook entries, he had not actually implemented any of them in the program.

At that time, Albert was still working on programming the de-tails of the front view of the haunted house, and had not put fig-ures into this scene. On March 12, Albert began his first consider-ation of changes regarding the cast of game actors. Returning from the computer pods, he wrote that "I didn't have any problems. I made one change. I am going to make creatures ask you problems and if you don't solve them you die." Albert was talking about a change he made in his plans about the game, not the actual implementation.

He continued March 13, with "I will make a guy on shapes and make him do something." Then on March 26, he wrote, "I am going to make a bully and his gang on shapes and they'll ask you a fraction question and if you get it right, you quit or chicken out." He announced on March 27 that "I need to make a gang of punks and they will ask you a question and if the answer is wrong they kill you." At the end of that day, he wrote, "I need to finish the gang and make them ask you a question. I have to finish the out-come of what happens when you get the right answer and wrong answer." The notebook entries on March 28 were exemplary for his thinking back and fourth about the actors (see Fig. 4.83).

On March 28, he changed the characters of the game again: "I need to make a gang of punks for chicken. I also am thinking about not making the punks but working a magic user come and ask you a question. If you get it wrong he turns you into a chicken." At the end of the day, he decided that "I changed the punks into a magic-user. I made this change because it is less vio-lent," and his plans for the next day confirmed this decision: "I am planning to work on the question that the magic user asked. If you get it wrong he turns you into a chicken." Next, Albert started specifying the specific features of his "guy" or "creature."

After that he started thinking about the specifics of the interactions between the player and the actors.

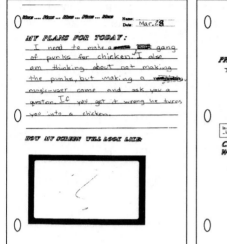 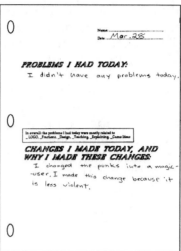

**FIG. 4.83.** Albert's designer notebook entries from March 28.

**Explanations of Why Albert Spent So Much Time Exploring Different Actors in His Game.** First, designing shapes took less work and was less risky than the programming scenes and worlds. Even if Albert redesigned or modified a shape the next day, it would not require him to change the whole setting of the game. Also, animation of shapes might have had more appeal for Albert than designing backgrounds. A second explanation might be connected to the development of a narrative in the game. While Albert was still working on a game that emphasized the environment (a haunted house) he was already preparing to move toward a story-oriented game. Albert changed his story so that the characters were more central than the locations. In support of this explanation, Albert mentioned openly in his plans for May 7 that he intended to change the plot of the story. His PLANS FOR TODAY stated, "I plan to make...to change the story ????" (see Fig. 4.84).

Several factors played a role in Albert's change of the game plot, and the explorations of different characters was the initial factor. Another was his interactions with the third graders in the first evaluation session (April 11), who told him to put more emphasis on the monsters, which was a clear indication to move away from the design of screens to the design of the creatures. A third factor was probably the impact of games designed by his other classmates, in particular Barney's game Fraction World (see chapter 3), which strongly emphasized the story idea. Many other classmates, in fact, started adopting the story format in their games at the same time. In a narrative game format, actors play an important role. They are the protagonists and they structure the actions: Things happen to them and they make things happen. What most students implemented in their games had more the character of a play. Other cultural media, such as video games, television and toys, also make extensive use of the narrative (Kinder, 1991). Albert's planning of the characters, his thinking and variations, were playful as he explored different ideas. None of them were implemented.

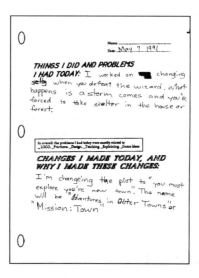

FIG. 4.84. Albert's designer notebook entry from May 7 which indicates his shift in game concept from graphics to narrative.

What are the implications of this change in Albert's game? First, he had to rewrite his introductions to accommodate the new story line. Second, it marked the definite turn from the world-oriented approach to the storyoriented approach of the coming scenes. The haunted house became an adventure/science fiction story where the player explored other worlds with rules. In Albert's world, the player explored houses and planets and defeated monsters by answering fractions questions correctly. Albert may have chosen to include fractions in this fashion because it was easier than his original idea of exploring fractions of the house. His concern about fractions might have been in the background, while he was exploring different characters and programming the front view of the house.

## March–June: Thinking about the Inside of the House—The Demon Scene

On March 14, Albert mentioned for the first time an idea that occupied him for the next three months. In his PLANS FOR TOMORROW, he stated, "Finish chicken and inside. I want to make a demon on shapes and make him jump out of a chest or a door." On March 20, he outlined the details for this scene (see Fig. 4.85).

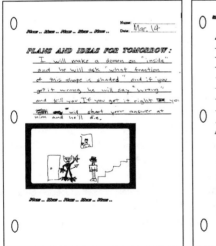
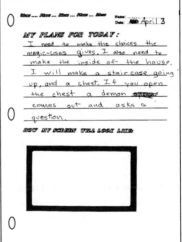

FIG. 4.85. Albert's entries from March 14 and April 3.

Albert considered different issues about this scene while he worked in parallel on the CHICKEN procedure in which the fraction wizard asked a fraction question. On April 3, he described the scene again (see Fig. 4.85). By the end of April (April 23 and 26), he gave further details on the demon scene (see Fig. 4.86).

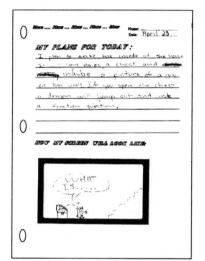

**FIG. 4.86.** Albert's designer notebook entries from April 23 and 26.

**Overview on Albert's Planning and Implementations for the Demon Scene.** Fig. 4.87 provides an overview on the different strands of Albert's thinking and programming on the demon scene during the period of March 20 to June 12. The first column describes Albert's ideas about the demon scene. Note that for the month of May, Albert mentioned in his notebook entries every day that he needed to work on this scene. The whole month of May had essentially the same statement written in his plans: "I need to make a demon jump out of a chest and ask a question . . . " During this same month, Albert worked on implementing other aspects of his game.

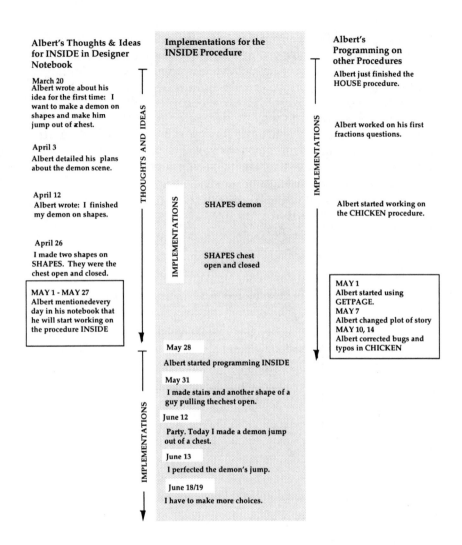

FIG. 4.87. Overview of Albert's thoughts, ideas and implementations for the INSIDE procedure. The period from March 20 until May 28 displays how Albert thought and worked in parallel on the INSIDE and the CHICKEN procedures.

The second column describes his actual implementations for the demon scene as they occurred durng the project. One can see that long before Albert actually programed his first line of the

`INSIDE` procedure, he implemented different aspects of it. For example, in April he worked on different shapes that became part of this scene. Beginning May 28, the notebook entries began reflecting Albert's actual implementation in Logo code. It took him less than a week to program and accomplish all features of this scene (one week in June was dedicated to rehearsals and performances of the annual Headlight theater play, in which he participated). The third column summarizes the main themes of scenes that Albert programmed while he planned the demon scene and before he started implementing his designs.

Albert's notebook entry from June 12 expressed clearly his joy over finishing a scene that took him nearly three months to conceive, design, and implement (see Fig. 4.88).

**FIG. 4.88.** Albert's designer notebook entry from June 12.

Let us take a look at the procedure `INSIDE`, in which Albert programmed the demon scene (Fig. 4.89). An explanation of the shapes can be found in Figure 4.89.

```
to inside
rg cc ct ht tell 1 pu setpos [-130 -85]
setsh 30 st tell 0 pu setpos [-30 -90]
seth 0 pd fd 30 seth 90 fd 20 seth 180
fd 30 pu setpos [-15 -84] setsh 13 st
tell 2 setsh 10 pu setpos [-25 -75] pd
```

```
repeat 20 [fd .5 rt 18] pu setpos [70
-90] seth 0 pd repeat 8 [fd 10 rt 90 fd
10 lt 90] pr [You go inside the house]
wait 50 ct tell 0 seth 270 pr [You see
a chest and a staircase.  You can a.
look and see what's in the chest or b.
go up the stairs]
name readchar "user.input
if user.input = "a [ct repeat 11
[wait 3 setsh 12 fd 3 wait 3 setsh 14 fd
3 wait 3 setsh 13 fd 3] wait 30 setsh
11 wait 40 setsh 10 tell 1 setsh 29
tell 0 seth 45 fd 15 seth 135 fd 20
setsh 12 tell 3 pu setpos [-120 -75]
setsh 20 st seth 45 fd 12 seth 135 fd 17]
```

**FIG. 4.89.** Albert's Logo code for the demon scene.

The player is represented by the following shapes:
    SHAPE 12: The walking player with left leg stretched out,
        arms half raised
    SHAPE 13: The standing player, arms stretched out
    SHAPE 14: The walking player, with both legs extended in air
    SHAPE 11: The player kneeling down, turned to left
    SHAPE 10: The player jumping in the air, with arms and legs extended

The demon is represented by the following shapes:
    SHAPE 20: The demon with trifork
In case of a wrong answer, the following shapes were added:
    SHAPE 18: The demon standing, with fork pointed to right
    SHAPE 19: The demon walking right, with fork pointed to right
In case of a correct answer, the following shape was added:
    SHAPE 21: The exploding demon

The chest is represented by the following shapes:
    SHAPE 29: The chest open
    SHAPE 30: The chest closed

**FIG. 4.90.** Overview of SHAPES used in the demon scene.

**Analysis of the Animation Programming.** In order to render justice to the complexity of this scene, I split up the different animation actions and placed the corresponding Logo code next to them (see Fig. 4.91a–h). Here is a recapitulation of the action using the different shapes and different turtles in the demon scene: The player went toward the chest (shapes 12, 13, and 14). This sequence was carefully timed.

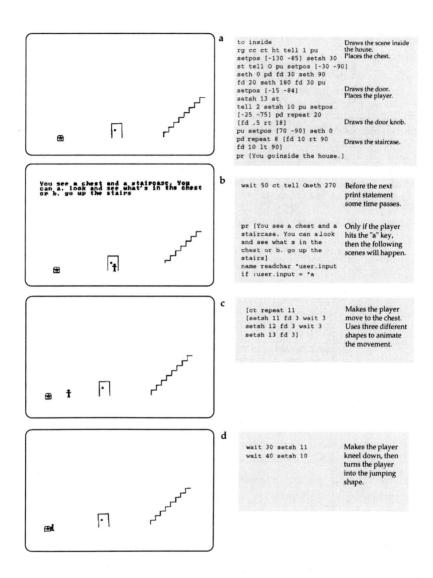

**FIG. 4.91a–d.** Albert's program: commented Logo code and animation for the `INSIDE` procedure, which displays a demon jumping out of a chest and asking a fraction question.

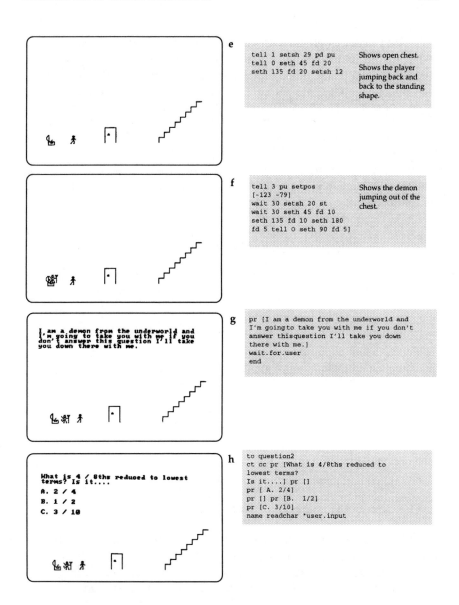

**e**

```
tell 1 setsh 29 pd pu
tell 0 seth 45 fd 20
seth 135 fd 20 setsh 12
```
Shows open chest.

Shows the player jumping back and back to the standing shape.

**f**

```
tell 3 pu setpos
[-123 -79]
wait 30 setsh 20 st
wait 30 seth 45 fd 10
seth 135 fd 10 seth 180
fd 5 tell 0 seth 90 fd 5]
```
Shows the demon jumping out of the chest.

**g**

```
pr [I am a demon from the underworld and
I'm going to take you with me if you don't
answer thisquestion I'll take you down
there with me.]
wait.for.user
end
```

**h**

```
to question2
ct cc pr [What is 4/8ths reduced to
lowest terms?
Is it....] pr []
pr [ A. 2/4]
pr [] pr [B.  1/2]
pr [C. 3/10]
name readchar *user.input
```

**FIG. 4.91e–h.** Albert's program: commented Logo code and animation for the INSIDE procedure, which displays a demon jumping out of a chest and asking a fraction question.

Then the player knelt down in front of chest (shape 11), waited for a moment, and turned into jumping player (shape 10). Then the chest changed to an open chest (shape 29). After this, the player jumped up in surprise in a half circle and turned into the standing player (shape 12). The demon (shape 20) jumped out of the chest. All of this happened in split seconds: the switch among turtles, character shapes, and the sequence of actions. Albert's use of different turtles allowed him to manipulate several characters easily and keep them in play. As long as a turtle was visible, there was no need for stamping it (a command that leaves a permanent trace of the shape on the screen).

The scene shown in Figs. 4.91 is one of the most complicated that Albert had programmed. A total of 11 shapes, more than one third of all the shapes he used (see Fig. 4.92), are involved.

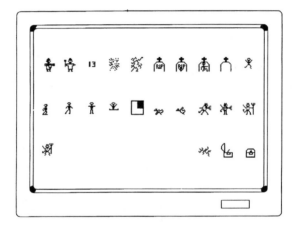

**FIG. 4.92.** SHAPES page of Albert's game.

Albert's final changes in the Logo code to perfect the jump showed once again, his sense for fine-tuning. They also illustrated that design decisions do not always concern big issues, but also apply to small details. The implemented changes (put in bold) in the visual effects were minimal, but necessary to satisfy Albert's personal aesthetics:

```
if user.input = "a [ct repeat 11 [
wait 3 setsh 12 fd 3 wait 3 setsh 14 fd
3 wait 3 setsh 13 fd 3] wait 30 setsh
```

```
11 wait 40 setsh 10 tell 1 setsh 29
tell 0 seth 45 fd 20 seth 135 fd 20
setsh 12 tell 3 pu setpos [-123 -79]

wait 30 setsh 20 st wait 30 seth 45
fd 10 seth 135 seth 180 fd 5]
```

Changed FD 15 to FD 20.
Changed [-120 -75] to
[-123 -79].
Inserted WAITs.
Changed FD 12 to FD 10;
inserted SETH and
changed FD 10 to 5.

The demon scene was the core of Albert's game. The number of shapes dedicated and used in this particular scene compared to others, the intricacies of the programmed animation, and the time spent on planning and implementing his ideas provide ample evidence. Animation seemed to be a general motivating force for programming (and this applied to all of Albert's classmates). Besides the visual appeal of animation sequences, I believe that another factor appeals to students, the control and programming of movements. In the same way that programming the turtle steps can resonate with one own's body movements, programming and controlling animations asks students to focus on the intricacies of their own body movements. Papert (1980) called this aspect of turtle programming "body syntonicity." The programming of animations is body syntonic, but on a different level. What resonates with students is the programming of movements of imaginary figures in the most realistic possible way (e.g., jumping out of the chest) or in a way that defeats all physical realities (e.g., shooting to the moon). The decomposition of Albert's demon scene (see Fig. 4.90a-h) showed the details of movement that Albert coordinated. In fact, what Albert had to do for this animation sequence was to analyze and decompose the movements of the two figures and the chest, and then compose them, using the right shapes and turtles, later again. This was programming in the most extreme sense through mastering the control flow, but on a visual level.

Another central feature of the demon scene was Albert's planning ahead. Already on the second day of the project, Albert foresaw as his biggest challenge the programming of the animation (he ended up using "demons jumping" instead of "robbers coming"). Before he wrote one line of code of the actual procedure, he had outlined all its essential features. I think one of the reasons why Albert programmed this scene so late is that he decided to focus first on aspects of the game that he felt more confident and comfortable programming, such as the front view of the house. Much in the same way as Simon (1969) used the two different watchmakers as examples for different approaches of how to assemble the pieces of a watch, Albert decided to think about and implement some of the demon scene's features in advance before actually assembling all the pieces into one scene.

## April: The First Fraction

Fractions and their representations were not at the center of Albert's attention in the Game Design Project. During the first days of the project, Albert expressed the idea of exploring "fractions of the house," which he did not follow up further. Two weeks later, his notebook entry introduced fractions again with the "demon asking a fraction question" (see Fig. 4.93). This points out an important aspect of the way that fractions were situated in his game: in the form of a dialogue or interaction. Albert's focus was not on the representation of fractions but on the context in which they appeared. His messing around in the first months of the project dealt with different game features, but not fractions. This is very much in contrast to the Instructional Game Design Project (Harel, 1988), in which most students spent the first months creating different representations of halves and fourths before they moved on to more sophisticated representations of fractions.

The issue of fractions does not come up again until the first focus session on March 25, in which we discussed with the whole class what was difficult about fractions, and how one could represent fractions. I saw Albert's sudden engagement with the fractions part of the game as a direct consequence of this session. On the following days, March 26, 27, and 28, his notebook entries dealt more frequently with the context in which the fraction question would be asked and who would ask the questions (as I presented and explained in the previous section, "The Cast of Actors"). Albert evaluated different actors and outcomes ("to chicken out" or "they will kill you") and whether the fraction question had been answered correctly or not. On all these days, none of the designs in his notebooks or the shapes designed in LogoWriter dealt with the content and representations of the fraction itself.

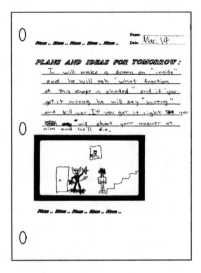

**FIG. 4.93.** Albert's designer notebook entry from March 14.

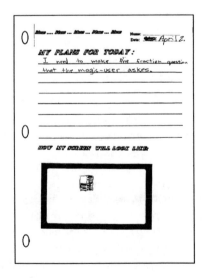
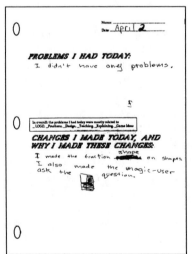

**FIG. 4.94.** Albert's designer notebook entries from April 2.

Albert introduced his first fraction representation on April 1 (see Fig. 4.94). On that day, Albert designed a shape (shape 15) that showed a square with 3/4 shaded in white. (LogoWriter shapes cannot be colored in different colors unless one composes a figure or area out of more than one shape). On April 2, Albert mentioned in his notebook that "I need to make the fraction question that the magic user asks." He then noted that "I made the fraction shape on shapes. I made also the magic user ask the 3/4 question" and that in his PLANS FOR TOMORROW he stated "I need to make the choices that the magic user asked. They will be A 3 4ths  B 2 3rds   C 2 4ths   D 5 8ths." Albert's entry into fractions used a natural entry point: standard representations (such as area) with fourths. In the weeks that followed, Albert mentioned fraction questions from time to time, but his main concern was with the implementation of the different choices, right and wrong, and how the actions were connected to each choice.

On April 11, the students had their first evaluation session. Before the students went out to start their games, we asked them to write down three or four questions or topics they wanted to discuss with their users. Albert wrote in his notebook the following questions for his game evaluators. Note that not one of these questions dealt with fractions.

Do I have enough graphics?
Are these questions easy?
Do you think I need more monsters or people?
Do you have any suggestions?

During the session, I captured Albert for a short moment on videotape with one of the third graders, who was looking at the front view on the house. Albert told him [as his user tried to follow the instructions printed on the screen]: "You cannot go in now because I haven't anything right now." He referred to the different options, such as the inside of the house, which he hadn't programmed yet. As a matter of fact, most game designers did not want to show their games to the third graders because of that reason: "We aren't done yet" or "I have nothing to show" were some of the many comments I heard when I asked students about choosing a date for the evaluation. I did not realize at that time that a game must have a sequence of actions for the player. A single screen is not enough to look at and does not provide enough simulation. (In the same way, linear arrangements of different screen shots on paper do not really provide a sense of the dynamics of the animated scenes.)

At the end of the evaluation session, when Albert returned to the class, I asked what he had heard from the students. He said: "They liked my game. The students made suggestions, to have choices for the answers and to have more monsters." A few days later, during a class discussion with his classmates, Albert previewed his visitors: "Well, the first person, he liked my game. He didn't have any suggestions when I asked him. And then I got the girl, Montoba, I think, she didn't have much to say. She just kind of sat. But the last people I had, they kind of, they asked questions about how this happened. They started talking about what I could do like . . . I could start working on other procedures."

Albert's case provides a typical example of how game design initiated the students' contact with fractions. Albert designed and programmed four fractions questions in his game, each question dealt with a different issue, such as reducing to the lowest term, addition, and matching between symbols and pictorial representations of fractions. These representations seemed to replicate the content of the school curriculum rather than Albert's personal preferences of fractions. A look at Albert's SHAPES page provides an excellent view of how fractions were integrated in the game: Albert designed only one fraction shape. Fig. 4.95 shows Albert's four fraction questions.

Albert's first fraction question was presented in an interesting way. His question used numbers such as three fourths and two thirds to give the user choices but phrased them as spoken words: 3 4ths and 2 3rds. One could say that Albert was "talking fractions." Another feature that becomes apparent when analyzing all his fraction representations in the questions is that Albert did not touch the deep structure of fractions. He was more on the surface level, using standard representations of halves and fourths in areas (Harel & Papert, 1991). The following example makes this point clearer. Albert used a house as his game context for asking fraction questions. In the Instructional Software Design Project (Harel, 1988), Debbie also used a house in which she divided all objects into halves to show her users that everything can be a fraction. Fractions are accorded only brief moments of attention in Albert's design of the educational game.

First fraction question: "Hi Kid! Tell me what fraction of this
square is shaded? TELL ME FAST IF IT IS . . .
A. 3 4ths
B. 2 3rds
C. 2  4ths
[Shows shape of 3/4, Albert's only fraction shape]

Second fraction question: "What is 4/8ths reduced to the
lowest terms? Is it . . .
A. 2/4
B. 1/2
C. 3/10

Third fraction question: "I am an alien from planet Zarg. I am
going to ask you a fraction problem and if you don't answer
it right I will kill you.
What is 1/4 + 3/3. Is it . . .
a. 1 whole
b. 1 and 1/4

Fourth fraction question: "WHAT IS 10/100 in lowest terms !!!!!!
YOU'LL  NEVER GET IT RIGHT, HA HA HA HA HA HA !!!!!!!!
IS IT . . .
A= 1/2  B = 1/10   OR C = 1/3 !!!!!!!

FIG. 4.95. Albert's four fraction questions in his game.

## June: Albert's Game at the End of the First Phase

At the end of the school year, Albert's program Mission: Town
had four LogoWriter pages: GAMES, GAMES2, GAMES3, and
GAMES4. A graphical representation of the program and the connection between the LogoWriter pages can be found in Fig. 4.96.

The GAMES page contained the credits and the general information and introduction to the game. GAMES2 drew the front
view of the haunted house and gave the user two options: to enter
the house (which calls GAMES4) or to chicken out (which goes to
page GAMES3). If the player decided to chicken out, a fraction
question appeared: "What fraction of the square is shaded?"
(correct answer is 3/4) and if the player chose a wrong answer
(choices b or c), the game provided instructions about how to start
the game again. The player who answered correctly had the
choice of "a" to go into the house or "b" to go to the back door.
Only option "a" was implemented and took the player to GAMES4.

Here, a staircase and a chest were displayed schematically and the user could decide whether to walk up the stairs (not implemented yet) or to look in the chest, which brought the demon from the underworld asking a fraction question: "What is 4/8ths reduced to the lowest term?" The incorrect answer called a procedure UNDERWORLD, whereas the choices for the other choices had not been implemented yet.

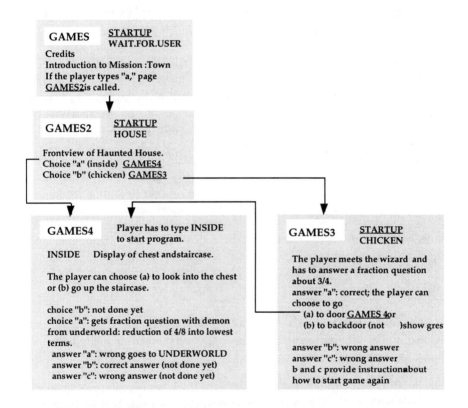

FIG. 4.96. Albert's GAMES pages as of June 19 and their connections with each other. Many features in the INSIDE procedure (GAMES4) had not been yet implemented.

In many ways, Albert's project was reminiscent of the students' projects in the Instructional Software Design Project (Harel, 1988), who stopped working on their instructional software after four months. Many of Albert's choices were still open; he did not have the time to complete the answers/actions for all the choices. This makes it clear that this was still a game in progress. On the other hand, one can recognize a basic structure in his game: an introductory screen with changing colors and music, the front view of the haunted house, the demon scene with the stairs and chest with two options, and two fraction questions.

## September–November: The Game Software's Organization in LogoWriter Pages

When the game designers came back after the summer, the students started with programming name poems. This second phase of the Game Design Project indicated a shift in the project's nature. The seven final weeks after the summer were dedicated to finishing the project, whereas the months before the summer were used by Albert to implement his demon scene and lay the framework for his game. By the end of June, Albert's program had four LogoWriter pages: one page GAMES with his introductions, the second page GAMES2 with the front view of the haunted house, a third page GAMES3 with the fraction wizard, and a fourth page GAMES4 with the demon scene. All pages were connected with each other; but several choices and options in the game had not been yet completed.

On September 25, I asked Albert about his plans for this second phase. His friend Shaun was sitting next to him.

> *Yasmin*: Albert, so what are your plans now?
>
> *Albert*: What I am going to do. OK. What happens, the guy comes up to the house and says "You go into the house" and it [the program] doesn't give you a chicken out [one of the choices]. It doesn't give an option to go away. So, then you have to go in there and you can go look at the chest or go up the stairs. And when you go up the stairs, there is a wizard and he asks you a fractions problem. If you get it right, he says, "Congratulations, you won the game. You've explored the house." And then he slices you in half with an axe and you go to heaven.
>
> *Shaun*: I gave him that!
>
> *Albert*: No, you didn't. He shoots you with a gun [he is refer-

ring to Shaun's game].

*Shaun*: No, I gave him [An exchange between them follows that is difficult to understand].

*Yasmin* [to both]: You have a variation on this theme.

*Albert* [continues]: So, and then if he gets it wrong, he slices him with an axe and goes to the underworld.

*Yasmin*: So now you are working on the underworld, is that it?

*Albert*: Yes, I am working on the, like when you and I have only two fraction problems.

Albert was detailing his plans about finalizing the demon scene in defining the different choices given to the player. He described how he thought the end of his game would look. Furthermore, he commented on the fact that he had "only two fraction problems." In sum, Albert outlined his line of work for the rest of the project: to design more fraction questions, program another scene with animations, and create the ending for his game. Once again, Albert showed himself to be careful and realistic in the ideas and plans that he would implement in his game.

## September–October: Reorganization of the Game Software

Another point of contention between Shaun and Albert dealt with Albert's use of LogoWriter pages to store his procedures. Logo is called a modular language because complicated problems can be broken down into simpler modules. The use of procedures is one of the main tools in programming to segment endless streams of code into more meaningful units. One must remember that Albert so far had not made use of procedures, even though he had been introduced to them before the Game Design Project. In the weeks that followed, Albert developed his own programming strategy to deal with the growing interactions and size of his game. For one, Albert used LogoWriter pages to store each individual scenes of his game. Furthermore, he segmented his program code into procedures (see Fig. 4.97). Before I describe this process in more detail, I return to the conversation between Shaun and Albert on September 25.

*Shaun*: He [Albert] wants to erase like a full, whole page of
   work!

*Yasmin*: What do you want to erase, Albert?

*Albert*: This! [He points out with his arm to the screen with the
   program code and tries at the same time to push Shaun
   away. Then he starts moving the cursor over the program
   code while highlighting it in red.] It's already on a
   different page.

*Shaun*: Function 1! [commenting on Albert's action of high-
   lighting]

*Albert*: I already moved it somewhere else.

*Yasmin*: So he doesn't really want to erase it.

*Shaun* [to Albert]: Albert, you are funny. So you are just going
   to use this whole page for the underworld?! [underworld
   is the procedure Albert is currently working on.]

*Albert*: Yes, it's the place to go when you . . .

*Shaun*: I know but you are gonna use . . . [his voice trails off;
   Shaun and Albert are wrestling and laughing.]

At a later point, Shaun joined the discussion again and argued
against Albert's idea of using an entire LogoWriter page for a single procedure.

*Albert* [turning to Shaun]: Shut up!

*Shaun*: I was trying to do the right thing. I was trying to help
   him save his game. Because I was trying to help him not
   being mean to him. He wants to erase [Shaun moves over
   to Albert's page]. Look at this [he says to me]. Wait, look
   at all of this! Look at all this work. He is putting it on
   whole pages and wants to erase it!

*Albert*: It's my work to erase it!

*Shaun*: No, I am trying to save your game.

*Albert*: It's not your game!

*Shaun*: Be quiet for a minute! If you want to be erased
   [laughing] I was showing him how to put it on a new page.
   So that it wouldn't be all wasted and he could have that
   problem somewhere else. But no, he doesn't want to. He
   just wants to mess up.

After finishing his name poem, Albert started working on his game project again. Albert was in the process of copying and cutting procedures and pasting them onto new pages. Shaun was complaining about Albert's intention "to erase a full, whole page of work." Shaun's statement "He just wants to mess up" expressed his disbelief at what he saw Albert doing: using a full page for one procedure. In the context of this project, students had been introduced to the use of GETPAGE, a command that allowed them to create links from one page to the next, hence extending the storage capacities of one page. LogoWriter projects can consist of several interconnected pages. This command is usually introduced when a student's page is filled up with procedures. However, Albert started turning this use of GETPAGE around: Instead of waiting until his page was filled up with procedures, he chose to use each single page as a repository for one scene.

On October 21, I had a similar conversation about the same topic with Albert and Shaun that confirmed my previous interpretation of Albert's effort.

> *Shaun*: I don't understand why his page can't hold more than 1,000. His pages aren't full. Why can't his page hold 1,000 mem . . . memory things?
>
> *Yasmin*: Are your pages full when you change?
>
> *Albert*: Because they are different, they are just different scenes. And I don't want to do two scenes on one page.
>
> *Yasmin*: On one page. So you decided to put each screen on a different page.
>
> *Albert*: Yes.

Here Albert stated most clearly why he chose this kind of organization, one scene per page: "I don't want to do two scenes on one page." Shaun interpreted Albert's action in light of memory limitations ("1,000 memory things") and compared it to his pages, which could hold much more. Shaun probably never understood the nature of Albert's reorganization.

Another important aspect in this conversation points to the emergence of a culture in the Game Design Project. By the time of that conversation, all the students were using more than one LogoWriter page to store their game programs. What in the beginning had been perceived as an impediment, opening a second page to continue the game, turned into a feature toward the end of the project. Students proudly told each other how many pages they needed to save at the end of each day. Shaun had adopted the more traditional stance that you only started a new page once the old one was full. Albert had turned this feature on its head by using individual pages for single scenes. The talk about procedures and pages had become the currency of conversation among the game designers.

In the remaining weeks, Albert continued working on his game. He reorganized his arrangement of procedures, created links between the different pages, and designed and programmed three more scenes (two of which included fraction questions). By the end of September (four days into the project's second phase), Albert's project was extended to six pages (Fig. 4.97). One of these pages was a copy of the page with the procedure CHICKEN whose place in the game he changed. His new page GAMES5 contained the followup to the UNDERWORLD procedure from GAMES4 where the game ended if the player answered the fraction question incorrectly. This is also the page about which the dispute between Albert and Shaun came up. The Logo code of GAMES5 is shown below:

```
GAMES5
to startup
rg ct cc Death
end

to Death
rg ct cc setc 0 pu setpos [-150 -100] pu seth 45 pu setc 4 pd
fd 100 rt 50 fd 20 seth 45 fd 56 rt 50 fd 70 seth 45 fd 16 rt
50 fd 56 seth 180 fd 103 pu setpos [57 -74] pd fill tell 0 pu
setpos [-8 86] setsh 14 seth 180 repeat 16 [wait 4 fd 10]
setsh 13 fd 10 pr [You better get used to fried foods!!! If
you want to play again type the a key.]
name readchar "user.input
if :user.input = "a [getpage "games]
```

As an additional feature, Albert designed the interactions with the player in such a way that if the player typed the A-key, he or she returned automatically to the beginning of the game. His page GAMES5 became one of the central pages in the game where all (except for the CHICKEN procedure) wrong answer choices wre directed.

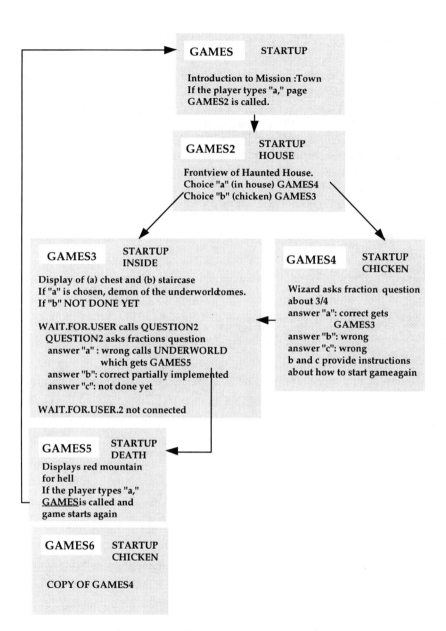

FIG. 4.97. Albert's GAMES pages as of September 25, and their connections with each other. Note that LogoWriter page GAMES3 has been duplicated.

## October: Creating Links Between Pages

By October 11, seven pages constituted his project, including a new page with the new procedure MASTER (see Fig. 4.99) where the player met the leader of all Zarks. Again, he segmented this scene in different subprocedures: MASTER, which included the landing of the ship on planet Zarg; FRACTION, which introduced the leader and question asker; DUH, in which he asked the fraction question; and SUM, which provided the feedback to the different answer choices. He completed the programming on this scene on October 15. The Logo code is shown in Fig. 4.98.

```
GAMES8
to startup
master wait.for.user
fraction duh sum
end

to master
rg cc ct tell 0 ht setsh 23 pu setpos [-100 85] seth 180
setc 13 st repeat 17 [wait 3 fd 10] tell 1 pu setpos [-90
-75] setsh 10 st seth 90 repeat 5 [ fd 3 rt 25] setsh 13
seth 180 fd 2 pr [You have landed on the Planet Zark.]
wait 100 cc ct tell 2 setc 2 pu setpos [155 -85] setsh 24
st seth 270 repeat 19 [wait 4 fd 10] tell 3 pu setpos [-
50 -85] setsh 27 st setc 10
end

to wait.for.user
cc type [Type any key to go on ...]
ignore readchar
end

to ignore :key
end

to fraction
cc ct pr [I am the leader of all the Zarks. I am going to
destroy you if you answer this problem wrong.]
wait.for.user
end

to duh
cc ct pr [WHAT IS 10/100 in lowest terms!!!!!!! YOU'LL
NEVER GET IT RIGHT, HA HA HA HA HA HA HA!!!!!!!!!!]
wait.for.user cc type [IS IT....... A = 1/2 B = 1/10 OR C
= 1/3!!!!!]
```

```
end

to sum
name readchar "user.input

if :user.input = "a [ cc ct pr [You have failed boy! The
right answer is B because 10/100 = 1/10!!! Now you
DIE!!!!] wait.for.user tell 3 seth 270 repeat 3 [wait 3
fd 10 wait 3 ] tell 1 setsh 22 tell 3 repeat 3 [ wait 3
bk 10 wait 3] cc ct pr [HA HA HA!!! I knew you could
never defeat me!! The right answer is B because 10/100 is
reduced to 1/10!!! You should study your fractions!!!]
wait.for.user getpage "games5 ]

if user.input = "b [ct cc pr[I can't belive it!!! You got
it right!!!!! AAAAARRRRGGGGGHHHHHH!!!!] wait.for.user
tell 2 wait 10 setsh 4 setc 4 tell 3 setsh 4 wait 15 ht
tell 2 ht wait.for.user ct cc pr [You have killed the
evil fraction aliens. You have won the game so you get in
your spaceship and blast home      (warp speed)]
wait.for.user tell 1 ht tell O seth 0 repeat 10 [wait 2
fd 11] ht getpage "games9]
if :user.input = "c [ cc ct pr [You have failed boy! The
right answer is B because 10/100 = 1/10!!! Now you
DIE!!!!] wait.for.user tell 3 seth 270 repeat 3 [wait 3
fd 10 wait 3 ] tell 1 setsh 22 tell 3 repeat 3 [wait 3 bk
10 wait 3] cc ct pr [HA HA HA!!! I knew you could never
defeat me!! The right answer is B because 10/100 is re-
duced to 1/10!!! You should study your fractions!!!]
wait.for.user getpage "games5 ]
end
```

FIG. 4.98. Logo code of Albert's page GAMES8.

But on October 11, Albert also continued rearranging the procedures of his project. His first step had been to copy procedures for individual scenes on single pages. His next step was to rearrange the place of the CHICKEN procedure of GAMES3. He started earlier on October 6 to duplicate this page on another page, GAMES6. On October 11, page GAMES6 was linked to the rest of the project (see Fig. 4.99). Albert's program created links between pages and connections between procedures or scenes: Instead of a linear narrative structure, Albert created a complex, branched, and linked story. Each narrative event in a story consisted of several interrelated and interactive events. The print medium was an inadequate medium for representing the dynamic structure of these events.

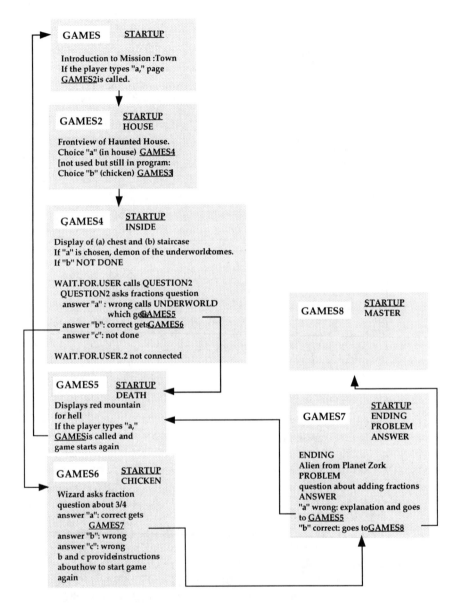

**FIG. 4.99.** Overview of Albert's GAMES pages as of October 11 and their connections with each other. Most procedures and pages have been connected with each other.

On the computer screen, the protagonists and objects were animated. They moved in relation to each other. They seemed to interact with each other according to the story told. These protagonists were interacting with the user/ player as well, because certain events were triggered only, if the player pressed a particular key or chose a particular answer.

Albert's development in this second phase began in June, but was not yet very pronounced. In June, Albert had already began to use individual Logo pages as repositories for single scenes, but I would never have understood the extent and intentions behind his organization without having seen his final project in November: eight pages connected in a hypertextlike fashion, representing a circle with an entry point and an exit point for the ending.

## October: Programming Style

By October 2, Albert's game extended to six pages, one page had been erased (the one with the double CHICKEN procedure), and a sixth page GAMES7 with the beginning of a new procedure ENDING which he will finish on October 11 (see Fig. 4.100). The Logo code for page GAMES7 is shown below:

```
GAMES7
to startup
rg cc ct ending problem answer
end

to ending
rg cc ct setbg 0 tell O pu setpos [155 -85] seth 270 setsh 13
repeat 8 [wait 3 setsh 12 fd 5 wait 3 setsh 14 fd 5 wait 3
setsh 13 fd 5] tell 1 pu setpos [-145 85] setsh 7 st repeat
30 [setc 1 + random 15 wait 1.5] setc 9 pu seth 90
repeat 10 [wait 4 fd 15 ] seth 180
repeat 14 [wait 4 fd 12 ]  fd 3 setsh 6
wait 20 setsh 5 tel 1 O repeat 2 [wait 3 bk 5 setsh 12 wait 3
bk 5 setsh 14 wait 3 bk 5 setsh 13] tell 1 setsh 25 tell 2 pu
setpos [15 -75] setsh 9 st setc 10 repeat 4 [rt 45 fd 8] fd 3
tell 3 pu
setpos [34. 3136 -86] setsh 8 setc 9 st end

to problem
pr [I am an alien from the Planet Zark. I am going to ask you
a fraction problem and if you don't answer it right I will
```

```
kill you.] wait.for.user
ct pr [What is 1/4 + 3/3. ]
wait.for.user

ct pr [Is it.......]
pr []
pr [a. 1 whole]
pr []
pr [b. 1 and 1/4]
end

to answer
name readchar "user.input
if :user.input = "a [cc ct pr [You're wrong!!! The right an-
swer is B because 3/3 = 1 whole and then you add 1/4. So the
right answer is 1 and 1/4!! ]
wait.for.user tell 3 seth 90 fd 10 wait 9 fd 10
tell 0 setsh 22 setc 15 tell 3 bk 10 wait 9 bk 10 cc ct pr
[HA HA HA HA HA!!!!!!!!!] wait 30 getpage "games5]]
[AAAAARRRRRGGGGGHHHHHH!!!!!!!] wait.for.user tell 2 setsh 4
wait 20 ht tell 2 ht tell 3 ht tell 1 setsh 23 cc ct pr
[You've destroyed an alien and his ship has changed. You go
in it.] wait.for.user tell 0 repeat 8 [wait 3 setsh 14 fd 5
wait 3 setsh 12 fd 5 wait S tell 1 pu tell 0 wait 3 ht tell 1
seth 0 cc ct repeat 6 [fd 8 wait 3 fd 8 wait 3] ht getpage
"games8] end

to wait.for.user
cc type [Press any key to go on....] ignore readchar
end

to ignore :key
end
```

A closer look at the LogoWriter page GAMES7 reveals an important change in Albert's programming style using procedures.
During the first four months, Albert's pages were characterized by
having one superprocedure, usually called STARTUP, which prepared the page and command center (clearings) and called only
one procedure. In the second phase of the Game Design Project,
Albert still used a superprocedure STARTUP that cleared text and
graphics (RG CC CT), but then the STARTUP procedure called
other procedures individually. Each of these procedures segments
contained pieces that were originally in one big procedure.

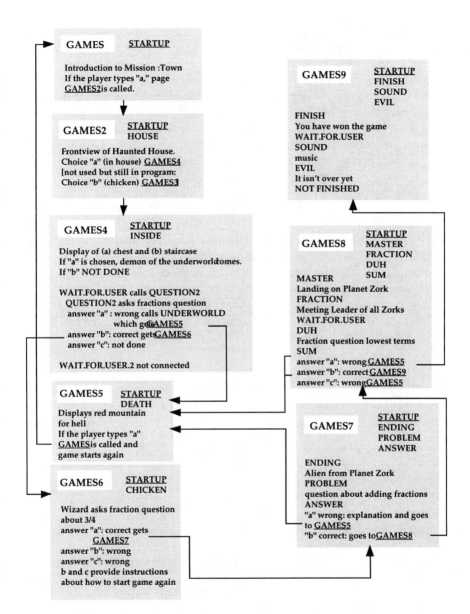

**FIG. 4.100.** Albert's GAMES pages as of October 25 and their connections with each other. Some procedures were still unconnected on pages GAMES4 and GAMES9.

For example, on page GAMES7, he had a number of different subprocedures in the following order: ENDING, which included an animation scene with meeting and alien from planet Zark; PROBLEM, which posed the fraction problem; and ANSWER, which took the player's choice and provided feedback corresponding to the correctness of the answer. Compared with his previous programming, this was the first time that Albert also segmented a scene into separate procedures in his programming.

Unfortunately, I do not have Albert's explanation for this change in programming with procedures. He also programmed the procedures on the next two pages, GAMES8 and GAMES9, in a similar fashion. One of my explanations is that Albert's organization of his game project into Logo pages found an equivalent in his organization of procedures. It may have been that suggestions and complaints from the teacher and myself had an impact on this change. As all students' games increased in size and became increasingly complex in their interconnections, we often asked students to segment their programs into smaller units. We introduced this measure as a debugging tool to help them and us locate and repair bugs in the program.

## October–November: Dramatic Moments

By October 17, Albert had eight pages including another page GAMES9 with a new procedure FINISH (see Fig. 4.101). He then started working on his closing screen. He concluded his adventure story with a return to the home base: "You have landed in your backyard," and then summarized the exploits of the player during the game: "You've globed ghosts, defeated demons and mashed Martians. Basically you've won the game!!!!!!" He congratulated the player with a message on the screen, "YOU'VE WON !!!!!!!" which he underlined with music and animation. But like a good story teller, Albert delayed the final scene for a moment of surprise, "This isn't over yet!!!! HA HA HA HA HA HA!!!!!!! THAT'S WHAT YOU THINK!!!" before he showed the THE END sign. Albert employed a technique called *prolongation* or *delayed ending*, often used in movies or musical composition, to further the climax of his story.

**GAMES9**

```
to startup
rg cc ct setbg 1 finish sound evil
end

to finish
tell 0 setpos [-45 85] seth 180 setsh 23 setc 13 repeat 17
[wait 4 fd 10] tell 1 pu setpos [-35 -80] setsh 10 st seth 90
repeat 4 [fd 3 rt 25] setsh 13 pr [You have landed in your
backyard.] wait.for.user ct cc tell 0 repeat 17 [wait 4 bk
10] ht pr [Your ship blasts off.] wait.for.user ct cc
pr [You've globed ghosts, defeated demons and mashed
Martians. Basically you've won the game!!!!!!]
end

to wait.for.user
cc type [Press any key to go on ...]
ignore readchar
end

to ignore :key
end

to sound
wait.for.user cc ct pr [YOU'VE WON !!!!!!!] tell 1
repeat 2 [tone 585 14 tone 590 1 tone 734 9 tone 806 9 tone
967 5 wait 35 tone 876 14 tone 734 10 tone 585 10 tone 485 5
tone 400 5 tone 400 3 wait 10 tone 400 2 wait 10 tone 400 2
wait 10 tone 440 16 wait 10 tone 400 2 wait 10 tone 400 4
wait 6 tone 410 4 wait 6 tone 400 4 tone 420 4  tone 450 17]
repeat 20 [wait 3 setsh 14 wait 3 seth 0  fd 10 wait 3 setsh
13 bk 10 ]
end

to evil
tell O setpos [150 -85] setsh 24 setc 2 st tell 2 pu setpos
[-150 -85] setsh 23 pu setpos [125 -85] setsh 9 setc 10 st
wait.for.user ct cc pr [ This isn't over yet!!!! HA HA HA HA
HA HA!!!!!!!] wait.for.user ct pr [THAT'S WHAT YOU THINK!!!]
wait.for.user tell [O 2 3] setsh 4 setc 12 wait 25 ht ct pr
[THE END] repeat 2 [tone 585 14 tone 590 1 tone 734 9 tone
806 9 tone 967 5 wait 35 tone 876 14 tone 734 10 tone 585 10
tone 485 5 tone 400 5 tone 400 3 wait 10 tone 400 2 wait 10
tone 400 2 wait 10 tone 440 16 wait 10 tone 400 2 wait 10
tone 400 4 wait 6 tone 410 4 wait 6 tone 400 4 tone 420 4
tone 450 17]
end
```

**FIG. 4.101.** Albert's GAMES9 page.

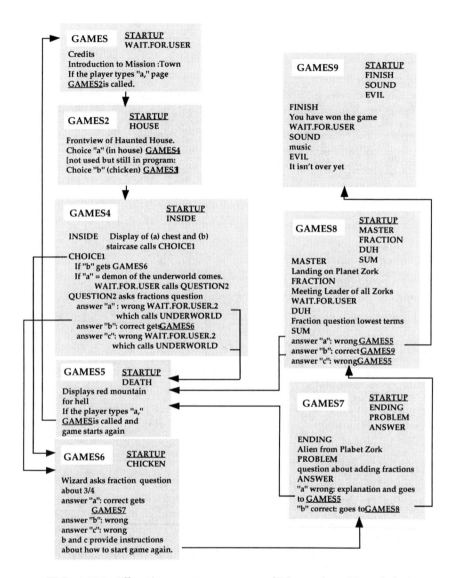

**FIG. 4.102.** Albert's GAMES pages as of November 15 and their connections with each other. Note that Albert had finished now the answer choice "c" in the INSIDE procedure on GAMES4.

By October 22, all his procedures were implemented; Albert began on correcting typos in his program. At the game fair day on November 14, he encountered a bug in his program: In his revisions, he must have accidentally erased the statement END in the startup procedure for CHICKEN. Because Albert's game, like those of his classmates, depended on a particular sequence to be followed, his game got stuck at this point and could not continue. After several searches through the program he eventually found the omission and fixed the bug (see the final program version in Figure 4.102).

## Summary and Discussion of Albert's Case

Different points can be made about Albert's case that concern his particular style of programming and design, and his approach to integrating ideas about fractions in his game. I decided to use Albert's project because of his development of programming skills and, in particular, his appropriation of modularization. Albert's project demonstrated that he was a skillful programmer. In the course of the project, we could observe two shifts in Albert's programming approach.

The first shift was of general nature and indicated his transition from using Logo for drawing to using Logo for powerful programming. During the first month of the project, Albert designed and implemented the front view of his haunted house. Albert started his game in a manner similar to his previous programming projects. He used the turtle very much like a drawing tool, with his foremost attention to fine graphic details. In the course of the project, Albert still kept his attention to details, but he moved to another level of programming. This came out clearly in the design and implementation of his animation scenes, in which Albert concentrated on coordinating and controlling the movements of different actors. His focus on programming graphical detail turned into programming interactions among actors with the user.

The second shift concerned his use of procedures and LogoWriter pages to control the growing complexity of his game program. All students had been introduced to the concept of procedures and superprocedures before the Game Design Project started. Yet, in the first phase of the project, Albert preferred to place one big procedure on each page without segmenting the different parts of his code into individual procedures. When Albert came back after the summer and started working on his game again, his initial "one big procedure on one page" programming style changed into "several procedures organized in one superprocedure on one page," in which each page was the repository for an event consisting of several scenes. In the same context, he also started using LogoWriter pages in a different way: to organize and structure his game, which in the meantime had grown to be dozens of different scenes distributed over eight pages. He used and manipulated the LogoWriter pages as procedures. His particular way of using LogoWriter pages in the second phase of the project showed that Albert still continued thinking in scene units. The summer break could have provided Albert and his classmates with an opportunity to step back, to evaluate their games, and to start anew. His closer familiarity with the game might have led him to modularize individual components of his scenes.

Albert was the only one in his class who came up with this kind of LogoWriter page organization. No other student created this kind of organization to control and arrange the flow of the program. Albert turned a limitation of LogoWriter (the amount of information available on each page) into a feature. In other words, what was first perceived by most students as an impediment (it was a threshold to think about two pages and the control flow among them) turned into a feature.

These two transitions document how Albert developed his personal approach to dealing with the complexity and the fine details of the project. He appropriated modularization for his own purposes. Albert's organization of LogoWriter pages raised issues of how students deal with complexity when a project grows and what kind of support we can offer, in terms of both computational tools and pedagogical tools. I discuss this question further in the conclusions (chapter 6).

Albert's involvement with fractions was rather limited. In the interview in the first days of the project, he talked about exploring "fractions of the house" that he would design. However, he never followed up to implement this idea. In the design of the representations of fractions in his questions, Albert remained attached to standard representations of fractions as area or in symbols by using halves and fourths. He still thought about fractions mainly in terms of part-whole relationships. In his design and program-ming, Albert was more concerned about the different features of his game.

For his crucial scene of the demon jumping out of chest, Albert spent three months on planning and preparations before eventu-ally implementing it. The number of shapes that Albert designed spoke for themselves. For one "actor," there were four to five dif-ferent shapes to simulate movements. Even objects such as the chest had different positions (open, closed, half motion).

Albert's approach in designing and programming his project pointed out interesting differences. His first ideas and plans about the game largely determined his game. I provided several incidents in which Albert laid out his ideas and implemented them. For example, the front view of the haunted house was sketched in one of his first notebook designs, and most of the fea-tures (such as the crack in the windows) were later implemented. Another example is his ideas and work on the demon scene over a period of three months. In fact, Albert was one of the very few students who implemented his first ideas, for the most part. What is most pervasive in Albert's approach is the adaptation of his plans to his programming abilities. In all his designs and ideas he proved to be a careful and realistic planner. But he also showed another side in his game development. For example, during the month of March, he messed around with ideas about his future actors, none of which were ever implemented. In May, he changed the plot of the story because it better suited his game's needs. The implementation of dynamic animation and graphical details reflected Albert's personal style and his sensitivity to aes-thetics.

# Chapter 5

# Learning Through Design:
# A Comparative Evaluation

The Game Design Project presented a rich learning environment for the students. As they were engaged in creating, implementing, revising, debugging, and presenting their games, they touched on many issues and subject areas. All 16 game designers who started this project in March accomplished a product, a software game, cover design, advertisement and documentation. Many questions could be raised about what the students learned during or as part of their participation. One way to understand this project better is by comparing it to other methods of learning through, or not through, design. The general goal of this comparative evaluation is to establish whether the game designers' skills in programming and knowledge of fractions differed from that of students taught by other pedagogical means.

In the Game Design Project, students used Logo as a tool of personal expression and knowledge reformulation. Game design, as used in my study, created a context that engaged students in complex programming over a long period of time. I wanted to know in which ways designing a game could contribute to the students' programming knowledge: to understand better the programming language and concepts, to generate a complex piece of software, and to debug and maintain the code. My interest in fractions focused on game design as an instructional strategy to engage students in the construction of fraction representations. Being placed in the position of an educational game designer, students asked themselves such questions as: What is important to learn about fractions? What is difficult? How can I teach these difficult things to other kids? But they also asked: How can fractions be integrated into games? What are good features of fractions to be included in games? My assumption was that through this process of thinking, designing, and programming fraction representations, students would become more deeply involved in knowledge about fractions and, hence, attain a better understanding of them.

The evaluation was designed to compare the students who participated in the Game Design Project (the experimental class) and their learning of Logo programming skills and fractions with students who learned these skills through other instructional means (the three control classes). The four classes that were included in this evaluation came from the same school, the same grade level, and participated in the same mathematics curriculum, but the teachers of each class used a different approach for integrating Logo with fractions (for a detailed description of the evaluation's objectives, procedures and instruments, I refer the reader to chapter 2). To facilitate the distinction between the classes, they have been labeled according to their different Logo programming instruction: the experimental class (N = 16) is also called Game Design; Control Class 1 (N = 17), Instructional Design; Control Class 2 (N = 18), Integrated Logo; and Control Class 3 (N = 16), Isolated Logo. I investigated not only the differences in the students' knowledge before and after their participation in the Game Design Project, but also compared their knowledge to that of three other classes taken from Harel's study (1988) (see Fig. 5.1).

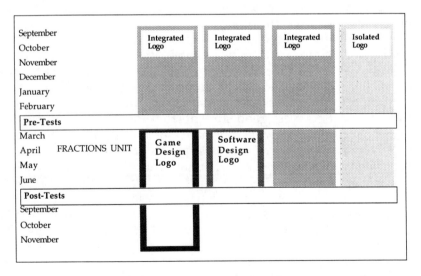

FIG. 5.1. Overview of evaluation procedures of the participating classes.

One of these three classes was a class of students who participated in another design activity, the Instructional Software
Design Project. This made it possible to compare two design
projects using Logo within the same school context: "instructional
design" and "game design." A major part of the discussion of the
results will analyze in which particular ways game design might
have contributed to students' engagement with programming and
fractions.

The following discussion presents selected results from the
comparative evaluation. Preference in the presentation of results
was given to data that was available from both pre- and posttests
for all classes. The results of this evaluation should be interpreted
with care for the following reason. The kind of environment that I
created with the teacher and the students in the Game Design
Project was complex and rich in many aspects. The evaluation's
focus on only two of these many aspects, the Logo programming
and fractions knowledge, represents one small portion of the
whole picture. To conclude causal relationships from these results
would do injustice to the intentions of the study to create a holistic environment with many interacting variables.

The nature of the evaluation and the use of data gathered four
years before the time of this study place some further constraints
on the interpretation. I tried to be as careful as possible adopting
the evaluation's design, procedures, and instruments for my research. However, there are two concerns with using the control
classes from Harel's study in my evaluation. One constraint on
the interpretation of results is imposed by the high pre-test scores
of the Game Design and Instructional Design students' Logo programming knowledge in some subtasks. These indicate that the
student designers were good students to begin with. Another constraint concerns the low performance of the Isolated Logo class
(Control Class 3) and raises questions about its inclusion as an
adequate comparative class. The fact that these students came
from a bilingual class must have had an impact on the test results,
even though this class shared many features with the other classes
(coming from the same school, the same grade, being an advanced
work class). Also, the one hour a week of Logo programming (23
hours in total, compared to the 70 hours of programming for the
other classes) cannot account alone for the differences found in
the pretest scores, in particular for the Logo assessment. In many
ways, perhaps, this bilingual class was much more like a "regular
class" than an advanced work class. Notwithstanding these limi-

tations, the following results provide rich material for discussion and allow important and interesting comparisons between the two design situations, "instructional design" and "game design".

## RESULTS OF THE COMPARATIVE EVALUATION

The general goal of the evaluation was to establish whether the students' skills in Logo programming and knowledge in fractions differed from those of students taught by other pedagogical means. For that purpose, the Game Design class was compared to three other classes. The results of the evaluation demonstrate that the game designers' knowledge improved significantly between the beginning and the end of the four-month project. The following presentation provides more detail to this statement and is divided into two sections: one dedicated to the results of the Logo programming tasks, the other to the results of the fraction knowledge assessment.

### Learning Logo Programming

Using a programming language involves many aspects besides writing code; among the essential ones are knowledge of the programming language commands and grammar, and the ability to read and transform given program code. In order to assess these skills, I used a paper-and-pencil test developed by Harel (1988). This test included several questions and tasks that focused on the students' knowledge of the programming language Logo. Students were asked to list and describe Logo commands, read and execute given Logo code, and transform Logo statements.

*Understanding of Logo Language, Commands, and Instructions.* This task covered the basic knowledge the students had about Logo command syntax and instructions. Students were asked to list as many Logo commands and instructions as they could remember and to explain the commands and/or provide examples. In so-called "computer literacy classes," major emphasis is placed on the students' acquisition of this knowledge. The task of listing Logo commands is a difficult one, because students use Logo mostly when working on the computer. As a simple measure, I

counted the number of correctly remembered and written-down
Logo statements.

**TABLE 5.1**
Number of Logo Commands Listed for Each Class in Pre- and Posttests
and the Results of the Two-Way Analysis of Variance for Repeated
Measurement

| | Number of Logo Commands | |
| --- | --- | --- |
| Group | Pretest | Posttest |
| Experimental Class **Game Design** | 18.9 | 22.1 |
| Control Class 1 **Instructional Design** | 22.6 | 27.9 |
| Control Class 2 **Integrated Logo** | 14.3 | 12.6 |
| Control Class 3 **Isolated Logo** | 9.3 | 8.3 |

| Source | d.f. | F-Statistics |
| --- | --- | --- |
| A (groups) | 3 | 22.58** |
| Subjects between | | |
| samples | 60 | |
| Within subjects | 63 | |
| B (pre–post) | 1 | 3.04 n.s. |
| A x B | 3 | 4.41** |
| B x subjects | 60 | |
| Between subjects | 64 | |
| Total | 127 | |

*Note.* **p<.01

The results indicate that the Game and Instructional Design
classes improved between and pre- and posttests, and list nearly

twice as many Logo commands than Control Classes 2 and 3 (Table 5.1). In contrast, the performance of the two control classes, integrated and isolated Logo, reached a plateau. These results are mitigated by the fact that the students of both design classes listed more commands in the pretest than the other control classes. In the statistical analysis, the differences between the groups (Factor A) is clearly expressed. One possible explanation for this improvement could be that these students advanced their Logo knowledge irrespective of the design activities because they were already better students. On the other hand, the daily work with Logo must have contributed to the students' Logo knowledge because, in contrast to the Integrated and Isolated Logo conditions, these students did not reach a plateau in their performance. Instead, they extended their knowledge of Logo, which was reflected in their higher posttest scores. However, the differences between the pre- and posttests are not significant, because of high variations and divergent patterns in the students. Furthermore, I evaluated the quality of the explanations and examples given by the students for each command in the pre- and posttest. I could observe a clear shift between the pre- and posttest for all students: The game designers became better in providing examples and explanations of Logo commands, although they were already good in the beginning.

*Classification of Logo Commands.* Students were asked to classify the list of their Logo commands in categories of their own choice. Although elementary students use classifications in a variety of subjects (e.g., science and language arts), they are usually are not asked to categorize programming language commands. In this situation, students had to transfer their knowledge from other experiences and apply it to Logo commands (see Table 5.2).

The number of categories built indicates to what extent students had a thorough understanding of the Logo programming language, could abstract features that are common to a number of commands, and could summarize them in a group. The interesting result of this analysis is that all students in both design classes consistently performed better on this task, whereas the students of the other classes seemed to reach a plateau. The analysis of variance confirms once again the differences between the groups, but also a clear distinction between the beginning of the project and four months into it.

**TABLE 5.2**
The Number of Categories with Logo Commands Created in Each Class
and the Results of the Two-Way Analysis of Variance
for Repeated Measurement

| Group | Number of Categories with Logo Commands | |
|---|---|---|
| | Pretest | Posttest |
| Experimental Class **Game Design** | 4.3 | 5.0 |
| Control Class 1 **Instructional Design** | 2.2 | 4.9 |
| Control Class 2 **Integrated Logo** | 2.9 | 3.1 |
| Control Class 3 **Isolated Logo** | 1.7 | 2.6 |

| Source | d.f. | F-Statistics |
|---|---|---|
| A (groups) | 3 | 6..21** |
| Subjects between | | |
| samples | 58 | |
| Within subjects | 61 | |
| B (pre–post) | 1 | 21.65** |
| A x B | 3 | 5.25** |
| B x subjects | 58 | |
| Between subjects | 62 | |
| Total | 123 | |

*Note.* **p<.01

A further analysis of the quality of the categories indicates that the students from both design classes also built more meaningful categories. For example, students composed categories for Logo commands that erased or deleted things, or Logo commands that moved the turtle on the screen. A comparison between pre- and posttest scores on this task revealed for the experimental students that they, at large, increased the quality of their classification which might be a further indicator for a better understanding of Logo. The longterm involvement in the context of one project might provide all students from different mathematical backgrounds with the opportunity to gain a better understanding of the Logo programming language.

*Drawing Pictures According to Someone Else's Code.* Students were asked to take a procedure called TO DESIGN, and draw on a grid the design the turtle would create on the monitor. The drawn picture—three aligned squares of different size—could be evaluated for correctness in regard to the number of squares and the correctness of scale and unit.

**TABLE 5.3**
Percentage of Students Who Correctly Executed
the Given Logo Code on the Pre- and Posttest

| Group | Correct Number of Squares | | Correct Scale & Consistent Unit | |
|---|---|---|---|---|
| | Pretest | Posttest | Pretest | Posttest |
| Experimental Class **Game Design** | 50% | 63% | 25% | 44% |
| Control Class 1 **Instructional Design** | 65% | 94% | 59% | 88% |
| Control Class 2 **Integrated Logo** | 44% | 56% | 28% | 39% |
| Control Class 3 **Isolated Logo** | 19% | 13% | 25% | 13% |

The results show that the students in both design classes were much better at this task (see Table 5.3). Students in the Integrated Logo class (Control Class 2) also improved their ability to deal with this task, in contrast to the students in the Isolated Logo condition. The drop in performance of the Isolated Logo class was unexpected. With no impact of the Logo programming instruction, the performance would have been expected to remain the same. A possible explanation may be that the students of both design classes and the Integrated Logo class were working daily with Logo, compared to the once-a-week exposure for the Isolated Logo students.

*Simplification of Given Logo Code.* Students were asked to take the procedure TO DESIGN and to simplify it with the goal of still producing the same picture on the screen.

**TABLE 5.4**
Percentage of Students Who Completed Each Level of
Simplification and Modularization of Logo Code

| Group | Level 1 Combination of commands | | Level 2 Using Repeat | | Level 3 Using sub-procedures | |
|---|---|---|---|---|---|---|
| | Pretest | Posttest | Pretest | Posttest | Pretest | Posttest |
| Experimental Class **Game Design** | 94% | 94% | 25% | 44% | 0% | 6% |
| Control Class 1 **Instructional Design** | — | 100% | — | 94% | — | 76% |
| Control Class 2 **Integrated Logo** | — | 78% | — | 22% | — | 6% |
| Control Class 3 **Isolated Logo** | — | 75% | — | 25% | — | 0% |

In this task, different levels could be distinguished: Level 1 indicates that students correctly combined commands (e.g., RIGHT 65 and RIGHT 25 to RIGHT 90); Level 2 indicates that the students wrote REPEAT procedures to combine Logo commands; and Level 3 indicates that students used subprocedures and/or input parameters. Table 5.4 gives an overview on all classes. These results show clearly the superior ability of the instructional designers to deal with this task. One could stipulate that the instructional designers were better in this task, because they also were better in executing the given Logo code and therefore were able to see the pattern, the three squares of different size. This could have improved their ability in simplifying and modularizing the code. Some of the instructional designers also used input variables in their procedures; an aspect to which the game designers and the other students were not introduced during their learning of Logo programming. It is important to remember that much of the programming instruction in the design classes was guided by the students' needs and experiences. The low performance of the Isolated Logo class can also be explained—most students did not understand the task because they were not very familiar with Logo.

*Number of Inputs for Logo Commands.* In this situation, students were asked to give an example for a given command and to write down the number of inputs the command required (see Table 5.5). For example, students were asked to name the number of inputs necessary for six Logo commands: FORWARD, LEFT, HOME, REPEAT, SETCOLOR, and SETPOSITION. Some of these commands are particularly difficult because they do not require an input (e.g., HOME) or because they work with lists (REPEAT, SETPOSITION).

Both design classes do well on this task. In general, all classes of Project Headlight (the experimental class and Control Classes 1 and 2) show better knowledge of the input parameters than does Control Class 3. The results of the analysis of variance confirm the differences between the groups in terms of providing the right input and example as well as the differences between the pre- and posttest results.

*Transforming Logo Procedures.* The last task of the Logo test dealt with the students' ability to transform given Logo statements. This task was not given in the pretest. Students were given a Logo code to draw a circle, square, or rectangle, and were asked how they could change this procedure to make a bigger circle or half a circle.

**TABLE 5.5**
Average Number of Correctly Listed Input Parameters for Logo
Commands (out of 6) and the Results of the Two-Way Analysis of
Variance for Repeated Measurement

| Group | Average Number of Input Parameters for Logo Commands | |
|---|---|---|
| | Pretest | Posttest |
| Experimental Class **Game Design** | 4.5 | 5.2 |
| Control Class 1 **Instructional Design** | 3.4 | 5.2 |
| Control Class 2 **Integrated Logo** | 3.0 | 2.8 |
| Control Class 3 **Isolated Logo** | 0 | 1.0 |

| Source | d.f. | *F*-Statistics |
|---|---|---|
| A (groups) | 3 | 54.01** |
| Subjects between samples | 59 | |
| Within subjects | 62 | |
| B (pre–post) | 1 | 21.52** |
| A x B | 3 | 6.85** |
| B x subjects | 59 | |
| Between subjects | 63 | |
| Total | 125 | |

*Note.* **p<.01

For example, the students were given the following Logo code
to draw a circle

```
to circle
repeat 360 [fd 1 rt 1]
end
```

and were asked how they could change this procedure to make a bigger circle or half a circle. In order to change the code, they had to know well the function of the individual parameters in the circle procedure. Changing FD 1 to FD 2 was the easiest change among other possible changes. For the third task, students were given a procedure SQUARE and asked to change the necessary parameters. The Instructional Design students were very clearly most able to handle this assignment, followed by the game designers and Control Classes 2 and 3 (see Table 5.6).

**TABLE 5.6**
Percentage of Correct Answers to the Transformation Tasks

| Group | Circle to Bigger Circle Posttest | Circle to Half-circle Posttest | Square to Rectangle Posttest |
|---|---|---|---|
| Experimental Class **Game Design** | 6% | 44% | 63% |
| Control Class 1 **Instructional Design** | 53% | 71% | 71% |
| Control Class 2 **Integrated Logo** | 56% | 28% | 0% |
| Control Class 3 **Isolated Logo** | 6% | 0% | 0% |

*Summary of Logo Test Results.* The results of the Logo paper-and-pencil test reveal a clear pattern in the subtasks: Both design classes handled these assignments better than did the students from Control Classes 2 and 3. It should be noted, however, that both design classes also have better scores on most subtasks in the pretest. The improvement observed in the Control Classes is smaller, and very often students who were part of these classes did not improve and reached a plateau in their performance.

## Learning Fractions

The students' knowledge of fractions was evaluated through two different measures: a version of the Rational Number Concept Test (Lesh, Landau, & Hamilton, 1983), and the mathematical section of the Boston Curriculum Reference Test.

*Results of the Rational Number Concept Test.* The results show that the game designers received higher scores on the posttest than Control Classes 2 and 3 did, but lower scores than the instructional designers (see Table 5.7). The main difference lies in the scores of the pretest, which were higher for the game designers. The students of Control Class 3 as a whole achieved in the posttest the results which the game designer's class received in the pre-test.

A closer look at the differences between the pre- and posttest scores reveals that the experimental class's performance (13% difference) on the rational number test increased compared to Control Class 3 (9% difference) and Control Class 2 (12% difference). Based on the differences between pre- and posttest, the Game Design class was much more similar in its performance to the Integrated Logo class than to the Instructional Design class. The analysis of variance indicates significant differences between the groups and between pre- and posttest results. The significant interaction points towards a specific combination of group and time point. This result is due to the Instructional Design class' high scoring on the pretest.

The items of the Rational Number Concept Test are composed of nine different categories, which are ordered according to their degree of difficulty from Level 1 to Level 9. These categories assess different aspects of the students' understanding of fraction representations and their flexibility in moving between the different levels. The test was also given to a wide range of students (n=650) from grade 4 to grade 8 (Lesh, Landau, & Hamilton, 1983). These scores make it possible to situate the students' performance in regard to a larger sample. In the following tables, the term *standard* always refers to the score achieved by the corresponding grade group.

**TABLE 5.7**

Rational Number Concept Test: Percentage of Correct Answers for
Students on Pre- and Posttests on Same 43 Items and Results of Two-way
Repeated Measurement Analysis of Variance

| Group | Percentage of Correct Answers | |
|---|---|---|
| | Pretest | Posttest |
| Experimental Class Game Design | 56% | 69% |
| Control Class 1 Instructional Design | 50% | 71% |
| Control Class 2 Integrated Logo | 53% | 65% |
| Control Class 3 Isolated Logo | 47% | 56% |

| Source | d.f. | F-Statistics |
|---|---|---|
| A (groups) | 3 | 3.65* |
| Subjects between samples | 63 | |
| Within subjects | 66 | |
| B (pre–post) | 1 | 207.00** |
| A x B | 3 | 7.95** |
| B x subjects | 63 | |
| Between subjects | 67 | |
| Total | 133 | |

*Note.* *p<.05; **p<.01

One difficult group of test items required translations from the
pictorial into the written mode. A compilation of all 14 test items
of this category shows that the experimental class as well as
Control Classes 1 and 2 were 10% above the standard score
(Table 5.8).

**TABLE 5.8**

Rational Number Concept Test, Level 7
(Translations From Pictorial Into Written Representations)

| Group | Percentage of Correct Answers | |
| --- | --- | --- |
| | Pretest | Posttest |
| Experimental Class Game Design | 51% | 64% |
| Control Class 1 Instructional Design | — | 68% |
| Control Class 2 Integrated Logo | — | 71% |
| Control Class 3 Isolated Logo | — | 51% |
| Standard | 56% | — |

*Note.* t-value for paired groups (d.f. = 15) 2.635, p<.05

Question 50 is one example for this category. It was the fifth most difficult item of the whole test (see Fig. 5.2). It is a polygonal representation of a discrete object with a perceptual distractor, the small triangle outside of the big triangle. To answer this question correctly, students had to go through several steps. First, they had to identify what fraction the shaded part of picture was and translate it into the words two-fifths, because the answer choices were given in written form. Then students had to read the question again and identify the denominator of the fraction in order to choose the correct answer.

50) What is the denominator of the fraction that tells us what part of the picture below is shaded?

a. five-thirds   b. five   c. three   d. two   e. not given

FIG. 5.2. Rational Number Test Question #50.


**TABLE 5.9**

Rational Number Concept Test, Level 7, Question 50
(Translations From Pictorial Into Written Representations)

| Group | Percentage of Correct Answers | |
|---|---|---|
| | Pretest | Posttest |
| Experimental Class **Game Design** | 13% | 31% |
| Control Class 1 **Instructional Design** | — | 66% |
| Control Class 2 **Integrated Logo** | — | 31% |
| Control Class 3 **Isolated Logo** | — | 27% |
| Standard | 26% | — |

The results (see Table 5.9) indicate clearly that the instructional designers, Control Class 1, were better than all the other classes, which were more centered around the standard score. One of the skills involved in answering this question was the decomposition of the given picture into its geometrical components, which is a common process in Logo programming and a skill that students acquired in their ongoing programming experience. A possible explanation of this result is that the perceptual distraction (the little triangle outside of the big triangle area) was probably not a distraction for instructional designers, who decomposed it with their Logo eyes into five geometrical objects. In fact, the students in the Instructional Software Design Project programmed fraction representations in Logo quite extensively, much more than the students in the other classes. (This particular difference in creating fraction representations is pursued in more detail in the discussion section.)

The most difficult group of questions in the test required translations of rational numbers' pictorial representations into symbolic representations (Level 9). Fourteen different items were included in this category. The experimental class was very similar in its performance to the other design class, whereas Control Class 3 was very similar to the standard performance, and Control Class 2 was midway between the two designer classes and the standard (Table 5.10).

Question 42 is one example (see Fig. 5.3) and was the 16th most difficult question of the test. In this question eight balls were shown, three of which were footballs, two were tennis balls, and three were basketballs. The students had to find out what fraction of the total balls were the tennis balls. To answer this question correctly, students had to translate the ratio represented by a picture into a symbolic representation.

**TABLE 5.10**
Rational Number Concept Test, Level 9
(Translations From Pictorial Into Symbolic Representations)

| Group | Percentage of Correct Answers | |
| --- | --- | --- |
|  | Pretest | Posttest |
| Experimental Class **Game Design** | 61% | 73% |
| Control Class 1 **Instructional Design** | — | 71% |
| Control Class 2 **Integrated Logo** | — | 64% |
| Control Class 3 **Isolated Logo** | — | 56% |
| Standard | 53% | — |

*Note.* t-value for paired groups (d.f. = 15) 2.332, p<.05

**42) What fraction of the balls are tennis balls?**

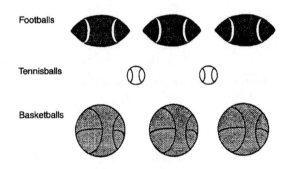

a. 2/8   b. 3/2   c. 2/6   d. 6/2   e. not given

**FIG. 5.3.** Rational Number Test Question #42.

**TABLE 5.11**

Rational Number Concept Test, Question 42
(Translations From Pictorial Into Symbolic Representations)

| | Percentage of Correct Answers | |
|---|---|---|
| Group | Pretest | Posttest |
| Experimental Class Game Design | 63% | 94% |
| Control Class 1 Instructional Design | — | 74% |
| Control Class 2 Integrated Logo | — | 60% |
| Control Class 3 Isolated Logo | — | 47% |
| Standard | 35% | — |

The game designer students were clearly very successful in answering this question (see Table 5.11). Both design classes were evidently better than were Control Classes 2 and 3.

*Summary of the Rational Number Test Results.* This test assessed the students' ability to translate between different modes of representations. One pattern was established through the analysis: The Game Design class performed better on this test than did Control Classes 2 and 3, but scored lower in some categories than did the Instructional Design class (Control Class 1). Although the students in both design classes were very similar in regard to their test performance, the higher starting scores of the experimental class accounted for the lower difference between the pre- and postassessments. This aspect is further evaluated in the general discussion of results, especially because both design classes scored consistently higher than did the students from the standard sample (Lesh, Landau, & Hamilton, 1983). *Results From the Boston Public School Mathematics Test.* To situate the game designers' performance in relation to a standard test of assessing mathematical knowledge, the mathematical section of the Boston Curriculum Reference Test was included in the pre- and posttests (the pretest version included only a subset of 12 questions relevant to fractions; these 12 also appeared in the posttest version among the 40 items). The major emphasis in this test is on algorithmic operations rather than on the representation of fractions.

TABLE 5.12

Boston Curriculum Reference Test: Posttest Results of the Complete Test and the Subsection Dealing With Fractions

| Group | Percentage of Correct Answers | |
| --- | --- | --- |
| | Complete Test (40 questions) | Subsection Fractions (15 questions) |
| Experimental Class **Game Design** | 81% | 76% |
| **Control Class 1 Instructional Design** | 87% | 89% |
| Control Class 2 **Integrated Logo** | 84% | 79% |
| Control Class 3 **Isolated Logo** | 75% | 69% |

*Note.* Chi square complete test = 0.9633 n.s.
Chi square subsection fractions = 2.637 n.s.

The percentage of correct answers shows the Game Design class to be much closer to Control Class 2 than to the Instructional Design class (see Table 5.12). This also holds true if one considers only the fractions component of the Boston curriculum reference test. In many ways, the students of the Game Design class behaved much more like the students of the Integrated Logo class and not like the Instructional Design class. However, the differences between the classes did not prove to be of significant order. Because the pretest version included only 12 items, those were compared with the posttest of the game designers (see Table 5.13). The Game Design class showed a significant increase in their ability to deal with fractions.

TABLE 5.13

Boston Curriculum Reference Test: Pre- and Posttest Results for the Game Design Class on the Same 12 Questions

|  | Percentage of Correct Answers | |
| --- | --- | --- |
| Group | Pretest | Posttest |
| Experimental Class Game Design | 55% | 70% |

*Note.* t-Value for paired groups (d.f. = 15) 3.796, p<.01

The analysis of five individual questions from the Boston Public School Curriculum Reference test dealt with different aspects of fractions, such as ordering of fractions, equivalence, and transformations. A clear pattern emerges in the results to these five questions: The instructional designers scored the highest with 79%, followed by the game designers, then Control Classes 2 and 3. The distinction between the design classes and the other classes was more pronounced. However, the general results in this test, which focuses less on the ability to translate between different representational modes than on the ability to perform algorithmic transformations of fractions, showed a more elaborate difference between the experimental class and the other design class.

# DISCUSSION OF RESULTS
# FROM THE COMPARATIVE EVALUATION

The results from the evaluation indicate that the game designers gained a better understanding of the Logo programming language. Furthermore, they improved in their understanding of fractions and became more flexible in translating between different modes of fraction representations. The participation in the Game Design Project proved to be of advantage when the game designers were compared to integrated and isolated Logo classes. However, when comparing the differences between pre- and posttest results, the growth of the game designers' knowledge was not of the same order as the instructional designers' performance. These results are moderated by two effects: the potential "ceiling" in their performance on the Rational Number test, and the high pretest scores of both design classes in many subtasks of the Logo programming test.

One interpretation of the results focuses on the students' performance on the Rational Number test. The difference between the pre- and posttests for the instructional designers was 21%, whereas for the game designers it was only 13% (compared to 12% and 9%, respectively for Control Classes 2 and 3). The major distinction lies in the amount of the pre- and posttest score differences. In order for the experimental class to have achieved the same change between pre- and posttest scores, they would have had to achieve an average of 77% of correct answers! One could argue that for fourth-grade students in general an average of 70% correct answers represented a "ceiling." This explanation gains further plausibility if one takes into consideration that the scores of both design classes and the Integrated Logo class are consistently higher than the standard scores from the Lesh, Landau, and Hamilton (1983) reference sample. This might also be explained by the fact that all students come from Advanced Work Classes in which only selected students participated.

The high pretest scores of the designers' Logo programming knowledge in some subtasks indicate that these were good students to begin with. A possible speculation could be that the students advanced their knowledge based on their good starting position irrespective of any participation in design activities. However, when looking at the programs that the students created in the design projects, it becomes clear that they were exposed to many aspects of programming the other students probably did not encounter in their Logo experience. For instance, students managed large programs; they programmed complex interactions between the computer and the player; and they dealt with branching, loops, and recursions to program features such as animation and feedback. These features, then, could be responsible for the improvement in results between pre- and posttest. A support for this argument lies in the little improvement or even stagnation that the students in the Integrated and Isolated Logo classes showed. A slightly different explanation says that students became, through their experience and participation in the design projects, more comfortable with tackling the tasks posed to them in the paper-and-pencil test. Both the increased familiarity and experience speak for the positive outcome of the design project participation.

In the following discussion, I deepen this analysis by including in the interpretation of results the students' processes and products from either the Instructional Software Design Project or Game Design Project.

## Comparison of Design Tasks:
## Game Design and Instructional Software Design

One of the initial expectations was that students in both design situations would perform equally well in understanding fractions and in their programming performance. The results of the evaluation did not provide a clear-cut answer and suggest that one must take a closer look at the nature of the design projects themselves—the software products as they were designed by the students and the processes that the students followed. From the outside, both design activities seem to offer similar opportunities for students to engage in Logo programming and fractions. However, it seems clear that the experience of participating in either the Instructional Software Design Project or the Game Design Project had a substantially different impact on the students' learning and thinking. The following discussion focuses on these differences as they expressed themselves in the students' processes and products: the centrality of fractions to the software product, the constructions of fraction representations in both design situations, and the processes involved in programming and designing. For that purpose, I included my observations and analyses of the students' work collected in the six months of the project.

*Centrality of Fractions to the Software Product.* The idea of fractions seemed to be situated differently in the Instructional Software Design Project compared to the Game Design Project. Although the game design task incorporated the instructional component (these were supposed to be educational games!), students situated their interactions with fractions in a different way. Both projects allowed students to personalize their products, but the Instructional Software Design Project clearly emphasized or foregrounded the idea of fractions. The teaching context provided a common framework for students to design their instructional screens and engaged them in thinking about teaching fractions, how to represent fraction knowledge to other children, and what was difficult about fractions, among other things. The screens designed by the students were very much like the pages of a textbook, except that all the work (thinking and learning) that went into the design of those occurred on the side of the student designer and not the teacher designer. The Instructional Software Design Project did not permit large degrees of latitude, which is at least one reason why the various products speak more directly to the idea of fractions. The Game Design Project, in contrast, gave children more latitude in determining how central the notion of fractions would be to the game. One way to examine the centrality of the fractions to the software product is to look at the format chosen by the students to introduce their learner/players to fractions.

In the Instructional Software Design Project, the students took the tutorial or "Show and Tell" format as the most used format for designing the instructional software and introducing their learners to fractions (see Figs. 5.4 and 5.5). An interesting observation here is that the student designers produced an instructionist type of software in a constructionist learning environment (see also Lehrer, 1992). One possible explanation might be that the instructional designers reflected in the adoption of the tutorial format their personal and current ideas on teaching. Their thinking about how one ought to be taught might intersect with their own experiences of the ways they are taught in school, at home, and through other cultural media. Many of these models emphasized the instructionist mode of teaching—passing knowledge on. Thus, the tutorials could be considered a reflection of the students' own experience and knowledge of teaching.

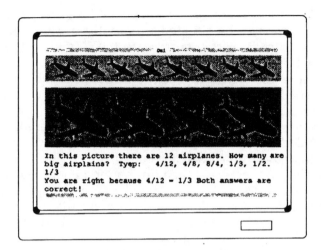

FIG. 5.4. Instructional Design Project: Oai's screen. Notice how Oai used pictorial representations of airplanes. When the learner gives an answer to the question, the program provided instructional feedback.

<u>Note</u>: From "Software Design as a Learning Environment" by I. Harel and S. Papert, 1991, *Constructionism*, (p. 66) Norwood, New Jersey: Ablex Publishing Corporation. Copyright 1991 by Ablex Publishing Corporation. Reprinted by permission.

In the Game Design Project, creating an interesting or playful game context was the most dominant feature. It drove the students' software products. There was a rich variety of game themes across all projects: 16 game designers in the project designed at least 16 different games. Different contexts were provided in the game themes for the instructions of fractions, such as skiing down a mountain, running in a maze, or battling with a spaceship. Nevertheless, there were some students who used fractions as their integral/central game idea. One example of a game in which fractions were tangential was Shaun's Fraction Killer: His game was about a person who has to find a hidden fraction wand—a tool that teachers use to teach fractions. In the game itself, the player had to answer fraction questions and could then shoot the attacking spaceship into pieces (see Figs. 5.6 and 5.7).

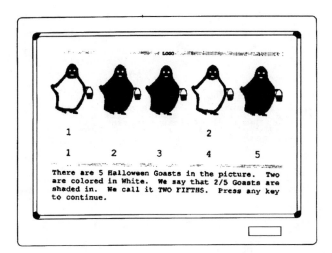

FIG. 5.5. Instructional Design Project: student's screen. This is an example for the "Show and Tell" format. The student explains the fraction to the player without any interactions.

<u>Note</u>: From "Software Design as a Learning Environment" by I. Harel and S. Papert, 1991, *Constructionism*, (p. 66) Norwood, New Jersey: Ablex Publishing Corporation. Copyright 1991 by Ablex Publishing Corporation. Reprinted by permission.

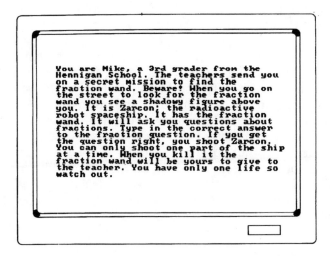

FIG. 5.6. Game Design Project: Shaun's introductory screen for his game Fraction Killer.

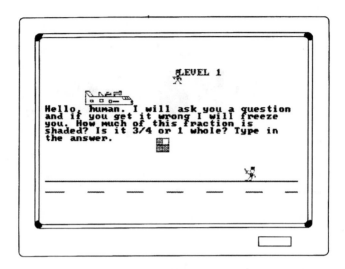

FIG. 5.7. Game Design Project: Shaun's first instructional screen. If the player answered the question correctly, then a shape moved toward the ship and the middle part of the ship exploded. If the question was not answered correctly, then a beam from the ship moved toward the player and transformed him or her into an ice block.

An example for a game in which the notion of fractions was central was Amy's Greek Myths. Her game was developed around the theme of a map ripped into four pieces (see Figs. 5.8 and 5.9). The player reassembled fourths of the map as he or she progressed through the game by answering fraction questions.

The striking similarity across all games was the role-playing aspect, which can be summarized the following way: As the player and learner, one took over a role in the game and experienced different situations (adventures, travels, activities, explorations). In the context of these situations, one was confronted to solve fractions problems. Most of the games did not center around the idea of fractions; the idea of fractions was in many cases external to the game, a process that could also be observed in the design development of the games.

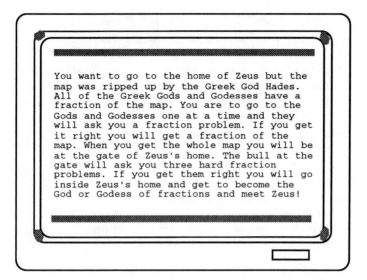

**FIG. 5.8.** Game Design Project: Amy's introduction to her game Greek Myths.

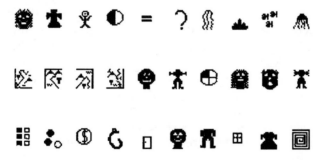

**FIG. 5.9.** Game Design Project: Amy's shapes. Once the player answered a question correctly, a screen appeared with the corresponding number of pieces (e.g., three questions correctly answered show 3/4 of the map) and a statement: "You have solved this question and now have 3/4 of the map. Please continue."

In the Instructional Software Design Project, all of the screens and the software products focused on the representation of fractions. Across projects, there was a similarity in format: The screen displayed one or more fraction representations, accompanied by either an explanatory text or a question to be answered. In the Game Design Project, however, the game context dominated the software product, interlacing it with the instructional screens. With a few exceptions, fractions were not central to the product. For most children, aspects of the game predominated (such as Shaun, who had hidden the fraction wand in a spaceship); for a few others (such as Amy, who created a map divided into fractions), the idea of fractions predominated.

The combination of fractions with games also raised the issue of competing design issues: Learning fractions is a subject that many students feel is rather boring (the statements in the pre-interviews were a testament to this; even students who were "good" in mathematics stated that they found schoolwork with fractions boring), whereas the playing of games is something "not like school"—it is "fun." The decision of many game designers was to focus more on the "fun" part of the game design task (meaning the design of the game) than on the fractions task. This preference may indicate that students were driven in their design by a simple motivation: They decided to invest their energies in the design of the game with the understanding that what makes a game exciting is when it is fun, and that learning fractions could only be fun in a fun context. As Shaun expressed in a reflection on the educational aspects of arcade games, they were concerned how to design a game that would be fun but at the same time also educational. In this context, the students also broke away from standard representations, but in a different way. They continued to use designs of fraction representations, but found nonstandard contexts (e.g., haunted houses, fraction killers, games with gods) to think about fractions. The games designed by the students point out how difficult it is to find a game idea that on one hand is central to fractions but on the other hand is also fun.

*Constructing Fractions Representations in the Context of Two Design Tasks.* One of the central conclusions from the Instructional Software Design Project (ISDP) (Harel, 1991; Harel & Papert, 1990) was that programming fraction representations in Logo contributed in an essential manner to the students' understanding of fractions. More precisely, instructional design provided students with an opportunity to engage with fractions on a new and different representational level: Through Logo programming, they were able to create procedural representations of fractions, thus extending their repertoire of symbolic, written, and pictorial representations. Creating fraction representations in Logo gave students a flexible and different medium to reformulate their knowledge on fractions. Students dealt with representations on different levels: they created representations in Logo, they accompanied them with symbols or words, they dealt with their own representations in a different medium (i.e., Logo), and they designed representations for the use of others. Students provided rich and various examples of representations coming from their own experiences, and in this process, their relationship between the everyday and practical side of mathematical knowledge evolved.

Several screens by instructional designers serve as an illustration. One example is Michaela's kitchen, which applied the ratio of water and juice to a fraction task (see Fig. 5.10).

FIG. 5.10. Instructional Design Project: Michaela's kitchen.

Note: From "Software Design as a Learning Environment" by I. Harel and S. Papert, 1991, *Constructionism*, (p. 63) Norwood, New Jersey: Ablex Publishing Corporation. Copyright 1991 by Ablex Publishing Corporation. Reprinted by permission.

A further example comes from Nicole's dollar screen (see Fig. 5.11). She used different representations (symbolic, pictorial, and

written) for money (one dollar bill, quarters) and combined them
with symbolic representations of fractions.

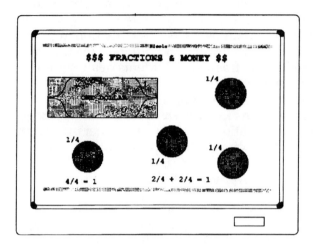

**FIG. 5.11.** Instructional Design Project: Nicole's money and fractions.

Note: From "Software Design as a Learning Environment" by I. Harel
and S. Papert, 1991, *Constructionism*, (p. 64) Norwood, New Jersey:
Ablex Publishing Corporation. Copyright 1991 by Ablex Publishing
Corporation. Reprinted by permission.

Another example is Sharifa who made the connection between
half an hour and the fraction one half while designing her fractions
clock (see Fig. 5.12).

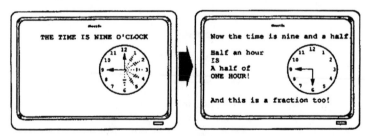

**FIG. 5.12.** Instructional Design Project: Sharifa's fraction clock.

Note: From "Software Design as a Learning Environment" by I. Harel
and S. Papert, 1991, *Constructionism*, (p. 65) Norwood, New Jersey:
Ablex Publishing Corporation. Copyright 1991 by Ablex Publishing
Corporation. Reprinted by permission.

The fraction representations that were created by the students of the Game Design Project were different in several aspects from the ones created by the students of the Instructional Software Design Project. For instance, all of Gloria's fraction shapes (Figs. 5.13 and 5.14) were pictorial representations of fractions on shapes.

FIG. 5.13. Game Design Project: Gloria's fraction shapes. Notice the shapes in the second and third rows, which represent 3/6, thirds, 5/12, 1/4, 1 whole, 1/2. The fraction shapes that Gloria designed are not all used in her game The Teacher.

FIG 5.14. Game Design Project: Gloria's instructional screen with the teacher, who was supposed to represent her classroom teacher. In the command center at the bottom of the screen the following question appears: "Can you tell me what fraction this is? Please type."

Another example is Gaby's shapes page, which included her fractions shapes (Fig. 5.15). As some other students did, she used shapes to create written fraction representations rather than using Logo commands such as PRINT or LABEL.

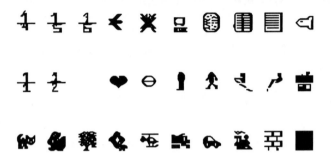

FIG. 5.15. Game Design Project: Gaby's Fraction Shapes. In contrast to most other students, Gaby used only a few shapes of her whole page for her game. Four shapes for fractions, 1/1, 1/2, 1/4, 1/5, 1/6, the fly, and the spider in the first row.

Barney's instructional screen used fractions and connected them to the use of money (see Fig. 5.16).

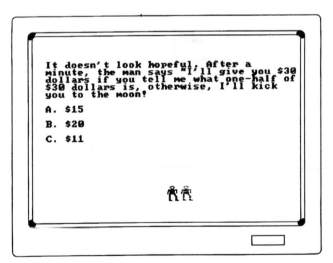

FIG. 5.16. Game Design Project: Barney's instructional screen, which appeared in the middle of his game story Jose in the Fraction World.

Here the contrast to Nicole's money screen, one of the instructional designers, emerged most clearly. Barney did not provide any pictorial representation of the money involved. Instead, he resorted to a more textbooklike representation in presenting a question and three choices. In contrast, Nicole created a screen with different representations of money and how these relate to fractions. The difference between these two design projects resided in the nature and content of creating the fractional representations in Logo.

*Process of Creating Fraction Representations.* The fraction representations in the Instructional Software Design Project were designed by programming the Logo turtle. The students of the Game Design Project did not use the turtle to draw these representations; instead, they used the shapes to represent fractions. (A shape in Logowriter is a form other than the turtle form that can be given to the turtle). In order to do so, students had to go to a special page where 30 slots for different shapes were given. In order to create new shapes, students selected a slot and then used the cursor and the space key to fill in an area consisting of 16 x 20 small squares. The process used by the game designers to create their fraction shapes resembled more the process that Streefland's (1991) students used to design representations on paper with pencils than the process of creating procedural representations with Logo. The question is, then, to what extent these external representations (e.g., Gaby's or Gloria's fraction shapes) are a reflection of the quality of internal representations built by the students. The test results do not provide us with clear-cut answers here in favor of the one or the other design situation.

The major reason why students designed fractions in the shapes mode and not in the turtle mode was that the nature of the games required animation. It was much easier to achieve impressions of real-time animation with shapes than with objects drawn by the turtle. The implications of this difference can be found in the interpretation of Question #50 from the Rational Number test (see Fig. 5.2). One of the skills involved in answering this question was the decomposition of the given picture into its geometrical components, a common process in Logo programming and a skill students acquired in their ongoing programming experience. Therefore, the perceptual distraction (the little triangle outside of the big triangle area) was probably not a distraction for students who decomposed it with their Logo eyes into five geometrical objects. The instructional designers' programming of procedural representations might have helped them in answering this question. The game designers, however, did not go through this process in designing their shapes and, hence, did not perform as well in answering this question. One conclusion is that students of the Game Design Project had a different learning experience with fractions, because they did not use the turtle to create procedural representations of fractions. This points out the importance of programming external representations of fractions for students' deep understanding of fractions.

*Content of Fraction Representations.* A further difference related to the content of the fraction representations created by students in both design groups. In the Instructional Software Design Project, students' screen designs centered around fractions: fraction clocks (see Fig. 5.9), measurement in fractions, house scenes, and halves; in contrast, in the Game Design Project, the students designed fraction representations that were geometrical areas cut into parts (see Fig. 5.15), some of them shaded in. Students did not establish the same connections between the everyday and practical side of mathematical knowledge. Personal preferences might have guided instructional designers in choosing particular situations or objects for representing fractions (e.g., Debbie's house scene, Sharifa's fraction clock, Michaela's kitchen). This is not to say that students in the Game Design Project did not show these preferences in the design of their games, but instead of displaying these preferences in their choice of fraction representations, they chose to focus on the game context.

*Processes of Designing and Programming Within Two Design Tasks.* Learning programming through designing instructional software or educational games proved to be a successful avenue for young designers. The results of the evaluation were clearly that using programming as a means for reformulating knowledge about fractions and personal expression enhanced students' understanding of the programming language Logo. In previous sections I touched on differences in programming between both design projects. One clear distinction, for example, referred to the programming technique in which instructional designers used the Logo turtle to program their fraction representations, compared to the game designers who used the shapes to make fraction representations.

Another distinction pointed toward the different formats that designers chose for their software products to present fractions. The instructional designers, for the most part, produced tutorial quizzes. In contrast, the game designers programmed instructional screens embedded in an interactive play mode. One interpretation might be that the tutorial format offered a complex yet not too complicated format to program. Students had to adjust their design ideas to their programming skills, because they learned programming as they went along in designing and implementing their projects. The design ideas of the tutorial could be a mix of what children knew from their previous Logo programming (i.e., to show something) and of what is easy to program. Incidentally, the progression of Debbie in Harel's study reflected this transition from the focus of showing things (e.g., house scene for 1/2, about 2/3 as a difficult fraction used most by teachers) to the scenes where she included the user and offered choices. Most of the instructional designers' products reflect the major emphasis on "Show, Tell, and Quiz," in contrast to the game designers' "Play and Quiz." This was a clear indication that different formats cultivated the development of different programming skills.

The game designers also used the instructional format to program their interactions with the player, but there was very little "Show and Tell." For the most part, the game designers preferred a dialogue format in which they asked questions and responded to the user's replies. For example, Shaun's and Barney's instructional screens showed this very clearly (see Figs. 5.7 and 5.16). In addition to this, the game designers embedded these interactions in the playing of the game. For example, in Shaun's game Fraction Killer, the player's correct response initiates an interaction between the figure on the screen (representing the player) and the battleship. Fig. 5.17 shows Shaun's program; Fig. 5.7 shows the corresponding screen.

```
To Question 1
wait.for.user ct pr [] pr [] pr        The instruction PR []
                                       places an empty
                                       line on the screen.
[] pr [] pr [] pr [Hello human.
I will ask you a question and if
you get it wrong I will freeze you.
How much of this fraction is
shaded?  Is it 3\/4 or 1 whole?]
pu setpos [-10 100] setsh 4
name readlistcc "a
```

```
if :a = [3/4]
```

If the answer is correct . . .

```
[cc tell 3 seth 270 rt 33 setc
```

Sets the direction and heading of turtle toward the battleship.

```
10 setsh 3 rt 1 setpos [85 -35]
ct st repeat 8 [pu fd 20 wait 5]
```

Moves the beam up to the battleship.

```
setpos [-55 50] setsh 2 setc 0
```

Sets the shape for the exploded middle part of the battleship.

```
pd stamp pu setc 8 setsh 5 pd
stamp pu wait 20 gp "games2
question2]
```

Gets the next page GAMES2 and the next question QUESTION2.

```
if :a = [1 whole]
```

If the answer is wrong

```
[seth 270 rt 30 ct setpos
```

Sets the shape to a ball that goes from the battleship to the player.

```
[-40 40] setsh 9 st setc 15
repeat 8 [pu bk 20 20 wait 5]
wait 10 pr [] pr [] pr [] pr
[A freeze ray hits you!]
```

Prints out statement on screen after hit.

```
setpos [100 -50] wait 5
setsh 2 setc 0 pd stamp pu
```

Sets the shape to an ice cube.

```
setsh 6 setc 11 pd stamp pu ct
wait 5 pr [] pr [] pr [] pr
[Now you are an ice cube fore
life!] pr [] pr [] pr [Better
get used to the north pole!
Pretty funny huh?] tone 200 10
tone 100 10 tone 200 10 cc rg
pr [Game over (You're dead)]
tone 100 5 tone 75 5 tone 25 5
setsh 30 setc 5 st pd stamp pu]
end
```

FIG. 5.17. Game Design Project: Shaun's Logo code for the first question. Notice also the indentations that Shaun included in his program.

Shaun's Logo code shows how he programmed the intricate interplay between the player and the interactive feedback on the screen. In this case, the right or wrong answer is not accompanied by direct instructional feedback (e.g., "Wrong answer") but with the corresponding action on the screen. In his programming, Shaun had to coordinate a number of aspects: the different positions of the shapes on the screen (the battleship and the player), the change of shapes (from player to player being destroyed to player turned into ice cube), and the timing of animation. Shaun's programming of the fraction representations, the instructional interaction, and the animation is exemplary of most other game designers.

One exceptional example to the instructionist format in the Game Design Project was Rosy, who devised a fraction design tool (see Fig. 5.18). Rosy's game included a hunt for a treasure, but in the middle of the game the player comes to a page that invites him or her to move around the turtle with the arrow keys on the screen. Afterward, the player is told "Now draw a fraction. When you are done press Q" without giving specific instructions about which fraction to do.

| | |
|---|---|
| `to startup`<br>`cc ct rg` | Clears the screen and command center. |
| `type se [Use the arrow keys to` | Appears in the command center. |
| `move the turtle. When you are`<br>`done press S.] char 13` | |
| `draw` | Calls procedure DRAW. |
| `end` | |
| `to draw`<br>`drive ascii readchar` | Starts the recursive procedure DRIVE, which reads in key strokes in ascii format. |
| `end` | |
| `to drive :key`<br>`pd if  :key = 72 [seth 0 fd 5]` | Arrow key up and five steps forward. |
| `pd if  :key = 80 [seth 180 fd 5]` | Arrow key down and five steps    forward. |
| `pd if  :key = 77 [seth 90 fd 5]` | Arrow key right and five steps forward. |
| `pd if  :key = 75 [seth 270 fd 5]` | Arrow key left and five steps forward. |
| `pd if  :key = 115 [rg cc DIR draw]` | Key "S" and calls procedures DIR and DRAW again. |
| `pd if  :key = 113 [gp "GAMES6 stop]` | Key "Q" gets a new page and stops the recursive DRIVE procedure. |

```
drive ascii READCHAR                    Procedure DRIVE calls
                                        itself again.
end

to dir
type se [Now draw a fraction. When
you are done press q] char 13
end
```

**FIG. 5.18.** Game Design Project: Rosy's code for the fraction design tool. My explanations of her programming are included in the right column. The numbers associated with the keys are the ascii code for the corresponding arrow keys up, down, left, and right, and the letters S and Q.

The following scene serves as a good example of how Rosy herself used the fraction design tool to explore fractions.

> [Rosy is moving the arrow keys and is in the process of drawing a rectangle divided into four smaller ones.]
>
> *Yasmin*: What fraction will this be?
>
> *Rosy*: Wait, I am not done yet [she divides up one of the rectangles into eight smaller ones by moving the arrow ].
>
> *Yasmin*: So what fraction is it now?
>
> *Rosy*: One fourths or ..... thirty twos .... [her eyes are on the screen and her lips move silently before she continues] It is eight thirty seconds, eight thirtytwos.

Rosy was the only one in the game design project who had programmed a fraction design tool; as she learned how to program keys on the keyboard, she turned them into a tool for making fractions. Besides her powerful conceptual teaching idea, this program segment also showed the complexity of her programming to give the player/learner at the same time freedom to explore fractions as well as to keep him or her in the context of the game (once the player decided he or she has enough of "drawing fractions" and pressed the Q-key, the program took care of bringing the player back into the game by calling LogoWriter page GAMES6).

The conclusions to be drawn from these analyses are that the given design task makes a difference, not only in terms of the design product and process but also to a certain extent for the learning experience. The results of this evaluation indicate that the instructional design context integrated not only the students' programming and design of fraction representations in a different way but also integrated the idea of fractions into the software product.

# Chapter 6

# Discussion of Conclusions

With the Game Design Project, I created one model of a constructionist learning environment that placed children in charge of their own learning and thinking. Sixteen students were engaged for a period of six months designing video games to teach fractions to younger children. The project did not follow any preset routines, but instead was developed together with the students and the teacher. My overall goal in the project's evaluation was to find out what children can learn when designing games and, similarly, what we can learn about them in this process. Programming games was seen as a medium for children's personal and creative expression: In the design of their games, children could engage their fantasies and build relationships with other pockets of reality that went beyond traditional school approaches.

A further purpose of this project's implementation was to analyze and discuss the value and implications of a new pedagogy called *learning through design*. I considered ideas about learning and about designing under the assumption that making something is a powerful way of learning. My goal was to explore how both theories could contribute to our understanding of what the students were doing. I investigated how students approached this task of designing a computer game and how they worked on a daily basis, encountered and mastered challenges, and learned programming concepts and fractions. Learning through design provided an example of how programming could be integrated with other classroom work. It considered learning programming not only valuable for its computational and technological knowledge, but also for its support of other learning.

The project offered also the opportunity to investigate the development of students' thinking and learning in the context of a long-term learning enterprise. I looked for insights into the different ways in which students engaged in designing a complex piece of interactive software and what knowledge they build and connect to in this process. In this context, I focused on two areas: learning programming and understanding mathematical concepts. I was interested in the students' understanding of the programming language, how they mastered particular programming concepts, and how they developed programming strategies. Furthermore, my investigation addressed the conceptual development of students' dealing with fractions, the students' ability to represent different concepts, and their flexibility in moving between different form of representations. My descriptions and analyses of students' Logo programming and thinking about fractions were intended to provide educators and researchers with portraits of what students can accomplish in this context.

In this book, I pursued these research goals on different levels. Chapter 3 looked at the class of game designers as a whole. I outlined the students' understanding of game design and how their conceptions changed during the project. I also analyzed the students' design approaches at different time points in the project. The variability in students' approaches to starting the project, dealing with the upcoming problems, and arranging the game design task for themselves was not something unique to a particular phase of the project; instead, it proved to be a consistent phenomenon at all time points. In chapter 4, I selected three students and documented their conceptual development in regard to their understanding of programming concepts and styles, game ideas, and fractions. The cases of Amy, Sid, and Albert provided examples of the diverse ways in which students approached this task and made this project their own. Each student chose to develop different aspects in designing a game. Chapter 5 compared the students from the Game Design Project to three control classes who were taught Logo programming and fractions by other pedagogical means. I focused on the comparison with another design environment—instructional software design—to point out differences how the design task itself situated students' thinking and learning.

The results from these different investigations provided a rich and multifaceted picture of what happened in the Game Design Project. They demonstrated that the students in the project were able to handle this complex and challenging task in an efficient manner. They indicated in which ways students significantly improved their understanding of Logo programming and fractions when compared to other students. The three case studies supported these results by providing an in-depth look at individual students' development, problems, and successes. The design, implementation, and maintenance of a complex program made students develop programming strategies to deal with complex interactions and to create a linked and coherent program. In this process, students were able to maintain long-term goals and use those as guidelines for their daily work.

In the following sections, I reexamine the major themes and discuss to what extent the project succeeded and the implications of the results for further research and educational practice. In Conclusion 1 I discuss the particular merits of making games for learning. Conclusion 2 looks at the issue of individual styles in learning and thinking and their pedagogical implications. Conclusions 3, 4, 5, and 6 discuss issues related to the social culture of the learning activity, implications of the design task, learning programming as a tool for personal expression, and learning through constructing mathematical representations. Conclusion 7 provides some ideas for the development of future environments for design and learning.

## Conclusion 1:
## Making Games for Learning

The special merits of making games for learning lie foremost in the integration of seemingly opposing activities: learning and designing, and learning and playing. I proposed an activity in which these different activities merged into one in the context of the Game Design Project. One of the central assumptions behind making games for learning was that making something is a good way of learning. I outlined commonalties that both theories of design and theories of learning share when they talk about designing or learning as an act of constructing meaning. The analysis of the students' work during the project showed that students actually learned about many things by making and playing games.

One of my intentions was to find out what theories of design could contribute to our understanding of learning through design. If design and learning can both be considered processes of constructing meaning, then these were the processes in which the students were involved in the Game Design Project. As the students were trying to give meaning to the task of designing a game (by finding out what game they would design and what features it would include), they were also involved in understanding what they were learning (i.e., constructing the meaning of fractions and how to make an educational game), while they were implementing their games (by thinking about what fractions to represent, by writing and using Logo programming, and by thinking about teaching strategies). Designing and learning contributed to each other in this process. This complimentary function of design and learning has been overlooked for a long time because of the overwhelming interest that the research community has in the processes in which designers are involved. This focus on processes allows design theorists to neglect the knowledge that designers acquire in the context of the design task. Many designers are able to see the learning as a function of designing when directly asked, but they tend not to think about designing this way. Only with recent efforts to reorganize design education have researchers and practitioners started paying more attention to the different applications of design (see, for example, Shannon, 1990).

Students displayed many of the behaviors of professional designers in the design of their games while they were learning about programming, and about design and fractions. In fact, the observations in the Game Design Project could be considered a case in point for a study of designers at work. Students started out with a design assignment that asked them to integrate two seemingly opposing domains, games with fractions. The students developed a piece of game software, the product, from the beginning to the end. In this context, they generated many ideas for their games but did not implement all of them; they solved problems related to programs, their game ideas, design, and fractions; they developed design strategies to deal with the complexity of the task at hand; and they modified and adapted their games in the ongoing development. Making games offers an example of how design can be brought into public education.

A second line of inquiry combined two other activities that are considered to be rather far apart: learning and playing. My initial assumption was that children's interest in playing games could be a motivation for making them. During the project, it became clear that students were strongly engaged in accomplishing their designs; engaged enough to spend six months on implementing and finalizing their products (many even continued after the official end of the project). When Turkle (1984) spoke about the "holding power" of playing games, she emphasized that this attraction is different for each player because particular features of programming or playing video games resonate with each player's personal desires and needs. Can we speak about a holding power of making games? Definitely, the parts that students enjoyed most in making their games were designing the graphics, creating the characters and story, and programming the animation and manipulations for the player. Many of these choices were guided by personal preferences in the same way that playing video games resonates with personal preferences. Students were having "hard fun," the kind of motivation that combines the pleasure of accomplishing something with the intense concentration and motivation involved in achieving it. Hard fun is intense concentration coupled with passion.

When Perkins spoke about the design nature of knowledge, he offered design as a framework for thinking about learning in a purposeful way. When Harel introduced learning through design, she adopted the perspective that creating something for the use of others invites inquiry and search for knowledge. When Papert assumed that making something is a good context for learning, then he saw that through direct interaction, the "objects" in the world can become the "objects" in our mind with which to think. Hence, design for learning was a natural integration and extension of all these approaches. Making games offered one way to integrate learning and designing in a powerful and stimulating way.

## Conclusion 2:
## Individual Styles Developing Over Time

The extended time frame of the Game Design Project made it possible to see the transition and shifts, not only in students' individual development but also in the project as a whole. One of the conclusions is that design activities allow for students' personal interests and styles of thinking, learning and designing. In this context, gender differences expressed themselves clearly in the choices of game themes and features. The long-term involvement in the project was essential for students' learning.

One of the most general statements I can make based on the results of my case studies is that Amy, Sid, and Albert came to the project with different backgrounds and expressed different levels of engagement and interest in the project. Yet, this environment allowed all of them to work on the same task, to play each other's games, and to share ideas with each other. In short, they all became members of the same community of practice in spite of their individual preferences and differences. The time frame of the project provided each of them with the opportunity to finish their games in their own way. Unlike typical school learning, students were not placed in different ability groups. Rather, they were part of the same activities but were all able to express themselves as they wished according to level of difficulty, style, or content in their games.

In my analysis, I followed the learning and thinking development of several students in regard to their programming, fractions, and design of their games. I captured two aspects: One focused on how students changed their understanding over time, the second investigated what concepts took root in their thinking as a result of this process. The results indicated that most students seemed to adopt different strategies when approaching the game design task: Some laid out features of their games ahead of time and followed through with their plan; whereas others were guided by the flow of their stories and ideas. Although there were students like Barney and Gaby who followed one of these paths consistently, the majority of the game designers preferred to operate in both styles according to their needs. Amy and Albert, for example, started off with integrating fractions into their game, whereas Sid (like many of his classmates) was more concerned about his game design context. In comparing the game development, it became clear that each of them followed different paths. For most of the project, Albert and Amy worked in parallel on different aspects of their games, whereas Sid seemed to approach the game design task in a more linear fashion. He created one game after the other, and only toward the end became able to maintain different lines of thoughts regarding fractions, instructional quizzes, and game design. The long-term involvement also showed that some students, such as Amy and Albert, are able to work fast and go deeper in the subject matter from the beginning, whereas students like Sid needed more time to bring all aspects of their games together. Nevertheless, all of the students designed and accomplished a game in the end.

Individual differences were strongly pronounced. Amy's engagement with fractions was situated on different levels not only in the design of her representations but also in how she integrated fractions into her game in different ways. Albert's programming, in the end, underwent a conceptual change once he realized that he could use the LogoWriter pages as procedures to help him deal with the growing complexity of his game. Just like Albert, Amy and Sid learned the value of developing programming strategies (e.g., for the instructional quiz) in the process of programming a complex and large piece of software. The time frame of the project (six months for designing and implementing these games) had a considerable impact on the development of such programming strategies. This became especially clear in the comparison with the Instructional Software Design Project. In her conclusions of Debbie's case study, Harel (1988) made a point of valuing the "unfinished" state of Debbie's software; many procedures were never implemented or just begun, and many of her plans were never realized. The game designer projects at the end of June resembled Debbie's project. For example, Albert had not implemented all his choices, many parts were not connected, and the software itself was not completed. I can only speculate what would have happened if Debbie had had another seven weeks after the summer to finish her fractions project. Would she implement and finalize all those plans that she laid out in her notebook, or would she go ahead and start designing new instructional screens?

As students approached in their idiosyncratic ways the complexities of the project, gender differences emerged as another important aspect. The students' making of video games replicated many of the gender differences and preferences found in the literature about playing video games (Provenzo, 1991). Many of the boys adopted adventure and exploration game themes and violent feedback features that can be found in commercially available games such as Nintendo or Sega. However, girls preferred to program and implement different game themes and features, even though their designs and programming were as sophisticated as the boys' games. The girls' games centered more around activities as their main attraction (teaching, skiing, collecting pieces of the map, moving around a spider web, or landing on an airport) and preferred as feedback to hold back something or to have the player start over again. If this finding tells us something, it is that the designs of currently available video games do not include girls in their considerations. It was obvious that girls chose to create their own game worlds. This facilitated their entry into the design task and allowed them to personalize their game designs compensating for the sexism and violence found in most commercially available video games (Gailey, 1992). A future task for professional producers and designers of games will be to find themes and interaction features that accommodate the styles and preferences of all kinds of players, not just a subset of them.

The particular nature of the Game Design Project—its extended time frame and daily routines—created an environment in which the individual students followed their own paths in designing and programming a game. It allowed students of different styles and gender to express themselves, and provided a window into their thinking and preferences.

## Conclusion 3:
## Learning Culture of the Game Design Project

**The activities of the Game Design Project were also inspired by other learning contexts, the design studio and learning cultures. The instructional rationale of learning through design drew on theories from both learning and design; the project's implementations of daily routines and interactions combined aspects from both learning contexts. I created with the teacher and the students not only a rich and complex learning environment, but also a learning culture. In many aspects, the nature of this learning culture represented the complexities of the everyday world in which children learn.**

One of the purposes of the Game Design Project was to create a learning culture in which thinking and talking about fractions, games, and Logo would become the daily talk. Several indicators provided support for the appearance of a particular culture in the project. For example, Barney, Juan, Trevor, Albert, and Shaun founded a company called TCA (Teaching, Computer, and Arts). The reference to the company logo appeared in all their games and credit screens, advertisements, documentation, and cover designs. Another example was the way that the number of LogoWriter pages turned into a symbol of success. Each LogoWriter page contained a list of instructions. As the students' games became larger over the months, one page was no longer sufficient to hold all the necessary instructions, and many students ended the project with a game consisting of several pages. In the beginning, many students complained about having to use and save more than one page. But this attitude changed during the project; I overheard many conversations where students spoke among themselves proudly about the size of their project. What in the beginning was regarded an impediment turned toward the end into a symbol of program size and expertise. A further example referred to the evolution of the game format into the narrative. I documented how the narrative became the standard for most of the students' games in the course of the project.

An important insight of this investigation was that the creation of such a learning culture depends on many factors. One essential component of this learning culture was the different collaborative styles fostered in the context of the Game Design Project. The collaborative styles observed in the project could be described as optional collaboration, in which students could work alone on their own piece of software, but could also work with others on the same piece if they wished; and as flexible partnerships, in which students could decide with whom they wanted to work, when, and for what purposes. All the student designers had a common "umbrella" goal, using LogoWriter to design a game that taught about fractions—but each of them also expressed his/her own ideas, and produced his or her own projects. Everyone faced similar problems, and found occasions for sharing ideas, asking for help, or discussing technical problems. Students could choose to discuss problems with a partner, or even to work together on designing and implementing certain aspects of their game. In other words, in these projects, students could move between both collaborative styles according to their own needs and desires (see also Kafai & Harel, 1991a, 1991 b). These styles of collaboration stand in contrast to more traditional approaches, where the teacher assigns students to teams that will work together toward one goal or product (Johnson & Johnson, 1989; Slavin, 1983). Students in the Game Design Project worked in multiple roles as users, designers, and consultants in addition to their roles as writers, teachers, and programmers while accomplishing their projects. Students also fulfilled these multiple roles toward each other when they evaluated, tested, or read each other's games. Different educational theories and practices have stressed over and over the importance of social interactions for learning

(Collins, Brown, & Newman, 1990; Palincsar & Brown, 1984; Rogoff, 1990; Vygotzky, 1978).

Another feature of the learning culture concerned the roles taken by the researcher and teacher. Even projects that share many features, such as the Instructional Software Design Project and the Game Design Project, can develop in different directions. For example, while analyzing my data (i.e., videotapes, notebooks, field notes, and personal communication with Harel), it became clear to me that Harel focused strongly on children's development of fractions in the Instructional Software Design Project. Harel's main goals were to provide students with the opportunity to create and express a different kind of representation—procedural ones—in addition to the symbolic, written, spoken, and visual ones they knew already. However, it may be that the culture and interactions of the Game Design Project emphasized games more than fractions. I was much more concerned with the game design aspects and the programming components (which proved in some instances to be a more challenging task than anticipated).

Therefore, as two "intervenors" we interacted differently with the students during each of our projects. Whereas Harel's questions prompted her students to think about representations of fractions, my questions probably prompted my students to think about dynamic games and sophisticated programming. The researcher's and teacher's agenda play an important role as we create learning environments around such complex learning projects, and as we analyze our data and make generalizations and pedagogic recommendations. These two studies may provide evidence that the researcher's actions during the so-called "action research" are important in directing the project culture along certain routes. Thus, even though we are looking at two very similar projects, we still must look carefully at the outcomes and the results, and reason accordingly about the components and influences of each project.

The intersection of different roles in the game designers and the different interactions of participants provided the backbone for the project's learning culture. They are an essential component to be considered when attempting to implement the learning through design activities in other places.

## Conclusion 4:
## Learning about "Learning through Design"

Learning through design provided a powerful opportunity for learning. One goal of this study was to define its further characteristics. The comparison between game design and instructional software design pointed out two important features of learning through design activities: students' degrees of freedom or latitude in determining the centrality of the subject matter to the software, and students' perception of the final product and how it guided their design process. Each design task had a considerable impact on the students' learning and thinking. For future research, it is important to explore which particular features can engage students in making intrinsically integrated educational games.

The results of the Game Design Project specified further characteristics of the pedagogy of learning through design. The task faced by students was to translate their game ideas via programming into a computational product—a rather challenging and complex enterprise. Most of the games could be divided into two categories: extrinsic and intrinsic integration of subject matter in games. The former was exemplified most simply in games where the player had to answer a question in order to proceed in the game. In contrast, intrinsic integration was exemplified in a game where the designer took care of integrating the subject matter with the game idea. Amy's game, in which the player had to assemble different parts (i.e., fractions) of the map to arrive at the goal, is a good example. It is a strength and a weakness of the extrinsic integration that domains of knowledge become almost interchangeable. It is a strength because the integration is relatively easy: When answering a question correctly is what allows the next move in a game, the question can be on any topic. But this is also a weakness, because it causes the designer to loose the incentive to think deeply about the particular piece of knowledge.

One of the factors having an impact on either intrinsic or extrinsic integration of knowledge can be identified comparing two design situations— instructional software (Harel, 1988) or educational computer games. Students in both situations were designing software. Yet, there appeared to be a substantial difference in how the idea of fractions was integrated in the software. The instructional software projects demonstrated more clearly the intrinsic integration approach as all the screens and questions designed by the students focused on fractions. When the game designers were asked to construct an educational game to teach fractions, most of them used the extrinsic integration method. As in commercially made games, the greater number chose the easiest extrinsic integration by stopping the action at key places to ask the player a question. A conclusion to be drawn from this difference is that the instructional design did not permit large degrees of latitude, which is at least one reason why the various products speak more directly to the idea of fractions. The game projects, in contrast, gave children more latitude in determining how central the notion of fractions would be to their games. This was particularly true for the integration of fractions into their game design. For most children, aspects of the game predominated (e.g., Shaun, who hid the fraction wand in a spaceship); for others, the idea of fractions predominated (e.g., Amy, who created a map divided into fractions).

The given design problem also situated students' perception of the final project. Students tended to think of their "project" in different ways: in terms of the entire software or in terms of individual screens. There was a stronger incentive for the games to be thought of as a whole. One indicator of this was the story format chosen for the game design by most students. For a typical narrative, the designer introduced the story in the beginning of the game and led the player through a number of adventures before bringing the game to a conclusion, hence resolving the tensions. In contrast, Debbie considered each instructional screen a project in itself. For example, Debbie's house scene took only a few days to implement (March 26–30) and could be evaluated separately from other screens that she had designed before or after. There was no interdependency among the different screens in regard to the instructional purpose or the player's ability to use the software. A game, however, even though it consists of different scenes, cannot be played until it is finished. The instructional software was in the form of an interactive lesson with the purpose of teaching something, whereas the educational game was a piece of software that performed its instructional purpose in the context of a game. It is my interpretation that students' thinking about the game as final product instead of individual scenes made the design task an even more challenging enterprise. The degrees of freedom accorded to the game designers placed a heavier emphasis on the game aspect to the detriment of the subject matter.

The lessons learned from this analysis spell out some suggestions for the "design" of future design tasks. Students might be faced with competing design issues when the task is too complex. The conclusion to be drawn from this finding is that the openness of the design task can vary according to its specifications. The question remains how to engage students in more dialogue about making intrinsically integrated educational games. In a first take, I explored whether game design combined with a different subject matter would result in better integration. In a follow-up study of the game project, I asked a class of fourth graders to design games to teach third graders about the solar system. One of my reasons for this choice was that there are many well-known games, plays, and stories around the theme of space. I assumed that this particular choice would facilitate intrinsic integration of knowledge about the solar system into the game theme. A preliminary analysis of my data gathered during the five-month-long project led me to the following observation: Yes, children's game themes were all centered around the space theme, but a majority of students were still creating games with extrinsic integration. One of the pedagogic goals of future work is to encourage wider use of the more difficult but epistemologically more rewarding process of intrinsic integration. An essential step in the direction of encouraging intrinsic integration is creating a culture in which this approach is recognized and valued by teachers and well represented in attractive example games made available to the students.

## Conclusion 5:
## Programming as a Tool for Personal Expression and Knowledge Reformulation

Logo programming was used in the Game Design Project as a tool for knowledge reformulation and personal expression. Designing a complex piece of software such as a computer game to teach younger students about fractions was an effective way of learning the Logo programming language. The analysis of the programming processes and products showed that students were able to master complex programming concepts, to create sophisticated products, and to develop efficient programming strategies. There was less support for the role of knowledge reformulation because only a few students succeeded in integrating fractions into their games. However, programming games allowed students to express their personal fantasies and ideas.

In the Game Design Project, students used the programming language Logo to design games for the purpose of teaching fractions to younger students. The approach to programming used in this project applied many of the features whose importance has been discussed in the research literature (Harel, 1988; Palumbo, 1990): extended time frame, complexity and size of program code, integration of programming into a meaningful context, and the personalization of products. Sixteen students designed 16 different games; each game carried the personal imprint of its designer. All game designers significantly improved their understanding of Logo syntax, programming constructs, and concepts. Students were involved in programming interactions, creating animation, and designing opportunities for user manipulation and feedback. The differences between the Game Design class and Control Classes 2 (Integrated Logo) and 3 (Isolated Logo) had been predicted from the beginning, based on the results of a prior study with the Instructional Design class. Yet, in comparative terms, these results have to be interpreted with care, because both design classes were better in their Logo knowledge from the onset.

Furthermore, students developed different programming strategies to deal with the complexity and size of their games. Game design fostered styles of modularization and created different programming needs. One example of the programming strategies were the "blueprints" that students developed for the programming of their instructional quizzes. Many students implemented programming code segments for one fraction question, which they then applied to the subsequent questions, modifying only the necessary parts. Another example concerned the creation of organizational structures to manage procedures and LogoWriter pages. Most of the students' programs consisted of several pages by the end of the project. The sheer size of these programs forced students to remember on which page they had placed which procedure and how these procedures were connected to the rest of the program. In contrast to other learning-through-design approaches (Perkins, 1986; Soloway, 1988), the learning of these skills was not directly built into the design task.

Instead, tools like the Designer's Notebook prompted students to reflect on their ideas and learning experiences. However, many other cues were given through social occasions for exchange with others.

The results point out one important difference in regard to the initial claim about Logo programming as a tool for knowledge reformulation and personal expression. The role of programming as knowledge reformulation is less clearly supported in the game design context. There appears to be a substantial difference in how the idea of fractions was integrated into the instructional or game design. Both projects offered students the opportunity to appropriate fractions and evoked many ideas around fractions; however, with a different emphasis. In the instructional design class, students used Logo to design procedural representations of fractions. Fractions were central to all their screen designs and programming. Most games, however, did not integrate fractions into their design, even though students obviously thought about it in the beginning. When I analyzed the students' conceptual development of fractions, it became apparent that many students still remained attached to stereotypical representations of fractions. The students' concern with fractions was of rather secondary interest. Albert was a particularly good case in point. He definitely learned a lot of programming by designing his game, but he did not use Logo to explore and extend his knowledge about fractions. Only some students came up with ideas to create fraction microworlds in which the player could learn in two ways about fractions: The design of fraction representations by some students, such as Amy and Rosy, showed more support for this point because they either integrated fractions in their game design or provided exploratory fraction tools for the player.

The variety of game themes chosen by the students speak clearly for the role of programming as personal expression. Programming of actors, animations, dialogues, and shapes was strongly influenced by students' individual preferences and how these resonated with their personal interests. Students chose to develop a narrative to integrate the fractions. The students' thinking went into creating seemingly fantastic and imaginary relations to fractions such as "becoming the God of Fractions" (Amy) or "finding the fraction wand" (Shaun). In game design, students' thinking about fractions was related more to fantasy and less to explaining and defining fractions, as in the instructional design task.

For future research, the aspects of personal expression and knowledge reformulation merit further consideration in the design of programming tasks. What are other tasks that could promote both aspects? An equally important issue is how students will be able to carry over their learned skills into other areas or design experiences. One step in this direction was proposed on an earlier occasion, when I made a group of software designers consultants to a new generation of software designers (Kafai & Harel, 1991b). In this context, students were able to benefit from their earlier learning experience and communicate their knowledge and insights to the inexperienced designers.

## Conclusion 6:
## Constructing Mathematical Representations for Learning

The Game Design Project presented an uncommon approach to learning about fractions. Students' learning was made instrumental to a larger intellectual and social goal by creating an educational game that would teach fractions to younger students. In designing their games, students constructed their own representations. Foremost, students thought and dealt with fractions in their games through invented stories and fantasies—contexts that are rarely promoted in mathematics textbooks or worksheets. The comparison with another design situation, the Instructional Software Design Project, indicated that students' conceptual development differed in terms of creating translations between different representational systems, even though both projects involved students in the construction of fraction representations. Game design did not promote the same richness and incentive for students to think through and create representations as did instructional design.

The Game Design Project investigated the construction of fraction representations as a way for students to reflect on their current knowledge and to build on their understanding of fractions. Students were expected to work on fractions through combining and translating between different representations of fractions while designing their educational games. In contrast to previous research efforts, I did not generate the situations or questions in which students dealt with fractions; the students were the ones who decided on which representations to use, which questions to ask, and which context to provide.

In general terms, the evaluation indicated that the students improved significantly in their understanding of fractions and flexibility in moving between different representational modes. This is particularly important, because the pre- and posttest assessments dealt with much more sophisticated representations than students actually addressed in the design of their games and instructional quizzes. These results confirm the value of constructing mathematical representations as it has been discussed (but little researched) in the community of mathematics educators and psychologists (Goldin, 1991; Janvier, Bednarz, & Belanger, 1987; Kaput, 1991; Streefland, 1991; von Glasersfeld, 1991). The comparison with the instructional software design situation pointed out three important differences in the students' learning experience: the conceptual development of fraction representations, the contexts in which representations were situated, and the processes through which the representations were constructed.

The conceptual development of fraction representations indicates an important difference between the two design situations. The game designers did not progress in the way they made fraction representations in the same fashion as did the instructional designers (Harel, 1988). At the beginning of the project, most instructional designers messed around with different ideas related to fraction concepts. Many students spent several weeks with stereotypical representations (as did Debbie with halves) before they progressed beyond those and created more interesting designs. In contrast, many of the game designers offered representations of fractions that were integrated into their game design from the very beginning. Amy's map, Miriam's Mr. Fraction, and Rosy's world map are just a few examples. However, most students (except for Amy) did not follow through on these initial ideas. For most of their fraction representations, the game designers chose stereotypical representations of fractions as area and used halves or fourths. Some students choose more sophisticated representations, such as group representations or combining different representational modes. In contrast, the instructional designers moved beyond the stereotypical representations; their designs clearly expressed the connections students had made between school-like fractions and personal everyday objects. One could conclude that the game designers' explorations of ways to represent fractions were limited as a result of their growing involvement with programming aspects related to game design.

The students encountered a different quality of knowledge and experience with fractions in the Game Design Project. The game design task made students think about creating a context of their personal interest to represent fractions, and express their fears and thoughts about fractions. In most games, the fractions problems to be solved were built in as "obstacles" to be overcome by the players. This instructional design strategy might reflect some of the students' own feelings toward fractions—seeing them as obstacles or impediments in their thinking and learning. The variety in themes and approaches provides evidence for the students' personalization of their products. This process of building personal relationships with knowledge, also called *concretizing*, is one important feature of mathematical knowing (Wilensky, 1991, p. 13). The game designers concretized their relationship to fractions through references to fantasy. This revealed one of their differences from the instructional software designers, who concretized their relationship to fractions by constructing representations of everyday objects. The instructional designers' representations of fractions could be considered a reflection of deep mathematical thinking, whereas fantasy stories seem to be less connected to mathematics, especially if we consider the formal and abstract nature of mathematics. However, the results of the evaluation pointed out that one important aspect of students' constructing representations is that it provokes students' thinking about them.

A further point concerned the process of constructing fraction representations used by students. In the Game Design Project, students did not program the fraction representations by using turtle graphics. Instead, they resorted to designing shapes and dividing areas into parts. The use of shapes limited the students in their design and implementation of representations, because it did not allow for the construction of complex representations. In the Instructional Software Design Project, students programmed procedural representations of fractions in Logo. Students used a new kind of representation, the programming code of pictorial representations, to create fractions. In doing so, they were free to work on whichever representation that interested them. The products and processes of constructing these representations provided compelling evidence that the instructional designers built relationships with the deep structure of fractions knowledge. The

game designers' products and processes indicated that these
students focused on the context and dialogue to situate fractions
in their games rather than on the content and type of fraction
representations. The most prominent feature of the game
designers' engagement with fractions was the emergence of the
narrative in their games, which contained the instructional
dialogue about fractions.

The comparison between the instructional and game design
situations allowed us to see more clearly some of the factors involved, such as task and process, in the construction of mathematical representations. Future research in this area should concentrate on settings that might help to stimulate the students'
thinking about fractions and help them create closer relationships
with fractions. For example, one could ask under which circum-
stances the game task would have been more conducive to students' exploration of fractions. A further point concerns the way
in which the designers invited the players to engage with fractions.
The majority of designers in both design situations employed
rather instructionist methods to teach about fractions, even though
they were themselves engaged in a constructionist learning experience. One of the interesting results of the game design task was
that the game format seemed to free some students from the restrictions of the instructionist teaching format. Some examples
were Rosy's fraction design tool and the manipulation of Amy's
player to collect the pieces (i.e., fractions) of the map. This seems
to be an interesting avenue to pursue.

## Conclusion 7:
## Some Thoughts about Future Computational Learning Environments for Young Designers

The Game Design Project raised interesting issues and provided ideas for future learning environments based on the
analysis of the game designers' processes and products. Some
of these suggestions are (a) the integration of new programming paradigms such as concurrent and object-oriented programming, (b) the integration of design support structures, (c)
tool kits for game design, and (d) building LEGO game worlds.
The goal of my projections is to create more integration in

subject matters and technology. Better tools for design will also allow for better learning and research.

In the Game Design Project, students created impressive products during the six months of the project. They created these games within the constraints of the existing environment, technological as well as human. I already discussed in the individual chapters and in the previous conclusions some of my thoughts about what could be done to augment and improve the human side of support. The following ideas grew out of my conversations with the young designers and my analysis of the data. Some of these are specifically related to game design; others present more general issues and concerns related to computational environments.

### Integrating New Programming Paradigms

Students used the programming language Logo to design and implement their games. Like most other traditional programming languages, Logo is sequential: It allows the user to control a single computational process or sequence of actions at a time. In contrast, multiprocessing allows the programmer to coordinate multiple processes at the same time. These processes can be "faked" in current Logo versions, but only at the expense of more complicated programming.

Many students asked for multiprocessing features in some of their initial game ideas and in the course of the design process. Students wanted to have "two things happen at the same time." Consider Shaun's description of his initial plans for his game Fraction Killer:

> *Shaun*: See, at first, I was gonna make a fraction come to you and you have to shoot it before it hits you and that's why I . . . I went way down with my game but I restarted the whole game because that didn't work. So what happens is that the fraction goes [makes movement with hands and then imitates a beeping sound] dit . . . dit . . . dit . . . and if it hits you, you're dead. But you are also dead. See you have to type . . . there is no way you can do this in Logo because there are two things happening at once. While the thing is mov-

ing you have to type in the answer and shoot the fractions. If your answer is wrong, you just have to type it in again until you get it right. But if it hits you, you die.

Shaun was clear about what he wanted to implement: "While the thing is moving, you have to type in the answer and shoot." Parallel processes could accommodate his plan very easily. His classmate Jero participated in the discussion and described his very similar plans:

> *Jero*: This was the same thing with my first idea. I had the fractions, I mean with my second idea, I had the fractions come towards you and you had to shoot at it. You had to put in the answer. But you can't do two things at the same time.

Another example was Darvin's game Run. In his game, Darvin wanted to have ghosts appear in random order at different places in the maze while the driver would move through the maze (see Sid's case study for a printout of his screen). A fourth example is Gaby's game Spider Web. She wanted to have her spider run at the same time as the player moved the fly from one fraction block to the next.

These are just four examples among many others where students' ideas called for multiprocessing. A new version of Logo, called *Logo, has already been designed for massive multiprocessing (see Resnick, 1990, 1992). Users can program parallel processes of thousands of individual turtles. Imagine a scenario in which students used *Logo to program their games. Darvin, Gaby, Jero, and Shaun could all implement their ideas in an environment that allowed the use of multiprocessing. Students could program the actions of each character involved in the game and have them act and interact in parallel. Game design provides a situation in which the exploration and implementation of parallel processes would occur in an unobtrusive way. Students could acquire understanding about parallel processes that underlie many complex systems in the world, and their programming products could also become more sophisticated.

## Integration of Design Support Structures

The size and complexity of the students' games by the end of the project raised the question of what kind of support we can offer to students in the process. Albert's case provided one compelling example of how the growing complexity of his game created his need for structure in the form of LogoWriter page organization.

A number of research efforts have been dedicated to helping software designers, especially beginners, deal with the complexity of their programs and to supporting them in their learning of proven design strategies (Guzdial et al., 1991; Soloway, 1988). What is pertinent to most of these approaches is that they include features in their programming environments that have been deduced from observing expert programmers at work. The reasoning behind this approach is that beginning programmers need to learn these strategies in order to become experts. Analysis of experts' work habits and processes has shown that experts make extensive use of these tools to organize their work more efficiently. Although many experts share common strategies and knowledge, they did not necessarily achieve their expertise in the same fashion. This raises the substantial issue that whatever "training wheels" are built into a design environment, such as libraries, prompts, or multiple linked representations, might not have their complement in the designer's learning process.

The important point about Albert's case was that he himself created the organization of LogoWriter pages. I do not think that if we had provided him with this tool in advance he would have taken advantage of it. This structure developed in Albert's understanding through the long-term programming process in which he was involved. His recognition of its usefulness represented one of his crucial learning moments in his learning history. Maybe now, after the Game Design Project, Albert might be ready to work with different structures to help him organize his next project. Of further importance is that even beginning programmers use a variety of approaches in dealing with their problems. Hence, I leave the issue of design support structure open, but it is important that the designers of future environments take the previous aspects into consideration.

## Providing Tool Kits for Game Design

This research presented a new angle on the issue of video game playing: Students were making their own games as well as playing them. The energy and motivation that students dedicated to this task led me to believe that this is a promising avenue to pursue. There have been several attempts in this direction, such as the Pinball Construction Set (see Greenfield, 1984), which provides users with a blank board and all the necessary tools and parts to install flippers, backgrounds, and controllers for their own pinball game. The user can design innumerable versions of pinball games. Eventually, the user can play her or his own game alone or with others. One of the drawbacks of designing pinball games is that certain feelings and sensations from the mechanical world (such as the tilting of the machine) cannot be replicated in the computational environment. A further limitation is that the designer must work with a given set of parts.

One continuation of the Game Design Project would be, then, to think about an environment that provides children with a video-game-design tool kit. They could create their own characters, design their own environments or worlds, and determine the rules of the game. Children could be provided with libraries of primitives for rules, actions, and characters, and could adapt the parameters according to the game's needs and their desires. The sharing of ideas and strategies that is already an essential part of the existing video game culture could continue in such an environment, in which children could invite each other to play their designed games (Gailey, 1992).

## Building LEGO Game Worlds

A different version on the Game Design Project would move game design from the two-dimensional space of the computer screen back into the three-dimensional space of the real world, while retaining the valuable connection to the computational domain. A first step into this direction would be to build games with LEGO/Logo (Resnick & Ocko, 1991), a construction kit that includes LEGO bricks as well as sensors and motors that can be connected via wires and controlled through programs written in Logo. In this process, children would not only build mechanical objects such as cars or robots, but also environments such as houses, gardens, or mazes. Children would then program the interactions between the environment and the mechanical objects. The design of the environment and the programming of interactions are interdependent with the design of the mechanical object. Each design decision influences construction and programming decisions and vice versa. If we imagine a game world, then the gates through which a robot has to move have to be large enough for the robot to pass, and yet, the robot has to be engineered in such a fashion that allows for certain flexibility in its movements. Although building a game world in this fashion increases the complexities of the design task, it also adds valuable learning experiences not gained through computational game design alone. For example, when designing and programming a video game, one does not actually have to know how given things work in the real world. In a video game, a designer could draw a car and animate it without the constraints of the real world. In a LEGO game world, on the other hand, children would have to build a working car and learn about steering mechanisms and transmissions to make it move around.

An extension of LEGO/Logo, called the *programmable brick* (Resnick, 1993), allows users to integrate the domain of computation within the "physical" domain. In this situation, the robots or gates of the environment are no longer connected through wires with the computer; instead, each brick can control its own set of motors and sensors and interact independently with the world. One could imagine, then, a game world consisting of dozens of these bricks, each carrying its own programs and interacting with each other. In contrast to a LEGO/Logo game world, where each interaction is controlled through a program, with the programmable brick interesting, unforeseen responses and interactions could be observed.

Each of these suggestions for new computational features of game-related activities for learning is just a first step to support young designers in their efforts. But they are important steps in the direction of turning children from consumers into producers of games and to allow them to take charge of their own learning and thinking.

# Coda

Designing games for learning offered a rich learning environment for children to become engaged in a variety of issues and to learn about many more aspects than I was able to pursue in detail in the context of this thesis. It is my hope that future projects of this kind will provide the "in play" of students' minds. Without discounting the seriousness of problems that schools, teachers, and students face in today's society, it seems to me that the "playful" and "whimsical" side of learning is equally necessary, as Sara Lawrence Lightfoot stated succinctly:

> A lot of learning has lost its play and has become very concrete and literal, very exacting. It moves towards an end or a conclusion rather than turning ideas on their sides and considering them and laughing about them and being whimsical about them. Some of the best teachers are humorous teachers who see the playfulness of the language and are quick and intuitive. Learning is at its best when it is deadly serious and very playful at the same time. When I say deadly serious, I mean that learning should be disciplined and that people should find ways of learning how to ask questions, how to think about evidence, and how to find out the truths that are out there. That's a very serious pursuit. On the other hand, in every serious thought there's a line of laughter. In my own teaching, I am at my best when I have something that I feel passionate about and talk seriously about but at the same time, that I can find a way of presenting the play in (1988, p. 212).

The students in the Game Design Project obviously found ways of "turning ideas on their sides" in the design of their games.

# Acknowledgments

Seven years ago, I came to the United States with many questions on my mind about learning, thinking, and computational media. During these seven years, I have gained many new friends and colleagues who all share the responsibility that made this book happen. Thanks to all of you.

This book is based on my thesis research conducted at the MIT Media Laboratory and at the Harvard University Graduate School of Education. My thesis committee—David Perkins, Idit Harel, Seymour Papert, and Terry Tivnan—has been always there. Many thanks to Idit Harel, who brought me into the Epistemology and Learning Group at the MIT Media Laboratory and Project Headlight. Her wonderful ideas, comments, energy, and support throughout the last three years have made this happen. I enjoyed working with you, sharing ideas, having discussions, and writing papers. Thanks also to David Perkins, who joined as my thesis advisor at Harvard School of Education. His careful readings of my writing and extensive comments were always right on the spot. But I also want to thank him for his understanding and support in guiding me in various ways through the graduate obstacle course at Harvard and showing me that this can be a gratifying experience after all. Additionally, thanks go to Seymour Papert, who was always there and contributed to my thinking; who was willing to untangle my thoughts and ideas and give them shape.

If there is one person who has been present from the beginning, it has been Elliot Soloway. Seven years ago, Elliot invited me to spend a year in his research group, the Cognition and Programming Project at Yale University (now the Highly Interactive Computer Environments at University of Michigan). His family and research team welcomed me with open arms and have remained friends over time and long distances. All these years, he has been there with his advice, support, and, most important, his humor. Jeannine Pinto, Ken Ewing, Robin Lampert, and Warren Sack started out with me at Yale. Mark Guzdial joined later at the University of Michigan, and has been a fellow graduate student since. It has been a pleasure working and sharing ideas over e-mail.

The former Epistemology and Learning Group at the MIT Media Laboratory (now: Learning and Common Sense) provided me with my intellectual home for the last five years at Cambridge. For all the discussions and suggestions, I want to thank Edith Ackerman, Aaron Brandes, Michele Evard, Nira Farber, Greg Gargarian, Fred Martin, Mitchel Resnick, Ricki Goldman Segall, Alan Shaw, Carol Sperry, Carol Strohecker, and Uri Wilensky. Robert Rasmussen and Lars Bo Jensen from LEGO have been attentive observers and visitors of the Game Design Project from the beginning to the end. And thanks to Jacqueline Karaslaanian, Mai Cleary, and Wanda Gleason, who provided much more than just administrative support. Jacqueline provided the fun, and became a friend in this process.

Project Headlight has been another home for the last three years and a constant source for new ideas. Joanne Ronkin, Marquita Minot, and Gwen Gibson gave me the opportunity to work with them. I am grateful to Joanne and her wonderful class of fourth (and then fifth) graders, who designed and implemented the games discussed in this thesis.

But MIT was not my only home: My Harvard community shares equal responsibility. Shep White has always had an open ear and gave many good pointers on where to start my investigations. Catherine Krupnick showed me the diverse facets of video work in the classroom. But most of all, my student colleagues and friends provided a supportive and warm environment at Harvard. In particular my QP group—Nathalie Vandepool, Hester Brooks, and Sharon Levad—helped with their comments and readings to get things going and to get through the administrative mills of Harvard. In the Gutman Library, Gladys Dratch and Patricia Moskow helped me navigate through the databases.

My editor, Wyn Snow, tried to bring me on the paths of correct English and make my thesis more readable. She kept her humor, yet sometimes she must have been desperate; innumerable pink marks on the margins were a sign of it. Amy Pierce, Lawrence Erlbaum Associates, guided the book manuscript through various stages. Two anonymous reviewers of my manuscript offered valuable comments.

Before I came to the United States, I studied at the Technical University of Berlin under the direction of Klaus Eyferth, a professor of psychology. For me, he set the example that one needs not to be limited to one area of interest. He supported my first investigations into thinking, learning, and computational technologies. Detlef Widowski became a very good friend and shared many discussions over the years.

My parents and friends in Germany were there, all these years, waiting patiently for life signs from the other side of the ocean. My father also came to a foreign country to pursue his graduate studies. He probably understands best about the trials and tribulations involved in this work.

Los Angeles, August 1994

Yasmin Kafai

This book describes research conducted at the MIT's Media Laboratory. Support for this research was provided by LEGO Systems, Inc., the National Science Foundation (Grants #MDR-8751190, #TPE-8850449, and #MDR-9153719), Nintendo Co., Ltd., and the MacArthur Foundation (Grant #874304). The ideas expressed here do not necessarily reflect those of the supporting agencies.

# References

Akin, O. (1984). An exploration of the design process. In N. Cross (Ed.), *Developments in design methodology* (pp. 189–208). New York: Wiley.

Anderson, J. (1983). *The Architecture of Cognition*. Cambridge, MA: Harvard University Press.

Au, W. K., & Leung, J. P. (1991). Problem solving, instructional methods and Logo programming. *Journal of Educational Computing Research, 7*(4), 455–467.

Avedon, E. M., & Sutton-Smith, B. (Eds.). (1966). *The Study of games*. New York: Wiley.

Baugham, S. S., & Clagett, P. D. (Eds.). (1983). *Video games & human development. Research agenda for the '80s*. Cambridge, MA: Harvard Graduate School of Education.

Behr, M., Post, T. R., Silver, E. A., & Mierkiewicz, D. (1980). Theoretical foundations for instructional research on rational numbers. In R. Karplus (Ed.), *Proceedings of the Fourth International Group for the Psychology of Mathematics Education* (pp. 60–70). Berkeley, CA: University of California.

Behr, M. J., Wachsmuth, I., Post, T. R., & Lesh, R. (1984). Order and equivalence of rational numbers: A clinical teaching experiment. *Journal for Research in Mathematics Education, 15*(5), 323–341.

Block, J. H., & King, N. R. (Eds.). (1987). *School play*. New York: Garland.

Bride, J. W., & Lamb, C. E. (1991). Using commercial games to design teacher-made games for the mathematics classroom. *Arithmetic Teacher, 38*, 14–22.

Bruner, J. (1987). Life as narrative. *Social Research, 54*(1), 11–32.

Bruner, J. (1990, June). *Narratives and the construction of realities*. Invited address given at the Piaget Society, Philadelphia, PA.

Burns, B., & Hagerman, A. (1989). Computer experience, self-concept and problem-solving: The effect of Logo on children's ideas of themselves as learners. *Journal of Educational Computing Research, 5*(2), 199–212.

Carpenter, T. P., Matthews, W., Lindquist, M. M., & Silver, E. A. (1984). Achievement in mathematics: Results from the national assessment. *Elementary School Journal, 84*(5), 485–495.

Carver, S. M. (1987). *Transfer of LOGO debugging skills: Analysis, instruction and assessment.* Unpublished doctoral dissertation. Carnegie-Mellon University, Department of Psychology, Pittsburgh, PA.

Clements, D. H. (1985, April). *Effects of LOGO programming on cognition, metacognitive skills and achievement.* Paper presented at the American Educational Research Association, Chicago.

Clements, D. H. (1990). Metacomponential development in a Logo programming environment. *Journal of Educational Psychology, 82*(1), 141–149.

Clements, D. H. (1991). Enhancement of creativity in computer environments. *American Educational Research Journal, 28*(1), 173–187.

Cobb, P., Yackel, E., & Wood, T. (1992). A constructivist alternative to the representational view of mind in mathematics education. *Journal for Research in Mathematics, 23*(1), 2–23.

Collins, A. S., Brown, J. S., & Newman, S. (1990). Cognitive apprenticeship: Teaching the craft of reading, writing and mathematics. In L. B. Resnick (Ed.), *Cognition and instruction: Issues and agendas.* Hillsdale, NJ: Lawrence Erlbaum Associates.

Dalton, D. W., & Goodrum, D. A. (1991). The effects of computer programming on problem-solving skills and attitudes. *Journal of Educational Computing Research, 7*(4), 483–506.

diSessa, A. (1985). Learning about knowing. In E. Klein (Ed.), *Children and computers. New directions in child development 28.* San Francisco: Jossey-Bass.

diSessa, A., & Abelson, H. (1986). Boxer: A reconstructible computational medium. *Communications of the ACM, 29*(9), 859–868.

Dominick, J. R. (1984). Videogames, television violence, and aggression in teenagers. *Journal of Communication, 34*, 136–147.

Dreher, M., & Oerter, R. (1987). Action planning competencies during adolescence and early adulthood. In S. L. Friedman, E. K. Scholnick, & R. R. Cocking, (Eds.), *Blueprints for thinking* (pp. 321–355). Cambridge, England: Cambridge University Press.

Falbel, A. (1991). Computer as a convival tool. In I. Harel & S. Papert (Eds.), *Constructionism* (pp. 29–40). Norwood, NJ: Ablex.

Fennell, F., Houser, L. L., McPartland, D., & Parker, S. (1984, February). Ideas. *Arithmetic Teacher, 31*, 27–33.

Feurzeig, W. (1988). Apprentice tools: Students as practitioners. In R. S. Nickerson & P. P. Zodhiates (Eds.), *Technology in education: Looking toward 2020*. Hillsdale, NJ: Lawrence Erlbaum Associates.

Friedman, S., L., Scholnick, E. K., & Cocking, R. R. (1987). Reflections on reflections: What planning is and how it develops. In S. L. Friedman, E. K. Scholnick, & R. R. Cocking, (Eds.), *Blueprints for thinking* (pp. 515–534). Cambridge, England: Cambridge University Press.

Gailey, C. (1992). Mediated messages: Gender, class, and cosmos in home video games. *Journal of Popular Culture, 25*(3), 44–53.

Gilligan, C. (1982). *In a different voice*. Cambridge, MA: Harvard University Press.

Goldin, G. A. (1991, June). The IGPME working group on representations. In the *Proceedings of the 15th International Conference on the Psychology of Mathematics Education*, Assisi, Italy.

Goldschmidt, G. (1988). Interpretation: its role in architectural designing. *Design Studies, 9*(4), 235–245.

Goldschmidt, G. (1990a). Problem representation versus domain of solution: Some examples from architectural design. *Journal for Architecture and Planning Research, 6*(3), 204–215.

Goldschmidt, G. (1990b). Development in architectural designing. In M. Franklin & B. Kaplan (Eds.), *Development and the arts*. Hillsdale, NJ: Lawrence Erlbaum Associates.

Greenfield, P. M. (1984). *Mind and media. The effects of television, video games, and computers*. Cambridge, MA: Harvard University Press.

Greenfield, P. M. (1990). Video screens: Are they changing the way children learn? *Education letter*. Cambridge, MA: Harvard Graduate School of Education.

Guindon, R., Krasner, H., & Curtis, B. (1987). Breakdowns and processes during the early activities of software design by professionals. In G. M. Ohlson, S. Sheppard, & E. Soloway (Eds.), *Empirical studies of programmers: Second workshop*. Norwood, NJ: Ablex.

Guzdial, M., Soloway, E., Blumenfeld, P., Hohmann, L., Ewing, K., Tabak, I., Brade, K., & Kafai, Y. (1991). The future of CAD: Technological support for kids building artifacts. In D. Balestry, S. Ehrmann, & D. C. Ferguson (Eds.), *Learning to design, designing to learn. Using technology to transform the curriculum* (pp. 75–117). Norwood, NJ: Ablex.

Harel, I. (1986, July). *Children as Software Designers*. Paper presented at the Logo'86 Internatinal Conference, Boston.

Harel, I. (1988). *Software design for learning: Children's construction of meaning for fractions and Logo programming*. Unpublished doctoral dissertation. MIT Media Laboratory, Cambridge, MA.

Harel, I. (1990, April). *Expanding the Logo environment: A review of research and development projects of multimedia programming environments for young learners*. Paper Presented at the annual meeting of the American Educational Research Association, Boston.

Harel, I. (1991). *Children designers*. Norwood: Ablex.

Harel, I., & Papert, S. (1990). Software design as a learning environment. *Interactive Learning Environment, 1*(1), 1–32.

Harel, I., & Kafai, Y. (1993). (Eds.). *Headlight Stories. Constructionist Teaching in a Computer Culture*. MIT Media Laboratory, Cambridge, MA.

Harris, M. B., & Williams, R. (1984). Video games and school performance. *Education, 105*(3), 306-309.

Hart, K. (1981). *Children's understanding of mathematics: 11–16*. London: John Murray.

Harvey, B. (1985). *Computer science Logo style. Volume 1: Intermediate programming*. Cambridge, MA: MIT Press.

Heller, R. S. (1986). *Different LOGO teaching styles: Do they really matter?* Paper presented at the First Workshop of Empirical Studies of Programmers, Washington, DC.

Hiebert, J., & Wearne, D. (1986). Procedures over concepts: The acquisition of decimal number knowledge. In J. Hiebert and P. Lefevre (Eds.), *Conceptual and procedural knowledge: The case of mathematics* (pp. 199–223). Hillsdale, NJ: Lawrence Erlbaum Associates.

Hoyles, C., & Noss, R. (1992). Deconstructing microworlds. In D. L. Ferguson (Ed.), *Advanced technologies in the teaching of mathematics and science.* New York: Springer.

Janvier, C. (Ed.). (1987). *Problems of presentation in the teaching and learning of mathematics.* Hillsdale, NJ: Lawrence Erlbaum Associates.

Janvier, J., Bednarz, N., & Belanger, M. (1987). Pedagogical considerations concerning the problem of representation. In C. Janvier (Ed.), *Problems of presentation in the teaching and learning of mathematics.* Hillsdale, NJ: Lawrence Erlbaum Associates.

Jeffries, R., Turner, A. A., Polson, P. G., & Atwood, M. E. (1981). The processes involved in designing software. In J. R. Anderson (Ed.), *Cognitive skills and their acquistion.* Hillsdale NJ: Lawrence Erlbaum Associates.

Johnson, D. W., & Johnson, R. (1989). Social skills for successful group work. *Educational Leadership, 47,* 29–31.

Jones, J. C. (1980). *Design methods. Seeds of human futures.* New York: Wiley.

Kafai, Y. B. (1992). *Design for learning: Exploration of design theories and their implications for educational computing.* Unpublished qualifying paper, Harvard Graduate School of Education, Cambridge, MA.

Kafai, Y. B. & Harel, I. (1991a). Childrens' learning through consulting: When mathematical ideas, software design, and playful discourse are intertwined. In I. Harel & S. Papert (Eds.), *Constructionism.* Norwood, NJ: Ablex.

Kafai, Y. B. & Harel, I. (1991b). Learning through teaching and design: Social aspects of constructionism. In I. Harel & S. Papert (Eds.), *Constructionism.* Norwood, NJ: Ablex.

Kalay, Y. (Ed.). (1987). *Computability of design.* New York: Wiley.

Kaput, J. (1991). Notations and representations as mediators of constructive processes. In E. von Glasersfeld (Ed.), Radical constructivism in mathematics education. Dordrecht, Netherlands: Kluwer.

Kaput, J. (1987). Representation systems and mathematics. In C. Janvier (Ed.), *Problems of presentation in the teaching and learning of mathematics.* Hillsdale, NJ: Lawrence Erlbaum Associates.

Keller, E. F. (1983). *A feeling for the organism*. New York: Freeman.
Keller, E. F. (1985). *Reflections on gender and science*. New Haven, CT: Yale University Press.
Kidder, L. H., & Fine, M. (1987). Qualitative and quantitative methods: When stories converge. In M. Mark & R. Shotland (Eds.), *Multiple methods in program evaluation*. San Francisco: Jossey-Bass.
Kieren, T. E., & Nelson, D. (1978). The operator construct of rational numbers in childhood and adolescence: An exploratory study. *The Alberta Journal of Educational Research, 24*(1), 22–30.
Kieren, T. E., Nelson, D., & Smith, G. (1985). Graphical algorithms in partitioning tasks. *Journal of Mathematical Behavior, 4*, 25–36.
Kinder, M. (1991). *Playing with power*. Berkeley, CA: University of California Press.
Kreitler, S., & Kreitler, H. (1987). Conceptions and processes of planning: The developmental perspective. In S. L. Friedman, E. K. Scholnick, & R. R. Cocking (Eds.), *Blueprints for thinking* (pp. 205–272). Cambridge, England: Cambridge University Press.
Krippendorf, K. (1989). On the essential contexts of artifacts or on the proposition that "design is making sense (of things)." *Design Issues, 5*(2), 9–39.
Kurland, M., & Pea, R. (1983). Children's mental models of recursive Logo programs. In *Proceedings of the Fifth Annual Cognitive Science Society*. Rochester, NY: Cognitive Science Society.
Lawler, R. (1985). *Computer experience and cognitive development. A child learning in a computer culture*. England: Ellis Horwood Unlimited.
Lefevre, P. (1984, October). *Rational number learning and instruction from a cognitive perspective*. Paper presented at the annual meeting of the Northeastern Educational Research Association, Ellenville, NY.
Lehrer, R. (1992). Book review. *Journal Educational Computing Research, 8*(2), 255–258.
Lehrer, R., Guckenberg, T., & Sancilio, L. (1988). Influences of Logo on children's intellectual development. In R. E. Mayer (Ed.), *Teaching and learning computer programming: Multiple research perspectives*. Hillsdale, NJ: Lawrence Erlbaum Associates.

Lepper, M. R., & Malone, T. W. (1987). Intrinsic Motivation and Instructional Effectiveness in Computer-Based Education. In R. E. Snow & M. J. Farr (Eds.), *Aptitude, learning and instruction. Volume 3: Conative and affective process analyses* (pp. 255–285). Hillsdale, NJ: Lawrence Erlbaum Associates.

Lesh, R., & Landau, M. (Eds.). (1983). *Acquisition of mathematics concepts and processes*. London: Academic Press.

Lesh, R., Landau, M., & Hamilton, T. (1983). Conceptual models and applied mathematical problem-solving research. In R. Lesh & M. Landau (Eds.), *Acquisition of mathematics concepts and processes*. London: Academic Press.

Light, R. J., & Pillemer, D. B. (1984). *Summing up*. Cambridge, MA: Harvard University Press.

Lightfoot, S. L. (1988). Interview. In B. Moyers (Ed.), *A world of ideas*. New York: Doubleday.

Loftus, G. R., & Loftus, E. F. (1983). *Minds at play*. New York: Basic Books.

Malone, T. W. (1981, December). What makes computer games fun? *BYTE*, pp. 258–277.

Malone, T. W., & Lepper, M. R. (1987). Making learning fun: A taxonomy of intrinsic motivations for learning. In R. E. Snow & M. J. Farr (Eds.), *Aptitude, learning and instruction. Volume 3: Conative and affective process analyses* (pp. 223–253). Hillsdale, NJ: Lawrence Erlbaum Associates.

Many, W. A., Lockard, J., Abrams, P. D., & Friker, W. (1988). The effect of learning to program in Logo on reasoning skills of junior high school students. *Journal of Educational Computing Research, 4*(2), 203–226.

Margolin, V. (1989). *Design discourse*. Chicago: University of Chicago Press.

Maxwell, J. A., Bashook, P.G., & Sandlow, L.J. (1986). Combining ethnographic and experimental methods in educational evaluation. A case study. In D. M. Fetterman and M. A. Pitman (Eds.), *Educational evaluation: Ethnography in theory, practice, and politics*. Beverly Hills, CA: Sage.

Mischler, E. G. (1990). Validation in inquiry-guided research: The role of exemplars in narrative studies. *Harvard Educational Review, 60*(4), 415–442.

Morlock, H., Yando, T., & Nigolean, K. (1985). Motivation of video game players. *Psychological Reports, 57*, 247–250.

Newell, A. & Simon, H. A. (1972). *Human problem solving*. Englewood Cliffs, NJ: Prentice-Hall.

Noelting, G. (1980). The development of proportional reasoning and the ratio concept: Part I: The differentiation of stages. *Educational Studies in Mathematics, 11*, 217–253.

Palincsar, A. S., & Brown, A. L. (1984). Reciprocal teaching. *Cognition and Instruction, 1*(1), 117–175.

Palumbo, D. B. (1990). Programming language/problem-solving research: A review of relevant issues. *Review of Educational Research, 60*(1), 65–89.

Papert, S. (1980). *Mindstorms.* New York: Basic Books.

Papert, S. (1986). *Constructionism: A new opportunity for elementary science education.* National Science Foundation proposal. MIT Media Laboratory, Cambridge, MA.

Papert, S. (1990a, November). Computer Criticsm vs. Technocentric Thinking. *Epistemology & Learning Memo, 1,* Cambridge, MA: MIT Media Laboratory.

Papert, S. (1990b, November). A critique of technocentrism in thinking about the school of the future. *Epistemology & Learning Memo, 2,* Cambridge, MA: MIT Media Laboratory.

Papert, S. (1993). *The Children's Machine.* New York: Basic Books.

Payne, J. N. (1984). Curricula issues: Teaching rational numbers. *Arithmetic Teacher, 31*(6), 14–17.

Pea, R. (1988). Putting knowledge to use. In R. S. Nickerson & P. P. Zodhiates (Eds.), *Technology in education: Looking toward 2020.* Hillsdale, NJ: Lawrence Erlbaum Associates.

Pea, R., & Hawkins, J. (1987). Planning in a chore-scheduling task. In S. L. Friedman, E. K. Scholnick, & R. R. Cocking, (Eds.), *Blueprints for thinking* (pp. 273–302). Cambridge, England: Cambridge University Press.

Pea, R. D., & Kurland, M. (1984). On the cognitive effects of learning computer programming. *New Ideas in Psychology, 2*(2), 137–168.

Perkins, D. N. (1986). *Knowledge as design.* Hillsdale, NJ: Lawrence Erlbaum Associates.

Perkins, D. N., & Martin, F. (1985). *Fragile knowledge and neglected strategies in novice programmers.* Technical Report 85-22. Cambridge, MA: Educational Technology Center, Harvard Graduate School of Education.

Piaget, J. (1929/1964). *The child's conception of the world.* London: Routledge.

Piaget, J. (1955). *The language and thought of the child.* New York: New American Library.

Piaget, J., & Inhelder, B. (1951/1975). *The origin of the idea of chance in children.* New York: Norton.

Post, T. R. (1981). Fractions: Results and implications from national assessment. *Arithmetic Teacher, 28*(9), 26–31.

Post, T. R., Behr, M. J., & Lesh, R. (1982). Interpretations of rational concepts. In L. Silvey & J. R. Smart (Eds.), *Mathematics for the middle grades, yearbook of the national council of teachers of mathematics.* Reston, VA: The Council, 59–71.

Priester, S. (1984, March). SUM 9.9: A game for decimals. *Arithmetic Teacher, 31,* 46–47.

Provenzo, E. F. (1991). *Video kids: Making sense of Nintendo.* Cambridge, MA: Harvard University Press.

Resnick, M. (1990). MultiLogo: A study of children and concurrent programming. *Interactive Learning Environments, 1*(3), 153–170.

Resnick, M. (1991). Xylophones, hamsters, and fireworks: The role of diversity in constructionist activities. In I. Harel and S. Papert (Eds.), *Constructionism.* Norwood, NJ: Ablex.

Resnick, M. (1992). *Beyond the centralized mindset. Explorations in massively-parallel microworlds.* Unpublished doctoral dissertation, MIT, Cambridge, MA.

Resnick, M. (1993). Behavioral Construction Kits. *Communications of the ACM, 36*(7), 64-71.

Resnick, M., & Ocko, S. (1991). LEGO/Logo: Learning through and about design. In I. Harel and S. Papert (Eds.), *Constructionism.* Norwood: Ablex.

Richards, J. (1991). Mathematical discussions. In E. von Glasersfeld (Ed.), *Radical constructivism in mathematics education.* Dordrecht, The Netherlands: Kluwer.

Rittel, H. W. J., & Webber, M. M. (1984). Planning problems are wicked problems. In N. Cross (Ed.), *Developments in Design Methodology* (pp. 135–144). New York: Wiley.

Robinson, J. W. (1986). Design as exploration. *Design Studies, 7*(2), 67–79.

Rogoff, B. (1990). *Apprenticeship in thinking.* New York: Oxford University Press.

Rowe, P. (1987). *Design thinking.* Cambridge, MA: MIT Press.

Schön, D. A. (1983). *The reflective practitioner.* New York: Basic Books.

Schön, D. A. (1988). Designing: Rules, types and worlds. *Design Studies, 9*(3), 181-190.

Selnow, G. W. (1984). Playing videogames: The electronic friend. *Journal of Communication, 34*, 148–156.

Shannon, M. J. (1990). Toward a rationale for public design education. *Design Issues, 7*(1), 29–41.

Silver, E. A. (1986). Using conceptual and procedural knowledge: A focus on relationships. In J. Hiebert and P. Lefevre (Eds.), *Conceptual and procedural knowledge: The case of mathematics* (pp. 181–196). Hillsdale, NJ: Lawrence Erlbaum Associates.

Silvern, S. B., & Williamson, P. A. (1987). The effects of videogame play on young children's aggression, fantasy and prosocial behavior. *Journal of Applied Developmental Psychology, 8*, 453–462.

Simon, H. A. (1969). *The sciences of the artificial*. Cambridge, MA: MIT Press.

Simon, H. A. (1984). The structure of ill-structured problems. In N. Cross (Ed.), *Developments in design methodology* (pp. 145–166). New York: Wiley.

Skypeck, D. H. (1984). Special characteristics of rational numbers. *Arithmetic Teacher, 31*(6), 10–12.

Slavin, R. (1983). *Cooperative learning*. New York: Longman.

Solomon, G., & Perkins, D. N. (1987). Transfer of cognitive skills from programming: When and how? *Journal of Educational Computing Research, 3*(2), 149–169.

Soloway, E. (1988). It's 2020: Do you know what your children are learning in programming class? In In R. S. Nickerson & P. P. Zodhiates (Eds.), *Technology in education: Looking toward 2020*. Hillsdale, NJ: Lawrence Erlbaum Associates.

Streefland, L. (1991). *Fractions in realistic mathematics education*. Dordrecht, The Netherlands: Kluwer.

Swan, K. (1991). Programming objects to think with: Logo and the teaching and learning of problem solving. *Journal of Educational Computing Research, 7*(1), 89–112.

Tierney, C. C. (1987). *Construction of fractions knowledge: Two case studies*. Unpublished doctoral dissertation. Cambridge, MA: Harvard Graduate School of Education.

Turkle, S. (1984). *The second self: Computers and the human spirit*. New York: Simon & Schuster.

Turkle, S., & Papert, S. (1990). Epistemological pluralism: Styles and voices within the computer culture. In. I. Harel (Ed.), *Constructionist learning*. Cambridge, MA: MIT Media Laboratory.

von Glasersfeld, E. (1987). Preliminaries to any theory of representation. In C. Janvier (Ed.), *Problems of presentation in the teaching and learning of mathematics*. Hillsdale, NJ: Lawrence Erlbaum Associates.

von Glasersfeld, E. (Ed.). (1991). *Radical constructivism in mathematics education*. Dordrecht, The Netherlands: Kluwer.

Vygotzky, L. S. (1978). *Mind in society: The development of higher psychological processes*. Cambridge, MA: Harvard University Press.

Wachsmuth, I., Behr, M., & Post, T. R. (1983, July). In R. Herskowitz (Ed.), *Proceedings of the Seventh International Group for the Psychology of Mathematics Education* (pp. 164–169). Jerusaleum, Israel.

Waldman, P. (1982). A primer of easy pieces: Teaching through typological narrative. *Journal of Architectural Education, 35*(4), 10–13.

Wearne-Hiebert, D. C., & Hiebert, J. (1983). Junior high students' understanding of fractions. *School Science and Mathematica, 83*(2), 96–106.

White, B. Y. (1984). Designing computer games to help physics students understand Newton's laws of motion. *Cognition and Instruction, 1*(1), 69–108.

Wilensky, U. (1991). Abstract meditations on the concrete and concrete implications for mathematics education. In I. Harel & S. Papert (Eds.), *Constructionism*. Norwood, NJ: Ablex.

# Author Index

# Subject Index